Thai

A ROUGH GUIDE
PHRASEBOOK

Compiled
by Lexus

Credits

Compiled by Lexus with David and Somsong Smyth

Lexus Series Editor:	Sally Davies
Rough Guides Phrasebook Editor:	Jonathan Buckley
Rough Guides Series Editor:	Mark Ellingham

This first edition published in 1996 by Rough Guides Ltd, 1 Mercer Street,
London WC2H 9QJ.
Reprinted in January 1998.

Distributed by the Penguin Group.

Penguin Books Ltd, 27 Wrights Lane, London W8 5TZ
Penguin Books USA Inc., 375 Hudson Street, New York 10014, USA
Penguin Books Australia Ltd, 487 Maroondah Highway, PO Box 257,
    Ringwood, Victoria 3134, Australia
Penguin Books Canada Ltd, Alcorn Avenue, Toronto, Ontario, Canada
    M4V 1E4
Penguin Book (NZ) Ltd, 182–190 Wairau Road, Auckland 10, New Zealand

Typeset in Rough Serif and Rough Sans to an original design by Henry Iles.
Printed by Cox & Wyman Ltd, Reading.

© Lexus Ltd 1996
272pp.

British Library Cataloguing in Publication Data
A catalogue for this book is available from the British Library.

ISBN 1-85828-177-6

CONTENTS

HELP US GET IT RIGHT

Lexus and Rough Guides have made great efforts to be accurate and
informative in this Rough Guide Thai phrasebook. However, if you feel
we have overlooked a useful word or phrase, or have any other
comments to make about the book, please let us know. All
contributors will be acknowledged and the best letters will be
rewarded with a free Rough Guide phrasebook of your choice. Please
write to 'Thai Phrasebook Update', at either Mercer Street (London) or
Hudson Street (New York) – for full addresses see opposite.
Alternatively you can email us at mail@roughguides.co.uk

Online information about Rough Guides can be found at our website
www.roughguides.com

INTRODUCTION

The Rough Guide Thai phrasebook is a highly practical introduction to the contemporary language. Laid out in clear A-Z style, it uses key-word referencing to lead you straight to the words and phrases you want – so if you need to book a room, just look up 'room'. The Rough Guide gets straight to the point in every situation, in bars and shops, on trains and buses, and in hotels and banks.

The first part of the Rough Guide is a section called **The Basics**, which sets out the fundamental rules of the language and its pronunciation, with plenty of practical examples. You'll also find here other essentials like numbers, dates, telling the time and basic phrases.

Forming the heart of the guide, the **English-Thai** section gives easy-to-use transliterations of the Thai words plus the text in Thai script, so that if the pronunciation proves too tricky, you can simply indicate what you want to say. To get you involved quickly in two-way communication, the Rough Guide also includes dialogues featuring typical responses on key topics – such as renting a car and asking directions. Feature boxes fill you in on cultural pitfalls as well as the simple mechanics of how to make a phone call, what to do in an emergency, where to change money, and more. Throughout this section, cross-references enable you to pinpoint key facts and phrases, while asterisked words indicate where further information can be found in the Basics.

The **Thai-English** section is in two parts: a dictionary, arranged phonetically, of all the words and phrases you're likely to hear (starting with a section of slang and colloquialisms); then a compilation, arranged by subject, of all the signs, labels, instructions and other basic words you might come across in print or in public places.

Finally the Rough Guide rounds off with an extensive **Menu Reader**. Consisting of food and drink sections arranged by subject (each starting with a list of essential terms), it's indispensable whether you're eating out, stopping for a quick drink, or browsing through a local food market.

เที่ยวให้สนุกนะ

têe-o hâi sa-nÒOk ná!

have a good trip!

The Basics

PRONUNCIATION

Throughout this book Thai words have been written in a
romanized system (see the Thai alphabet page 7) so that they
can be read as though they were English, bearing in mind the
notes on pronunciation below. There are, however, some
sounds that are unlike anything in English. In this
pronunciation guide, words containing these sounds are given
in Thai script as well; ask a Thai to pronounce them for you.

Vowels

a	as in **a**live
e	as in t**e**n
i	as in s**i**n
o	as in **o**n
u	as in f**u**n
ah	as the **a** in r**a**ther
ai	as in Th**ai**
air	as in f**air**
ao	as in L**ao**
ay	as in h**ay**
ee	as in s**ee**
er	as in numb**er**
er-ee	as in the Thai word **ner-ee** เนย (butter); the **r** is not pronounced
eu	as in the Thai word **meu** มือ (hand); like the English exclamation **ugh!**
ew	as in f**ew**
oh	as the **o** in n**o**
oo	as in b**oo**t
OO	as in l**oo**k
oy	as in b**oy**

Consonants

bp	sharp **p** sound (don't pronounce the **b**). It occurs in the word bpai ไป (go)
dt	sharp **t** (don't pronounce the **d**). It occurs in the word dtàir แต (but)
g	as in **g**ate
ng	as in ri**ng**

When **k**, **p** and **t** are at the end of a word, it may sound almost as if these consonants are not being pronounced. Ask a Thai to say:

lâhk	ลาก	drag (verb)
lâhp	ลาบ	minced meat
lâht	ลาด	cover; spread (verb)

When a final r is followed by a vowel, the r is not pronounced:

ner-ee	เนย	butter

Bangkok Thai

Among some Bangkok speakers, when there are two consonants at the beginning of a word, the second consonant sound is often omitted:

bplah (fish) becomes bpah
gra-tee-um (garlic) becomes ga-tee-um

Sometimes, words beginning with a kw sound are pronounced as if they began with an f instead:

kwǎh (right) becomes fǎh
kwahm sòòk (happiness) becomes fahm sòòk

TONES

Thai is a tonal language which means that the pitch at which a word is pronounced determines its meaning. The same combination of letters pronounced with a different tone will produce different words. In Thai there are five different tones: mid tone (no mark), high tone (´), low tone (`), falling tone (ˆ) and rising tone (ˇ). For example:

mai	ไมล์ (mid-tone)	mile	mài	ใหม่ (low tone)	new
mái	ไม้ (high tone)	wood	măi	ไหม (rising tone)	silk
mâi	ไม่ (falling tone)	not			

In Thai, the tone is as important a part of the word as the consonant and vowel sounds.

To help you get a clearer idea of how the tones sound, Thai script equivalents are given for the words in this section. Ask a Thai speaker to read the words for you so that you can hear the tonal differences.

Mid-tone: e.g. bpai (go). This can be thought of as normal voice pitch. The following are words pronounced with mid-tone:

mah	มา	come	mee	มี	have
bpen	เป็น	is	tum	ทำ	do
nai	ใน	in			

High tone: e.g. rórn (hot). The voice has to be pitched slightly higher than normal. Tones are relative, though, and a Thai with a deep voice will have no problem producing a high tone, even though it will not be as 'high' in absolute terms as a child's high tone.

The following are words pronounced with high tones:

sái	ช้าย	left	rót	รถ	car
cháo	เช้า	morning	lék	เล็ก	little
náhm	น้ำ	water			

Low tone: e.g. nèung (one). The voice should be pitched below the normal level:

yài	ใหญ่	big	jàhk	จาก	from
bpìt	ปิด	closed	gài	ไก่	chicken
tòok	ถูก	cheap			

Falling tone: e.g. **dâi** (can). The best way to convey a falling tone is to speak very emphatically, but this doesn't mean that Thai words with falling tones have to be shouted. English speakers tend to find this the most difficult tone and do not let the voice fall sufficiently. The secret is to start at a fairly high pitch in order to achieve a distinct fall:

têe	ที่	at	mâi	ไม่	not
hâh	ห้า	five	mâhk	มาก	much
chôrp	ชอบ	like			

Rising tone: e.g. **sŏrng** (two). The rising tone is like the intonation used when asking a question in English:

pŏm	ผม	I (said by a man)	kŏr ...	ขอ ...	may I ...
kwăh	ขวา	right	lăi	หลาย	several
mŏr	หมอ	doctor			

The relative positions of the five Thai tones can be represented graphically like this:

High Tone	Falling Tone	Mid Tone	Low Tone	Rising Tone

THE THAI ALPHABET

Vowels

-อ	-or	เ-อะ	-er
-ะ	-a	เ-ะ	-e
-ั	-u-	เ-า	-aw
-ัว	-oo-a	เ-าะ	-or
-า	-ah	เ-	-er
-ำ	-um	เ-ีย	-ee-a
-ิ	-i	เ-ียะ	-ee-a
-ี	-ee	เ-ือ	-eu-a
-ึ	-eu	แ-	-air
-ื	-eu	แ-็	-air
-ุ	-oo	แะ	-air
-ู	-oo	โ-	-oh
-เ	-ay	โ-ะ	-o
เ-	-e	ใ-	-ai
เ-ย	-er-ee	ไ-	-ai

Consonants

ก	g	ท	t
ข	k	ฒ	t
ค	k	ณ	n
ฆ	k	ด	d
ง	ng	ต	dt
จ	j	ถ	t
ฉ	ch	ท	t
ช	ch	ธ	t
ซ	s	น	n
ฌ	ch	บ	b
ญ	y	ป	bp
ฎ	d	ผ	p
ฏ	dt	ฝ	f
ฐ	t	พ	p

ฟ	f		ว	w
ภ	p		ศ	s
ม	m		ษ	s
ย	y		ส	s
ร	r		ห	h
ฤ	reu		ฬ	l
ฤๅ	reu		อ	consonant that is
ล	l			not sounded
ฦ	leu		ฮ	h
ฦๅ	leu			

NOTE

When appropriate, in the **Basics** and **English-Thai** sections of this book, the phrases include two forms, the second of which is in brackets.

Where you have pŏm (chún) ('I' or 'me') in a phrase, pŏm should be used by a male speaker and chún by a female speaker.

There are also different polite particle forms for male and female speakers (see the **Basics** section, page 18). Where you have krúp (kâ) or krúp (ká), the form in brackets should be used by a female speaker.

ARTICLES

There are no definite or indefinite articles in Thai. So, for example, rót (car) can mean either 'a car' or 'the car' depending on the context.

NOUNS

Gender and Number

There is no gender in Thai and nouns have a single fixed form for both singular and plural. So, for example, bâhn means either 'house' or 'houses', depending on the context. In most cases, this is enough to make it clear whether it is a single item or more than one item that is being referred to. Even so, the Westerner has to learn to live with apparently ambiguous statements like bpai gùp pêu-un which can mean: 'I'm going with a friend' or 'I'm going with friends'.

You can be more specific in Thai by using a number with a noun. However, if you use a number or word denoting quantity, you also have to use a special 'counting' word known as a 'classifier'.

CLASSIFIERS

Every noun in Thai has a specific classifier which is used when counting or quantifying that noun. Some classifiers can be readily translated into English while others cannot. The classifier for all human beings, for example, is kon which means 'person' and the classifier for cars is kun which means 'vehicle'; dtoo-a literally means 'body' but is the classifier for animals.

The most common classifiers are:

bai	fruit, eggs, cups, bowls, small bits of paper such as tickets
cha-bùp	letters, newspapers, papers, documents
chín	pieces of cake, meat or cloth
dtoo-a	animals, chairs, tables, clothing
hàirng	places, buildings
hôrng	rooms
kon	people (excluding monks and royalty)
kòo-ut	bottles
kun	vehicles
lôok	round objects such as fruit or balls
lêm	books, knives
lǔng	houses

Uncountable nouns such as coffee, tea, beer etc are counted by the container in which they are sold. So food can be counted by the 'plate', coffee by the 'cup', beer by the 'bottle' etc.

When referring to more than one item the word order is as follows:

noun	number	classifier	
dtǒo-a	hâh	bai	five tickets
dtôm yum gài	sǎhm	chahm	three bowls of chicken 'tom yam'
cháhng	sǒrng	dtoo-a	two elephants
gairng néu-a	sǒrng	jahn	two plates of beef curry
pôo-yǐng	sǎhm	kon	three girls
bee-a	sèe	kòo-ut	four bottles of beer
rót	sèe	kun	four cars

When only one item is being counted the order of number and classifier is reversed:

noun	classifier	number	
dtǒo-a	bai	nèung	one/a ticket
mǎh	dtoo-a	nèung	one/a dog
pôo-chai	kon	nèung	one/a man
bee-a	koo-ùt	nèung	one/a bottle of beer
gah-fair	tôo-ay	nèung	one/a cup of coffee

For some nouns, the classifier is the same as the noun itself. For example, hôrng means 'room', and is also the classifier for rooms. However, the word hôrng is not repeated and only the classifier is used with the number:

sèe hôrng
four rooms

hôrng nèung
a room

Similarly, kon means 'person' and is also the classifier for people:

mee sǎhm kon
there were three people

kon nèung
a person, one person

Units of time and measurement are used in the same way as hôrng above; that is the unit of time or measurement is the same as the classifer and is not repeated:

> **hâh wun**
> five days

> **sŏrng ah-tít**
> two weeks

pêu-un	**tóok**
friend	every/all
all my friends	

kon ung-grìt	**lăi**
English person	many
many English people	

rohng rairm	**bahng**
hotel	some
some hotels	

If you can't think of the right classifier for something, use the general classifier un:

> **pŏm (chún) mâi dâi kŏr ao un née**
> I didn't ask for this (thing)

> **un la tâo-rài?**
> how much are they each?

> **èek un nèung**
> another one, the other one, the other thing

> **deu-un nèung**
> one month

> **bpra-mahn yêe-sìp gi-loh-met**
> it's about 20 kilometres

Words such as 'all', 'every', 'many', 'several' and 'some' are also used with classifiers:

kon
classifier

kon
classifier

hàirng
classifier

ADJECTIVES AND ADVERBS

Adjectives are always placed after the noun to which they refer:

> **pôo-yĭng sŏo-ay**
> a beautiful girl

> **rót yài**
> a large car

> **ngern deu-un dee**
> a good salary

Thai adjectives also function as verbs: **sŏo-ay** thus means both 'beautiful' and 'to be beautiful' and **yài** means both 'big' and 'to be big'. The above examples might therefore just as readily have been translated as, 'the girl is beautiful', 'the car is big', and 'the salary is good'.

Note, however, that the Thai verb bpen (to be) cannot be used with adjectives and you cannot say:

pôo-yǐng bpen sǒo-ay* or rót bpen yài*

*incorrect sentences

Comparatives

To form the comparative (more ..., ...-er), add gwàh after the adjective:

yài	large
yài gwàh	larger
sǒo-ay	beautiful
sǒo-ay gwàh	more beautiful
dee	good, nice
dee gwàh	better, nicer

To say 'more ... than ...' or '...-er than ...', the word order is as follows:

adjective + gwàh ...

gr00ng-tâyp yài gwàh chee-ung mài
Bangkok is bigger than Chiangmai

dee gwàh un née rěu bplào?
is it better than this one?

bpai rót fai tòok gwàh bpai krêu-ung bin
going by train is cheaper than going by plane

Superlatives

To form the superlative, add têe sòOt after the adjective:

yài	large
yài têe sòOt	(the) largest
dee	good
dee têe sòOt	(the) best

wút sǔm-kun têe sòOt
the most important temple

tahng ray-o têe sòOt
the quickest route

Adverbs

Adverbs are placed after the verb as in English. The adverb is the same as the adjective in Thai:

rót ray-o
a fast car

káo wîng ray-o
he runs quickly

pêu-un dee
a good friend

kǎi dee
(it) sells well

Demonstrative Adjectives

The English demonstrative adjective 'this' is translated by née. 'That' is translated either by nún or nóhn. nún refers to something near the speaker and nóhn refers to something further away. Classifiers are also used with Thai demonstrative adjectives (see the section on Classifiers page 9):

noun	classifier	demonstrative	
dtó	dtoo-a	née	this table
gah-fair	tôo-ay	nún	that cup of coffee
dtum-ròo-ut	kon	nóhn	that policeman over there

PRONOUNS

Personal Pronouns

There are many more personal pronouns in Thai than there are in English. The most useful pronouns are listed below. There is no distinction between subject and object pronouns in Thai:

pǒm (said by a man)	I, me
chún (said by a woman)	I, me
dee-chún (said by a woman)	I, me (more formal)
kOOn	you
káo	he, him; she, her; they, them
ráo	we, us
mun*	it

*Thais tend to avoid this as it is regarded as impolite in formal spoken Thai.

When appropriate, in the Basics and English-Thai sections of this book, the phrases show both the male and female forms. Where you have pǒm (chún) ('I' or 'me') in a phrase, pǒm should be used by a male speaker and chún by a female speaker.

Frequently pronouns are omitted altogether and it is only from the context that you will know who or what is being referred to. This sentence, for example,

doo	nǔng	láir-o	glùp	bâhn
see	film	already	return	home

could mean, 'after seeing a film, I/we/he/she/they went home'.

If you know a person's name, the polite way to address them or to speak about them is to use their first name and to place the word **k00n** in front of it:

> **k00n Chârt-chai mah jàhk năi?**
> where are you from?
> where is Chartchai from?

> **k00n Sŏm-chai séu a-rai?**
> what did you buy?
> what did Somchai buy?

POSSESSIVES

The equivalent of possessive pronouns and adjectives in Thai is as follows:

> noun + **kŏrng** + pronoun

The word **kŏrng** (of) however, is optional and frequently omitted:

> **pêu-un kŏrng káo** or **pêu-un káo**
> his/her/their friend

> **bâhn kŏrng pŏm** or **bâhn pŏm**
> my house

> **nûn kŏrng káo**
> that's his/hers/theirs

> **kŏrng chún**
> it's mine

Relative Pronouns

There is only one relative pronoun in Thai – **têe** – which translates as either 'who', 'which', 'that' or 'where'.

Here are some examples of how it is used:

> **kroo têe sŏrn pah-săh tai**
> the teacher, who teaches Thai

> **pŏn-la-mái têe rao séu**
> the fruit which we bought

> **órp-fit têe káo tum ngahn**
> the office where he works

VERBS

Verbs in Thai have a single fixed form. That is, unlike European languages, the form of the verb does not change according to the person or the tense. So, for example, **káo bpai** can mean 'he goes', 'he will go', 'he went' or 'he has gone'. Usually, the context in which you hear the verb will make it clear whether the speaker is referring to the past, present or future. But when it is important to be more specific, the context can be made clearer by placing a 'time-marker' word in front of or after the verb.

The most common and useful of these time-marker words are as follows:

ja
ja is placed immediately in front of the verb to indicate the future tense. For

example:

> chún ja bpai prôong née
> I shall go tomorrow

> rao ja séu rót mài
> we shall buy a new car

ker-ee

ker-ee is placed in front of the verb to indicate the fact of having done something at least once in the past. It can also mean 'used to (do something)':

> rao ker-ee bpai têe-o Chee-ung-mài
> we have been to (visit) Chiangmai

> káo ker-ee ree-un pah-săh tai
> he used to study Thai

> pŏm mâi ker-ee gin
> I have never eaten it

láir-o

láir-o is placed at the end of a clause or sentence to indicate a completed action in the past:

> káo gin kâo láir-o
> he has eaten

> chún doo láir-o
> I've seen (it)

gum-lung

gum-lung is placed in front of the verb to indicate the continuous present or past:

> káo gum-lung doo tee wee
> he is watching TV or he was watching TV

These time-marker words are often omitted when the time context is specified or is otherwise obvious:

> pŏm séu bpee gòrn
> I bought (it) last year

> rao bpai bpee nâh
> we are going next year

Negatives

To form a negative sentence, place the word mâi in front of the main verb:

> ah-hăhn a-ròy
> the food is tasty

> ah-hăhn mâi a-ròy
> the food is not tasty

> pŏm (chún) mee way-lah wâhng
> I have some free time

> pŏm (chún) mâi mee way-lah wâhng
> I don't have any free time

Imperative

To make the imperative or command form, add si (pronounced sí, see or sée) after the verb:

> doo sí
> look!

ra-wung sí
look out!

bpìt bpra-dtoo sí
close the door!

For negative commands
(don't ...), the word yàh is
placed in front of the verb:

yàh tum	don't do it
yàh bpai	don't go
yàh gin	don't eat

QUESTIONS, ANSWERS, YES AND NO

... mái? questions

A statement can be made into
a question by adding the
question particle mái at the
end of the sentence:

jèp
(it) hurts

jèp mái?
does it hurt?

bâhn yài
the house is big

bâhn yài mái?
is the house big?

To answer 'yes' to this type of
question, you simply repeat
the verb:

jèp mái?
does it hurt?

jèp
yes

bâhn yài mái?
is the house big?

yài
yes

If you want to say 'no', place
the negative word mâi in front
of the verb:

jèp mái?
does it hurt?

mâi jèp
no

bâhn yài mái?
is the house big?

mâi yài
no

... châi mái? questions

To form tag-questions in
Thai, equivalent to the
English, 'isn't it?' or 'aren't
they?' etc, add châi mái? to the
end of a sentence:

káo mâi mah, châi mái?
he's not coming, is he?

soy sǎhm sìp sǎhm, châi mái?
soi 33, isn't it?

The châi mái question form is
extremely useful for checking
that you have understood
what is going on. A 'yes'
answer to a châi mái? question
is châi. A 'no' answer is mâi
châi:

bpai láir-o, châi mái?
he's gone, hasn't he?

châi/mâi châi
yes/no

... rĕu bplào?
questions

Another common question form tags **rĕu bplào?** on to the end of a statement. Literally it means '... or not?', but it is not nearly as abrupt as such a translation suggests; it simply demands a straight answer:

k00n bpai doo rĕu bplào?
are you going to see (it) or not?

mee rĕu bplào?
are there (any) or not?

If you want to say 'yes' to this, repeat the main verb – that is **bpai** in the first example, and **mee** in the second; if you want to say 'no', the answer is **bplào**.

Other question words: who? what? where? why? how? how much? how many?

Here are the remaining question words with examples; note that in almost every example the question word occurs at the end of the sentence.

krai
who?
k00n bpai gùp krai?
who are you going with?

krai mâi bpai?
who isn't going?

a-rai
what?
nêe arai?
what's this?

k00n pôot arai?
what did you say?

têe nǎi
where?
káo púk yòo têe nǎi?
where is he staying?

hôrng náhm yòo têe nǎi?
where's the toilet?

tum-mai?
why?
káo bpai tum-mai?
why is he going?

yung-ngai?
how?
k00n ja tum yung-ngai?
how will you do (it)?

tâo-rài?
how much?
nêe tâo-rài?
how much is this?

gèe
how many?
bpai gèe krúng?
how many times did (you) go?

POLITE PARTICLES:
krúp, kâ, ká

An important way of making your speech sound polite in Thai is to use polite particles, which are untranslatable words placed at the end of a sentence. A male speaker should add the particle krúp to the end of both statements and questions to make them sound more polite, while a female speaker should add the particle kâ to the end of a statement and ká to the end of a question:

pŏm bpai prôông née krúp
I am going tomorrow (said by a man)

chún mâi bpai kâ
I am not going (said by a woman)

káo bpai năi krúp?
where is he going? (said by a man)

kOOn tum a-rai ká?
what are you doing? (said by a woman)

It is important to get into the habit of using the appropriate polite particle at the end of every sentence and question. In the English-Thai section, most of the phrases have been given without these particles and the appropriate

particle should be added. Sometimes, depending on the situation and person addressed, it is acceptable to omit the polite particles but until you are more familiar with the Thai language, it is better to use them all the time.

DATES

Dates are expressed using the pattern:

wun (day) + ordinal number + month

Ordinal numbers are formed by placing têe in front of the cardinal number. A list of numbers is given on page 21.

the first of July wun têe nèung
ga-rúk-ga-dah-kom
วันที่หนึ่งกรกฎาคม
the twentieth of March wun têe
yêe sìp mee-nah-kom
วันที่ยี่สิบมีนาคม
the twenty first of June wun têe
yêe sìp èt mí-too-nah-yon
วันที่ยี่สิบเอ็ดมิถุนายน

Thais use both the Western Gregorian calendar and a Buddhist calendar – Buddha is said to have attained enlightenment in the year 543BC, so Thai dates start from that point: thus 1996 AD becomes 2539 BE (Buddhist Era).

DAYS

Monday wun jun วันจันทร์
Tuesday wun ung-kahn
วันอังคาร
Wednesday wun póot วันพุธ
Thursday wun pá-réu-hùt
วันพฤหัส
Friday wun sùk วันศุกร์
Saturday wun sǎo วันเสาร์
Sunday wun ah-tít วันอาทิตย์

MONTHS

January mók-ga-rah-kom
มกราคม
February gOOm-pah-pun
กุมภาพันธ์
March mee-nah-kom มีนาคม
April may-sǎh-yon เมษายน
May préut-sa-pah-kom
พฤษภาคม
June mí-tOO-nah-yon มิถุนายน
July ga-rúk-ga-dah-kom
กรกฎาคม
August sǐng-hǎh-kom สิงหาคม
September gun-yah-yon
กันยายน
October dtOO-lah-kom ตุลาคม
November préut-sa-ji-gah-yon
พฤศจิกายน
December tun-wah-kom
ธันวาคม

TIME

The Thai system of telling the
time seems rather complicated
at first because it uses
different words for 'o'clock'
depending on what time of day

it is:

from 1 a.m. to 5 a.m.   dtee
from 6 a.m. to midday   mohng
                           cháo
from 1 p.m. to 4 p.m.   bài
from 5 p.m. to 6 p.m   yen
from 7 p.m. to midnight   tôom

Here, then, is how the hours
are expressed in Thai:

1 a.m. dtee nèung ตีหนึ่ง
2 a.m. dtee sǒrng ตีสอง
3 a.m. dtee sǎhm ตีสาม
4 a.m. dtee sèe ตีสี่
5 a.m. dtee hâh ตีห้า
6 a.m. hòk mohng cháo
หกโมงเช้า
7 a.m. jèt mohng cháo
เจ็ดโมงเช้า
  or mohng cháo โมงเช้า
8 a.m. bpàirt mohng cháo
แปดโมงเช้า
  or sǒrng mohng cháo
สองโมงเช้า
9 a.m. gâo mohng cháo
เก้าโมงเช้า
  or sǎhm mohng cháo
สามโมงเช้า
10 a.m. sìp mohng cháo
สิบโมงเช้า
  or sèe mohng cháo สี่โมงเช้า
11 a.m. sìp èt mohng cháo
สิบเอ็ดโมงเช้า
  or hâh mohng cháo
ห้าโมงเช้า
midday têe-ung wun เที่ยงวัน
1 p.m. bài mohng บ่ายโมง

2 p.m. bài sŏrng mohng
บ่ายสองโมง

3 p.m. bài săhm mohng
บ่ายสามโมง

4 p.m. bài sèe mohng บ่ายสี่โมง

5 p.m. hâh mohng yen
ห้าโมงเย็น

6 p.m. hòk mohng yen
หกโมงเย็น

7 p.m. tôom nèung ทุ่มหนึ่ง

8 p.m. sŏrng tôom สองทุ่ม

9 p.m. săhm tôom สามทุ่ม

10 p.m. sèe tôom สี่ทุ่ม

11 p.m. hâh tôom ห้าทุ่ม

midnight têe-ung keun เที่ยงคืน

Note: There is no equivalent of
'it is ...' in Thai when stating
the time; **săhm tôom** means
both '9 p.m.' and 'it is 9 p.m.'.

To say 'half-past', use the
word **krêung** (half). There is
no special word for 'quarter
past' or 'quarter to' the hour;
these are translated by
'fifteen minutes (past)' and
'fifteen minutes (to)' the
hour:

11.30 a.m sìp-èt mohng
krêung สิบเอ็ดโมงครึ่ง

3.30 p.m bài săhm mohng
krêung บ่ายสามโมงครึ่ง

11.30 p.m hâh tôom krêung
ห้าทุ่มครึ่ง

1.15 p.m bài mohng síp hâh
nah-tee บ่ายโมงสิบห้านาที

1.45 p.m èek sìp hâh nah-tee

bài sŏrng mohng
อีกสิบห้านาทีบ่ายสองโมง

Note that when expressing
minutes past the hour, the
word order is:

> hour time
> number of minutes
> **nah-tee** (minutes)

2.10 p.m bài sŏrng mohng sìp
nah-tee บ่ายสองโมงสิบนาที

8.25 p.m sŏrng tôom yêe sìp
hâh nah-tee สองทุ่มยี่สิบห้านาที

To express minutes to the
hour, the word order is as
follows:

> **èek** (further, more)
> number of minutes
> hour time

4.50 p.m èek sìp nah-tee hâh
mohng yen อีกสิบนาทีห้าโมงเย็น

10.55 p.m èek hâh nah-tee hâh
tôom อีกห้านาทีห้าทุ่ม

what time is it? gèe mohng láir-
o? กี่โมงแล้ว

hour chôo-a-mohng ชั่วโมง

minute nah-tee นาที

two minutes sŏrng nah-tee
สองนาที

second wí-nah-tee วินาที

a quarter of an hour sìp hâh
nah-tee สิบห้านาที

half an hour krêung chôo-a-
mohng ครึ่งชั่วโมง

three quarters of an hour sèe sìp
hâh nah-tee สี่สิบห้านาที

NUMBERS

0	sŏon	๐	ศูนย์
1	nèung	๑	หนึ่ง
2	sŏrng	๒	สอง
3	săhm	๓	สาม
4	sèe	๔	สี่
5	hâh	๕	ห้า
6	hòk	๖	หก
7	jèt	๗	เจ็ด
8	bpàirt	๘	แปด
9	gâo	๙	เก้า
10	sìp	๑๐	สิบ
11	sìp-èt	๑๑	สิบเอ็ด
12	sìp-sŏrng	๑๒	สิบสอง
13	sìp-săhm	๑๓	สิบสาม
14	sìp-sèe	๑๔	สิบสี่
15	sìp-hâh	๑๕	สิบห้า
16	sìp-hòk	๑๖	สิบหก
17	sìp-jèt	๑๗	สิบเจ็ด
18	sìp-bpàirt	๑๘	สิบแปด
19	sìp-gâo	๑๙	สิบเก้า
20	yêe-sìp	๒๐	ยี่สิบ
21	yêe-sìp-èt	๒๑	ยี่สิบเอ็ด
22	yêe-sìp-sŏrng	๒๒	ยี่สิบสอง
30	săhm-sìp	๓๐	สามสิบ
31	săhm-sìp-èt	๓๑	สามสิบเอ็ด
40	sèe-sìp	๔๐	สี่สิบ
50	hâh-sìp	๕๐	ห้าสิบ
60	hòk-sìp	๖๐	หกสิบ
70	jèt-sìp	๗๐	เจ็ดสิบ
80	bpàirt-sìp	๘๐	แปดสิบ
90	gâo-sìp	๙๐	เก้าสิบ
100	nèung róy	๑๐๐	หนึ่งร้อย
101	nèung róy nèung	๑๐๑ หนึ่งร้อยหนึ่ง	

102	nèung róy sŏrng	๑๐๒ หนึ่งร้อยสอง
110	nèung róy sìp	๑๑๐ หนึ่งร้อยสิบ
200	sŏrng róy	๒๐๐ สองร้อย
201	sŏrng róy nèung	๒๐๑ สองร้อยหนึ่ง
202	sŏrng róy sŏrng	๒๐๒ สองร้อยสอง
210	sŏrng róy sìp	๒๑๐ สองร้อยสิบ
1,000	nèung pun	๑๐๐๐ หนึ่งพัน
2,000	sŏrng pun	๒๐๐๐ สองพัน
10,000	nèung mèun	๑๐๐๐๐ หนึ่งหมื่น
100,000	nèung săirn	๑๐๐๐๐๐ หนึ่งแสน
1,000,000	nèung láhn	๑๐๐๐๐๐๐ หนึ่งล้าน
100,000,000	nèung róy láhn	๑๐๐๐๐๐๐๐๐ หนึ่งร้อยล้าน

Ordinals

1st	têe nèung	ที่หนึ่ง
2nd	têe sŏrng	ที่สอง
3rd	têe săhm	ที่สาม
4th	têe sèe	ที่สี่
5th	têe hâh	ที่ห้า
6th	têe hòk	ที่หก
7th	têe jèt	ที่เจ็ด
8th	têe bpàirt	ที่แปด
9th	têe gâo	ที่เก้า
10th	têe sìp	ที่สิบ

BASIC PHRASES

yes
krúp (kâ); châi
ครับ(ค่ะ) ใช่

no
mâi
ไม่

OK
oh-kay
โอเค

hello
sa-wùt dee
สวัสดี

hi!
bpai nǎi?
ไปไหน

good morning
sa-wùt dee krúp (kâ)
สวัสดีครับ(ค่ะ)

good evening
sa-wùt dee krúp (kâ)
สวัสดีครับ(ค่ะ)

good night
sa-wùt dee krúp (kâ)
สวัสดีครับ(ค่ะ)

goodbye
lah gòrn ná
ลาก่อนนะ

bye
lah gòrn
ลาก่อน

see you!
jer gun mài ná!
เจอกันใหม่นะ

see you later
dĕe-o jer gun èek
เดี๋ยวเจอกันอีก

please
 (requesting something)
kŏr ...
 ขอ ...

 (offering)
chern krúp (kâ)
 เชิญครับ(ค่ะ)

(could you) please ...?
chôo-ay ... nòy dâi mái?
ช่วย ... หน่อยได้ไหม

yes please
ao krúp (kâ)
เอาครับ(ค่ะ)

thanks, thank you
kòrp-kOOn
ขอบคุณ

no thanks, no thank you
mâi ao kòrp-kOOn
ไม่เอาขอบคุณ

thank you very much
kòrp-kOOn mâhk
ขอบคุณมาก

don't mention it
mâi bpen rai
ไม่เป็นไร

how do you do?
sa-wùt dee krúp (kâ)
สวัสดีครับ(ค่ะ)

how are you you?
bpen yung-ngai bâhng?
เป็นอย่างไรบ้าง

fine, thanks
sa-bai dee krúp (kâ)
สบายดีครับ(ค่ะ)

nice to meet you
yin dee têe dâi róo-jùk gun
ยินดีที่ได้รู้จักกัน

excuse me
(to get past, to say sorry) kŏr-tôht
ขอโทษ

(to get attention) kOOn krúp (kâ)
คุณครับ (ค่ะ)

(to say pardon?) a-rai ná?
อะไรนะ

I'm sorry
pŏm (chún) sĕe-a jai
ผม(ฉัน)เสียใจ

sorry?/pardon (me)?
(didn't understand) a-rai ná krúp
(ká)?
อะไรนะครับ(คะ)

I see/I understand
kâo jai láir-o
เข้าใจแล้ว

I don't understand
pŏm (chún) mâi kâo jai
ผม(ฉัน)ไม่เข้าใจ

do you speak English?
kOOn pôot pah-săh ung-gr%ìt
bpen mái?
คุณพูดภาษาอังกฤษเป็นไหม

I don't speak Thai
pŏm (chún) pôot pah-săh tai
mâi bpen
ผม(ฉัน)พูดภาษาไทยไม่เป็น

could you speak more slowly?
pôot cháh cháh nòy!
พูดช้า ๆ หน่อย

could you repeat that?
pôot èek tee dâi mái?
พูดอีกทีได้ไหม

could you write it down?
chôo-ay kěe-un long hâi nòy,
   dâi mái?
ช่วยเขียนลงให้หน่อยได้ไหม

I'd like a ...
pǒm (chún) ao ...
ผม(ฉัน)เอา ...

I'd like to ...
pǒm (chún) yàhk ...
ผม(ฉัน)อยาก ...

can I have ...?
kǒr ... dâi mái?
ขอ ... ได้ไหม

how much is it?
tâo-rài?
เท่าไร

it is ...
bpen ...
เป็น ...

where is it?
yòo têe nǎi?
อยู่ที่ไหน

is it far?
yòo glai mái?
อยู่ไกลไหม

CONVERSION TABLES

| 1 centimetre = 0.39 inches | 1 inch = 2.54 cm |

1 metre = 39.37 inches =
  1.09 yards

1 foot = 30.48 cm

1 yard = 0.91 m

1 kilometre = 0.62 miles =
  5/8 mile

1 mile = 1.61 km

km	1	2	3	4	5	10	20	30	40	50	100
miles	0.6	1.2	1.9	2.5	3.1	6.2	12.4	18.6	24.8	31.0	62.1

miles	1	2	3	4	5	10	20	30	40	50	100
km	1.6	3.2	4.8	6.4	8.0	16.1	32.2	48.3	64.4	80.5	161

1 gram = 0.035 ounces   1 kilo = 1000 g = 2.2 pounds

g	100	250	500
oz	3.5	8.75	17.5

1 oz = 28.35 g

1 lb = 0.45 kg

kg	0.5	1	2	3	4	5	6	7	8	9	10
lb	1.1	2.2	4.4	6.6	8.8	11.0	13.2	15.4	17.6	19.8	22.0

kg	20	30	40	50	60	70	80	90	100
lb	44	66	88	110	132	154	176	198	220

lb	0.5	1	2	3	4	5	6	7	8	9	10	20
kg	0.2	0.5	0.9	1.4	1.8	2.3	2.7	3.2	3.6	4.1	4.5	9.0

1 litre = 1.75 UK pints / 2.13 US pints

1 UK pint = 0.57 l   1 UK gallon = 4.55 l
1 US pint = 0.47 l   1 US gallon = 3.79 l

centigrade / Celsius $C = (F - 32) \times 5/9$

C	-5	0	5	10	15	18	20	25	30	36.8	38
F	23	32	41	50	59	65	68	77	86	98.4	100.4

Fahrenheit $F = (C \times 9/5) + 32$

F	23	32	40	50	60	65	70	80	85	98.4	101
C	-5	0	4	10	16	18	21	27	29	36.8	38.3

English - Thai

A

a, an*

about: about 20 **bpra-mahn**
yêe-sìp
ประมาณยี่สิบ

it's about 5 o'clock **bpra-mahn** hâh mohng yen
ประมาณห้าโมงเย็น

a film about Thailand nǔng rêu-ung meu-ung tai
หนังเรื่องเมืองไทย

above kâhng bon
ข้างบน

abroad dtàhng bpra-tâyt
ต่างประเทศ

absolutely (I agree) nâir-norn
แน่นอน

absorbent cotton sǔm-lee
สำลี

accelerator kun rêng
คันเร่ง

accept rúp
รับ

accident oo-bùt-dti-hàyt
อุบัติเหตุ

there's been an accident mee oo-bùt-dti-hàyt
มีอุบัติเหตุ

accommodation têe púk
ที่พัก

see **room** and **hotel**

accurate tòok-dtôrng
ถูกต้อง

ache bpòo-ut
ปวด

my back aches bpòo-ut lǔng
ปวดหลัง

across: across the ... kâhm ...
ข้าม ...

adapter (for voltage) krêu-ung bplairng fai fáh
เครื่องแปลงไฟฟ้า
(plug) bplúk
ปลั๊ก

address têe-yòo
ที่อยู่

what's your address? koon púk yòo têe-nǎi?
คุณพักอยู่ที่ไหน

Thai addresses can be confusing, mainly because property is often numbered twice, firstly to show which real estate lot it stands in, and then to distinguish where it is on that lot. In large cities a minor road running off a major road is often numbered as a soi ('lane' or 'alley', although it may be a sizeable thoroughfare), rather than given its own street name. Sukhumvit Road for example – Bangkok's longest – has minor roads numbered Soi 1 to Soi 103, with odd numbers on one side of the road and even on the →

other. Addresses are written as follows:

215/3 Sukhumwit 31
Bangkok 10110

which means no.3 on lot 215 on soi 31.

address book sa-mòot tee-yòo
สมุดที่อยู่

admission charge kâh kâo
ค่าเข้า

adult pôo-yài
ผู้ใหญ่

advance: in advance lôo-ung nâh
ล่วงหน้า

aeroplane krêu-ung bin
เครื่องบิน

after lŭng
หลัง

after you chern gòrn
เชิญก่อน

after lunch lŭng ah-hăhn glahng wun
หลังอาหารกลางวัน

afternoon dtorn bài
ตอนบ่าย

in the afternoon dtorn bài
ตอนบ่าย

this afternoon bài née
บ่ายนี้

aftershave yah tah lŭng gohn nòo-ut
ยาทาหลังโกนหนวด

aftersun cream yah tah lŭng àhp dàirt
ยาทาหลังอาบแดด

afterwards tee lŭng
ทีหลัง

again èek
อีก

against: I'm against it pŏm (chún) mâi hĕn dôo-ay
ผม(ฉัน)ไม่เห็นด้วย

age ah-yóo
อายุ

ago: a week ago ah-tít nèung mah láir-o
อาทิตย์หนึ่งมาแล้ว

an hour ago chôo-a mohng nèung mah láir-o
ชั่วโมงหนึ่งมาแล้ว

agree: I agree pŏm (chún) hĕn dôo-ay
ผม(ฉัน)เห็นด้วย

AIDS rôhk áyd
โรคเอดส์

air ah-gàht
อากาศ

by air tahng ah-gàht
ทางอากาศ

air-conditioning krêu-ung air
เครื่องแอร์

airmail: by airmail sòng tahng ah-gàht
ส่งทางอากาศ

airmail envelope sorng jòt-măi

ah-gàht
ของจดหมายอากาศ

airport sa-nǎhm bin
สนามบิน

to the airport, please bpai sa-
nǎhm bin
ไปสนามบิน

airport bus rót sa-nǎhm bin
รถสนามบิน

aisle seat têe nûng dtìt tahng
dern
ที่นั่งติดทางเดิน

alarm clock nah-li-gah bplòok
นาฬิกาปลุก

alcohol lâo
เหล้า

alcoholic kon kêe lâo mao yah
คนขี้เหล้าเมายา

all: all the boys pôo-chai tóok
kon
ผู้ชายทุกคน

all the girls pôo-yǐng tóok
kon
ผู้หญิงทุกคน

all of it túng mòt
ทั้งหมด

all of them tóok kon
ทุกคน

that's all, thanks sèt láir-o
kòrp-koon
เสร็จแล้วขอบคุณ

allergic: I'm allergic to ... pǒm
(chún) páir ...
ผม(ฉัน)แพ้ ...

allowed: is it allowed? un-nóo-
yâht mái?
อนุญาตไหม

all right mâi bpen rai
ไม่เป็นไร

I'm all right pǒm (chún) sa-
bai dee
ผม(ฉัน)สบายดี

are you all right? bpen yung-
ngai bâhng?
เป็นอย่างไรบ้าง

almost gèu-up
เกือบ

alone kon dee-o
คนเดียว

alphabet dtoo-a uk-sǒrn
ตัวอักษร

already ... láir-o ...
แล้ว

also dôo-ay
ด้วย

although máir wâh
แม้ว่า

altogether túng mòt
ทั้งหมด

always sa-měr
เสมอ

am*: I am ... pǒm (chún)
bpen ...
ผม(ฉัน)เป็น ...

a.m.: at six/seven a.m. hòk/jèt
mohng cháo
หก/เจ็ดโมงเช้า

amazing (surprising) mâi nâh

chêu-a
ไม่น่าเชื่อ
(very good) wi-sàyt
วิเศษ

ambulance rót pa-yah-bahn
รถพยาบาล
call an ambulance! rêe-uk rót
pa-yah-bahn!
เรียกรถพยาบาล
see police

America a-may-ri-gah
อเมริกา

American (adj) a-may-ri-gun
อเมริกัน
I'm American pǒm (chún)
bpen kon a-may-ri-gun
ผม(ฉัน)เป็นคนอเมริกัน

among nai ra-wàhng
ในระหว่าง

amount jum-noo-un
จำนวน

amp: a 13-amp fuse few sìp
sǎhm airm
ฟิวส์สิบสามแอมป์

and láir
และ

angry gròht
โกรธ

animal sùt
สัตว์

ankle kôr táo
ข้อเท้า

anniversary (wedding) wun cha-
lǒrng króp rôrp
วันฉลองครบรอบ

annoy: this man's annoying me
kon née tum hâi pǒm (chún)
rum-kahn
คนนี้ทำให้ผม(ฉัน)รำคาญ

annoying nâh rum-kahn
น่ารำคาญ

another èek
อีก
can we have another room?
kǒr bplèe-un hôrng nòy dâi
mái?
ขอเปลี่ยนห้องหน่อยได้ไหม
another beer, please kǒr bee-a
èek kòo-ut nèung
ขอเบียร์อีกขวดหนึ่ง

antibiotics yah bpùti-chee-wa-
ná
ยาปฏิชีวนะ

antihistamines yah airn-dtêe
hít-dta-meen
ยาแอนตีฮิสตะมีน

antique: is it an antique? bpen
kǒrng gào taír táir rěu
bplào?
เป็นของเก่าแท้ ๆ หรือเปล่า

antique shop ráhn kǎi kǒrng
gào
ร้านขายของเก่า

antiseptic yah kâh chéu-a
ยาฆ่าเชื้อ

any: have you got any bread/
tomatoes? mee ka-nǒm-
bpung/ma-kěu-a-tâyt mái?
มีขนมปัง/มะเขือเทศไหม
do you have any change? mee

sàyt sa-dtahng mái?
มีเศษสตางค์ไหม

sorry, I don't have any kŏr-
tôht pŏm (chún) mâi mee
ขอโทษผม(ฉัน)ไม่มี

anybody krai gôr dâi
ใครก็ได้

does anybody speak English?
mee **krai** pôot pah-săh ung-
grìt dâi?
มีใครพูดภาษาอังกฤษได้

there wasn't anybody there
mâi mee **krai** yòo têe nûn
ไม่มีใครอยู่ที่นั่น

anything a-rai gôr dâi
อะไรก็ได้

•••••• DIALOGUES ••••••

anything else? ao a-rai èek mái?

nothing else, thanks mâi ao krúp
(kâ)

would you like anything to drink?
dèum a-rai mái?

I don't want anything, thanks mâi
krúp (kâ)

apart from nôrk jàhk
นอกจาก

apartment a-páht-mén
อพาร์ตเม้นท์

apartment block dtèuk a-páht-
mén
ตึกอพาร์ตเม้นท์

apologize kŏr-tôht
ขอโทษ

appendicitis rôhk sâi dtìng
โรคไส้ติ่ง

apple air-bpêrn
แอปเปิล

appointment nút
นัด

•••••• DIALOGUE ••••••

good morning, how can I help you?
sa-wùt dee krúp mee a-rai ja hâi
chôo-ay mái krúp?

I'd like to make an appointment with
... yàhk nút póp gùp ...

what time would you like? yàhk dâi
way-lah tâo-rài?

three o'clock bài săhm mohng

I'm afraid that's not possible, is four
o'clock all right? kít wâh kong mâi
dâi ao bpen way-lah sèe mohng
dâi mái?

yes, that will be fine krúp dtòk-long

the name was? chêu a-rai krúp?

apricot ay-pri-kort
เอพริคอท

April may-săh-yon
เมษายน

are*: we are rao bpen
เราเป็น

you are koon bpen
คุณเป็น

they are káo bpen
เขาเป็น

area bor-ri-wayn
บริเวณ

area code ra-hùt
รหัส

arm kăirn
แขน

arrange: will you arrange it for us? chôo-ay **jùt gahn** hâi nòy dâi mái?
ช่วยจัดการให้หน่อยได้ไหม

arrival gahn mah těung
การมาถึง

arrive mah těung
มาถึง

when do we arrive? rao ja **těung** mêu-a rài?
เราจะถึงเมื่อไร

has my fax arrived yet? fairks kŏrng pŏm (chún) **mah** rěu yung?
แฟกซ์ของผม(ฉัน)มาหรือยัง

we arrived today rao **mah těung** wun née
เรามาถึงวันนี้

art sĭn-la-bpà
ศิลป

art gallery ráhn kăi pâhp kěe-un
ร้านขายภาพเขียน

artist sĭn-la-bpin
ศิลปิน

as: as big as yài tâo gùp
ใหญ่เท่ากับ

as soon as possible yàhng ray-o têe sòot têe ja ray-o dâi
อย่างเร็วที่สุดที่จะเร็วได้

ashtray têe kèe-a bOO-rèe
ที่เขี่ยบุหรี่

Asia ay-see-a
เอเชีย

ask tăhm
ถาม

I didn't ask for this pŏm (chún) mâi dâi **kŏr** ao un née
ผม(ฉัน)ไม่ได้ขอเอาอันนี้

could you ask him to ...? chôo-ay **bòrk hâi** káo ... dâi mái?
ช่วยบอกให้เขา ... ได้ไหม

asleep: she's asleep káo norn lùp yòo
เขานอนหลับอยู่

aspirin airt-pai-rin
แอสไพริน

asthma rôhk hèut
โรคหืด

astonishing nâh bpra-làht jai
น่าประหาดใจ

at: at the hotel **têe** rohng rairm
ที่โรงแรม

at the station **têe** sa-tăh-nee rót fai
ที่สถานีรถไฟ

at six o'clock **way-lah** hòk mohng
เวลาหกโมง

at Noi's **têe** bâhn kOOn nói
ที่บ้านคุณน้อย

athletics gree-tah
กรีฑา

attractive sǒo-ay
สวย

aubergine ma-kěu-a
มะเขือ

August sǐng-hǎh-kom
สิงหาคม

aunt (elder sister of mother/father)
bpâh
ป้า
(younger sister of father) ah
อา
(younger sister of mother) náh
นา

Australia órt-sa-tray-lee-a
ออสเตรเลีย

Australian (adj) órt-sa-tray-
lee-a
ออสเตรเลีย
I'm Australian pǒm (chún)
bpen kon órt-sa-tray-lee-a
ผม(ฉัน)เป็นคนออสเตรเลีย

automatic ùt-dta-noh-mút
อัตโนมัติ
(car) rót ùt-dta-noh-mút
รถอัตโนมัติ

automatic teller bor-ri-gahn
ngern dòo-un
บริการเงินด่วน

autumn réu-doo bai-mái rôo-
ung
ฤดูใบไม้ร่วง
in the autumn dtorn réu-doo
bai-mái rôo-ung
ตอนฤดูใบไม้ร่วง

average tum-ma-dah
ธรรมดา
on average doy-ee cha-
lèe-a
โดยเฉลี่ย

awake: is he awake? káo **dtèun**
láir-o rěu yung?
เขาตื่นแล้วหรือยัง

away: go away! bpái!
ไป
is it far away? yòo glai mái?
อยู่ไกลไหม

awful yâir mâhk
แย่มาก

axle plao
เพลา

B

baby dèk òrn
เด็กอ่อน

baby food ah-hǎhn dèk
อาหารเด็ก

baby's bottle kòo-ut nom
ขวดนม

baby-sitter kon fâo dèk
คนเฝ้าเด็ก

back (of body) lǔng
หลัง
(back part) kâhng lǔng
ข้างหลัง
at the back kâhng lǔng
ข้างหลัง
can I have my money back?

kŏr ngern keun dâi mái?
ขอเงินคืนได้ไหม
to come/go back glùp mah/
glùp bpai
กลับมา/กลับไป

backache bpòo-ut lǔng
ปวดหลัง

bacon mŏo bay-korn
หมูเบคอน

bad mâi dee
ไม่ดี
a bad headache bpòo-ut hǒo-
a mâhk
ปวดหัวมาก

badly mâi dee
ไม่ดี

bag tǒong
ถุง
(handbag) gra-bpǎo těu
กระเป๋าถือ
(suitcase) gra-bpǎo dern
tahng
กระเป๋าเดินทาง

baggage gra-bpǎo
กระเป๋า

baggage check têe fàhk gra-
bpǎo
ที่ฝากกระเป๋า

baggage claim sǎi pahn lum-
lee-ung gra-bpǎo
สายพานลำเลียงกระเป๋า

bakery ráhn tum ka-nǒm-
bpung
ร้านทำขนมปัง

balcony ra-bee-ung
ระเบียง
a room with a balcony hôrng
mee ra-bee-ung
ห้องมีระเบียง

ball lôok born
ลูกบอล

ballpoint pen bpàhk-gah lôok
lêun
ปากกาลูกลื่น

bamboo mái pài
ไม้ไผ่

bamboo shoot(s) nòr mái
หน่อไม้

banana glôo-ay
กล้วย

band (musical) wong don-dtree
วงดนตรี

bandage pâh pun plǎir
ผ้าพันแผล

Bandaids® plah-sa-dter
พลาสเตอร์

Bangkok groong-tâyp
กรุงเทพฯ

bank (money) ta-nah-kahn
ธนาคาร

Banking hours are Monday to
Friday from 8.30 a.m. to 3.30
p.m., but exchange kiosks are
always open till at least 5 p.m.,
sometimes 10 p.m. Upmarket
hotels will change money 24
hours a day and the Don Muang
→

airport exchange counter also operates 24 hours, so there's little point in buying baht before you arrive, especially as it takes seven working days to order from most banks outside Thailand.

Anyone entering Thailand is officially required to bring a minimum amount of foreign currency with them, a sum that varies with the class of visa. If you import Thai money, you're restricted to a paltry B2000 cash per person or B4000 per family; when you leave you're supposed to export no more than B500/B1000 without prior authorization.

bank account bun-chee ngern fàhk ta-nah-kahn
ปัญชีเงินฝากธนาคาร
bar bah
บาร์

'Bars' to most Thais are places where foreign men go for alcohol and hired female company. In Bangkok, however, there are several 'yuppie' bars, where young, affluent Thai professionals drink expensive foreign →

whisky and brandy to a background of sentimental music, as well as a fair number of Western-style bars catering to serious drinkers of all backgrounds. Beer and whisky can be ordered at virtually any time of the day in food shops, coffee shops, guesthouses and restaurants.

barber's châhng dtùt pŏm
ช่างตัดผม
bargaining gahn dtòr rah-kah
การต่อราคา

Bargaining or haggling over the price of goods is essential in markets or at pavement stalls, but in most shops it is inappropriate. When travelling by tuk-tuk (three-wheeled motorized pedicab) it is important to negotiate a price before the journey begins. Most taxis in Bangkok have meters, but in provincial towns be prepared to haggle. It is important to remember, however, that bargaining should be carried out in a good-humoured manner. Losing your temper, or trying to drive an unreasonably hard →

bargain will not help to seal a deal, while an offended tuk-tuk driver will be only too willing to give the tight-fisted the scariest ride of their life.

•••••• DIALOGUE ••••••

how much is this? nêe tâo-rài?

500 baht hâh ròy bàht

that's too expensive pairng bpai nòy

how about 400? sèe róy dâi mái?

I'll let you have it for 450 kít sèe róy hâh sìp gôr láir-o gun

can't you reduce it a bit more?/OK it's a deal lót èek mâi dâi lěu?/oh kay, dtòk long

basket dta-grâh
ตะกร้า

bath àhng àhp náhm
อ่างอาบน้ำ

can I have a bath? kǒr àhp náhm dâi mái?
ขออาบน้ำได้ไหม

bathroom hôrng náhm
ห้องน้ำ

with a private bathroom hôrng norn têe mee hôrng náhm dôo-ay
ห้องนอนที่มีห้องน้ำด้วย

bath towel pâh chét dtoo-a
ผ้าเช็ดตัว

bathtub àhng àhp náhm
อ่างอาบน้ำ

battery bair-dta-rêe
แบตเตอรี่

bay ào
อ่าว

be* bpen
เป็น

beach chai hàht
ชายหาด

on the beach tee chai haht
ที่ชายหาด

Topless bathing/sunbathing is not something that will win a great deal of respect from Thais. Indeed, sunbathing is not to be recommended at all in Thailand because of the heat. Wearing protective clothing is a good idea when swimming, snorkelling or diving: a T-shirt will stop you from getting sunburnt in the water, while long trousers can guard against coral grazes. Thailand's seas are home to a few dangerous creatures, such as jellyfish, poisonous sea snakes, sea urchins, stingrays and stone fish, whose potentially lethal venomous spikes are easily stepped on because the fish look like stones. If stung or bitten you should always seek medical advice as soon as possible.

beach mat sèu-a bpoo chai-
hàht
เสื่อปูชายหาด

beach umbrella rôm gun dàirt
ร่มกันแดด

beans tòo-a
ถั่ว

beansprouts tòo-a ngôrk
ถั่วงอก

beard krao
เครา

beautiful sŏo-ay
สวย

because prór
เพราะ

because of ... neû-ung jàhk ...
เนื่องจาก ...

bed dtee-ung
เตียง

I'm going to bed now pŏm
(chún) bpai norn
ผม(ฉัน)ไปนอน

bedroom hôrng norn
ห้องนอน

beef néu-a woo-a
เนื้อวัว

beer bee-a
เบียร์

two beers, please kŏr bee-a
sŏrng kòo-ut
ขอเบียร์สองขวด

Beer is one of the few consumer items in Thailand that's not a bargain: it works out roughly the same as what you'd pay in the West. The most popular beers are the locally-brewed **Singha**, and **Kloster** and **Carlsberg**, which are brewed in Thailand under German licence and cost slightly more than Singha. Some places also stock a lighter version of Singha called **Singha Gold** and another beer called **Amarit**, though that's not widely available.

before gòrn
ก่อน

begin rêrm
เริ่ม

when does it begin? rêrm
mêu-a rài?
เริ่มเมื่อไร

beginner pôo rêrm ree-un
ผู้เริ่มเรียน

beginning: at the beginning
dtorn dtôn
ตอนต้น

behind kâhng lăng
ข้างหลัง

behind me kâhng lăng pŏm
(chún)
ข้างหลังผม(ฉัน)

Belgian (adj) bayl-yee-um
เบลเยียม

Belgium bpra-tâyt bayl-yee-um
ประเทศเบลเยียม

below dtâi
ใต้

belt kĕm kùt
เข็มขัด

bend (in road) tahng kóhng
ทางโค้ง

berth (on ship) têe-norn
ที่นอน

beside: beside the ... kâhng
kâhng ...
ข้างๆ ...

best dee têe sòot
ดีที่สุด

better dee gwàh
ดีกว่า

are you feeling better? kôy
yung chôo-a mái?
ค่อยยังชั่วไหม

between ra-wàhng
ระหว่าง

beyond ler-ee bpai
เลยไป

bicycle jùk-gra-yahn
จักรยาน

big yài
ใหญ่

too big yài gern bpai
ใหญ่เกินไป

it's not big enough yài mâi por
ใหญ่ไม่พอ

bike jùk-gra-yahn
จักรยาน

(motorbike) jùk-gra-yahn-
yon
จักรยานยนตร์

bikini bi-gi-nee
บิกินี

bill bin
บิล

(US) bai báirng
ใบแบ้งค์

could I have the bill, please?
chék bin
เช็คบิล

If you go out for a meal with a
group of people, it is normal for
the host or the most senior person present to pick up the bill.
It is not usual to split the bill.

bin tŭng ka-yà
ถังขยะ

bin liners tǒong ka-yà
ถุงขยะ

bird nók
นก

birthday wun gèrt
วันเกิด

happy birthday! oo-ay-porn
wun gèrt!
อวยพรวันเกิด

biscuit kóok-gêe
คุกกี้

bit: a little bit nít-nòy
นิดหน่อย
a big bit chín yài
ชิ้นใหญ่
a bit of ... ... chín
nèung ...
ชิ้นหนึ่ง
a bit expensive pairng bpai
nòy
แพงไปหน่อย
bite (by insect, dog) gùt
กัด
bitter (taste etc) kǒm
ขม
black sěe dum
สีดำ
blanket pâh hòm
ผ้าห่ม
bleach (for toilet) yah láhng
hôrng náhm
ยาล้างห้องน้ำ
blind dtah bòrt
ตาบอด
blinds môo-lêe
มู่ลี่
blister plǎir porng
แผลพอง
blocked (road, pipe, sink) dtun
ตัน
blond (adj) pǒm sěe torng
ผมสีทอง
blood lêu-ut
เลือด
high blood pressure kwahm

dun loh-hìt sǒong
ความดันโลหิตสูง
blouse sêu-a pôo-yǐng
เสื้อผู้หญิง
blow-dry bpào pǒm
เป่าผม
I'd like a cut and blow-dry
yàhk hâi dtùt láir bpào pǒm
อยากให้ตัดและเป่าผม
blue sěe núm ngern
สีน้ำเงิน
boarding pass bùt têe-nûng
บัตรที่นั่ง
boat reu-a
เรือ
body râhng-gai
ร่างกาย
boiled egg kài dtôm
ไข่ต้ม
boiled rice kâo sǒo-ay
ข้าวสวย
boiler môr náhm
หม้อน้ำ
bone gra-dòok
กระดูก
bonnet (of car) gra-bprohng rót
กระโปรงรถ
book (noun) núng-sěu
หนังสือ
(verb) jorng
จอง
can I book a seat? kǒr jorng
têe-nûng dâi mái?
ขอจองที่นั่งได้ไหม

•••••• DIALOGUE ••••••

I'd like to book a table for two yàhk
jorng dtó sǔm-rùp sǒrng kon
what time would you like it booked
for? ja jorng way-lah tâo-rài?
half past seven tóom krêung
that's fine dâi krúp
and your name? chêu a-rai krúp?

bookshop, bookstore ráhn kǎi
núng-sěu
ร้านขายหนังสือ

boot (footwear) rorng-táo
รองเท้า
(of car) gra-bprohng tái rót
กระโปรงท้ายรถ

border (of country) chai-dairn
ชายแดน

bored: I'm bored pǒm (chún)
bèu-a
ผม(ฉัน)เบื่อ

boring nâh bèu-a
น่าเบื่อ

born: I was born in Manchester
pǒm (chún) gèrt têe
Manchester
ผม(ฉัน)เกิดที่ Manchester
I was born in 1960 pǒm
(chún) gèrt bpee nèung pun
gâo róy hòk sìp
ผม(ฉัน)เกิดปีหนึ่งพันเก้าร้อย
หกสิบ

borrow yeum
ยืม
may I borrow ...? kǒr yeum ...

dâi mái?
ขอยืม ... ได้ไหม

both túng sǒrng
ทั้งสอง

bother: sorry to bother you kǒr-
tôht têe róp-goo-un
ขอโทษที่รบกวน

bottle kòo-ut
ขวด

bottle-opener têe bpèrt kòo-ut
ที่เปิดขวด

bottom (of person) gôn
ก้น
at the bottom of the hill
cherng kǎo
เชิงเขา
at the bottom of the street
bplai ta-nǒn
ปลายถนน

bowl chahm
ชาม

box hèep
หีบ

box office hôrng kǎi dtǒo-a
ห้องขายตั๋ว

boy pôo-chai
ผู้ชาย

boyfriend fairn
แฟน

bra sêu-a yók song
เสื้อยกทรง

bracelet gum-lai meu
กำไลมือ

brake bràyk
เบรค

brandy lâo brùn-dee
เหล้าบรั่นดี

bread ka-nŏm-bpung
ขนมปัง

break (verb) dtàirk
แตก

I've broken the ... pŏm (chún)
tum ... dtàirk
ผม(ฉัน)ทำ ... แตก

I think I've broken my wrist
pŏm (chún) kít wâh kôr meu
hùk
ผม(ฉัน)คิดว่าข้อมือหัก

break down sĕe-a
เสีย

I've broken down (car) rót
pŏm (chún) sĕe-a
รถผม(ฉัน)เสีย

breakdown service bor-ri-gahn
sôrm
บริการซ่อม

breakfast ah-hăhn cháo
อาหารเช้า

break-in: I've had a break-in mee
ka-moy-ee kâo bâhn
มีขโมยเข้าบ้าน

breast nom
นม

breathe hăi jai
หายใจ

breeze lom òrn òrn
ลมอ่อนๆ

bridge (over river) sa-pahn
สะพาน

brief sûn
สั้น

briefcase gra-bpăo
กระเป๋า

bright (light etc) sa-wàhng
สว่าง

bright red dairng jùt
แดงจัด

brilliant (idea) yêe-um
เยี่ยม

bring ao ... mah
เอา ... มา

I'll bring it back later ja keun
hâi tee lŭng
จะคืนให้ทีหลัง

Britain bpra-tâyt ung-grìt
ประเทศอังกฤษ

British ung-grìt
อังกฤษ

brochure rai la-èe-ut
รายละเอียด

broken dtàirk láir-o
แตกแล้ว

bronchitis lòrt lom ùk-
sàyp
หลอดลมอักเสบ

brooch kĕm glùt sêu-a
เข็มกลัดเสื้อ

broom mái gwàht
ไม้กวาด

brother (older) pêe chai
พี่ชาย

(younger) nórng chai
น้องชาย

brother-in-law (older) pêe kĕr-ee
พี่เขย

(younger) nórng kĕr-ee
น้องเขย

brown sĕe núm dtahn
สีน้ำตาล

bruise fók-chúm
ฟกช้ำ

brush (for hair) bprairng pŏm
แปรงผม

(artist's) bprairng
แปรง

(for cleaning) mái gwàht
ไม้กวาด

bucket tŭng
ถัง

Buddha prá-póot-ta-jâo
พระพุทธเจ้า

Buddhism sàh-sa-năh póot
ศาสนาพุทธ

Buddhism plays an essential part in the lives of most Thais, and Buddhist monuments should be treated accordingly – which means wearing long trousers or knee-length skirts, covering your arms, and removing your shoes whenever you visit one. All Buddha images are sacred, however small, and should never be used as a backdrop for a portrait photo, →

clambered over, or treated in any manner that could be construed as disrespectful.

Buddhist (noun) chao póot
ชาวพุทธ

buffet car rót sa-bee-ung
รถเสบียง

buggy (for child) rót kĕn dèk
รถเข็นเด็ก

building ah-kahn
อาคาร

bulb (light bulb) lòrt fai fáh
หลอดไฟฟ้า

bumper gun chon
กันชน

bungalow bung-gah-loh
บังกาโล

bureau de change bor-ri-gahn
lâirk ngern
บริการแลกเงิน
see bank

burglary ka-moy-ee kâo bâhn
ขโมยเข้าบ้าน

Burma bpra-tâyt pa-mâh
ประเทศพม่า

Burmese pa-mâh
พม่า

burn (noun) plăir mâi
แผลไหม้

burnt: this is burnt un née mâi
อันนี้ไหม้

burst: a burst pipe tôr dtàirk
ท่อแตก

bus rót may
รถเมล์
what number bus is it to ...?
rót bpai ... ber tâo-rài?
รถไป ... เบอร์เท่าไร
when is the next bus to ...? rót
têe-o nâh bpai ... òrk gèe
mohng?
รถเที่ยวหน้าไป ... ออกกี่โมง
what time is the last bus? rót
têe-o sòot tái òrk gèe
mohng?
รถเที่ยวสุดท้ายออกกี่โมง

Buses, overall the fastest way of
getting around the country,
come in two categories: ordinary
(rót tum-ma-dah) and air-
conditioned (rót air), with an
additional 'air-con' subsection
misleadingly known as tour
buses (rót too-a), which are
privately owned and ply the
most popular long-distance
routes. The orange-coloured ordinary buses are incredibly
cheap and cover most short-
range routes between main
towns, but they have frequent
stops. 'Air-con' buses stop a lot
less often (if at all) and cover
the distances faster and more
comfortably. On the downside,
→

they cost almost twice as much,
depart less frequently, and don't
cover nearly as many routes.
In rural areas, the bus network
is supplemented by songthaews
(literally: two rows), which are
open-ended vans with two facing benches, onto which the
drivers squash as many passengers as possible. (In the deep
south they do things with a little more style – the longer-dis-
tance songthaews there are
known as share taxis, and are
usually old limousines.)
Songthaews ply set routes
within and between towns; to
pick one up between destina-
tions just flag it down. As a general rule, the cost of inter-town
songthaews is comparable to
that of 'air-con' buses.

•••••• DIALOGUE ••••••
does this bus go to ...? rót kun née
bpai ... mái?
no, you need a number ... mâi bpai
koon dtôrng kêun mǎi-lâyk ...

business tóo-rá
ธุระ
bus station sa-tǎh-nee rót
may
สถานีรถเมล์

bus stop **bpâi rót may**
ป้ายรถเมล์

bust **nâh òk**
หน้าอก

busy (restaurant etc) **nâirn**
แน่น

I'm busy tomorrow **prôong née mee tóo-rá**
พรุ่งนี้มีธุระ

but **dtàir**
แต่

butcher's **ráhn néu-a**
ร้านเนื้อ

butter **ner-ee sòt**
เนยสด

button **gra-dOOm**
กระดุม

buy **séu**
ซื้อ

where can I buy ...? **pǒm (chún) séu ... dâi têe nǎi?**
ผม(ฉัน)ซื้อ ... ได้ที่ไหน

by: by bus/car **doy-ee rót may/rót yon**
โดยรถเมล์/รถยนต์

written by ... **kěe-un doy-ee ...**
เขียนโดย ...

by the window **glâi nâh-dtàhng**
ใกล้หน้าต่าง

by the sea **chai ta-lay**
ชายทะเล

by Monday **gòrn wun jun**
ก่อนวันจันทร์

bye **lah gòrn**
ลาก่อน

C

cabbage **ga-lùm-bplee**
กะหล่ำปลี

café see **coffee shop** and **restaurant**

cake **ka-nǒm káyk**
ขนมเค้ก

call (verb) **rêe-uk**
เรียก

(to phone) **toh-ra-sùp, toh**
โทรศัพท์, โทร

what's it called? **rêe-uk wâh a-rai?**
เรียกว่าอะไร

he/she is called ... **káo chêu ...**
เขาชื่อ ...

please call the doctor **chôo-ay rêe-uk mǒr hâi nòy**
ช่วยเรียกหมอให้หน่อย

please give me a call at 7.30 a.m. tomorrow **chôo-ay toh mah way-lah jèt mohng krêung ná**
ช่วยโทรมาเวลาเจ็ดโมงครึ่ง

please ask him to call me **chôo-ay hâi káo toh mah**
ช่วยให้เขาโทรมา

call back: I'll call back later dĕe-o
ja **toh mah mài**
เดี๋ยวจะโทรมาใหม่

call round: I'll call round
tomorrow prôong née ja
wáir mah hăh
พรุ่งนี้จะแวะมาหา

Cambodia bpra-tâyt gum-poo-
chah
ประเทศกัมพูชา

Cambodian (adj) ka-măyn
เขมร

camcorder glôrng bun-téuk
pâhp
กล้องบันทึกภาพ

camera glôrng tài rôop
กล้องถ่ายรูป

camera shop ráhn kăi glôrng
tài rôop
ร้านขายกล้องถ่ายรูป

---

camping

You can usually camp in a
national park for a minimal fee
and some national parks also
rent out tents. Unless you're
planning an extensive tour of
national parks though, there's
little point in lugging a tent
around Thailand: accommodation everywhere else is too
cheap to make camping a neces-
sity, and anyway there are
no campsites inside town
→

---

perimeters. Few travellers
bother to bring tents for beaches
either, opting for cheap bungalow accommodation or simply
sleeping out under the stars. But
camping is allowed on nearly all
islands and beaches, many of
which are national parks in their
own right.

---

can gra-bpŏrng
กระป๋อง
a can of beer bee-a gra-
bpŏrng
เบียร์กระป๋อง

can*: can you ...? kOOn ... dâi
mái?
คุณ ... ได้ไหม
can I have ...? kŏr ... dâi mái?
ขอ ... ได้ไหม
I can't ... pŏm (chún) ... mâi
dâi
ผม(ฉัน) ... ไม่ได้

Canada bpra-tâyt kairn-nah-
dah
ประเทศแคนาดา

Canadian (adj) kair-nah-dah
แคนาดา
I'm Canadian pŏm (chún)
bpen kon kair-nah-dah
ผม(ฉัน)เป็นคนแคนาดา

canal klorng
คลอง

cancel ngót
งด

candies tórp-fêe
ท็อฟฟี่

candle tee-un
เทียน

can-opener têe bpèrt gra-
bpòrng
ที่เปิดกระป๋อง

cap (hat) mòo-uk
หมวก

car rót yon
รถยนต์

by car doy-ee rót yon
โดยรถยนต์

carburettor kah-ber-ret-dtêr
คาร์บูเรเตอร์

card (business) nahm bùt
นามบัตร

here's my card nêe nahm bùt
pŏm (chún)
นี่นามบัตรผม(ฉัน)

cardigan sêu-a năo
เสื้อหนาว

careful ra-mút ra-wung
ระมัดระวัง

be careful! ra-wung ná!
ระวังนะ

caretaker kon fâo bâhn
คนเฝ้าบ้าน

car ferry pair chái bun-
tóok rót-yon kâhm
fâhk
แพใช้บรรทุกรถยนต์ข้ามฟาก

car hire bor-ri-gahn rót châo
บริการรถเช่า

see **driving** and **rent**

carnival ngahn
งาน

car park têe jòrt rót
ที่จอดรถ

carpet prom
พรม

car rental bor-ri-gahn rót châo
บริการรถเช่า

see **driving** and **rent**

carriage (of train) dtôo rót fai
ตู้รถไฟ

carrier bag tŏong hêw
ถุงหิ้ว

carrot hŏo-a pùk-gàht dairng
หัวผักกาดแดง

carry (something in the hands) tĕu
ถือ

(something by a handle) hêw
หิ้ว

(a heavy load on the back or shoulder)
bàirk
แบก

(a child, in one's arms) ôom
อุ้ม

carry-cot dta-grâh sài dèk
ตะกร้าใส่เด็ก

carton glòrng
กล่อง

carwash bor-ri-gahn láhng rót
บริการล้างรถ

case (suitcase) gra-bpăo dern

tahng
กระเป๋าเดินทาง

cash (noun) ngern sòt
เงินสด

(verb) kêun ngern
ขึ้นเงิน

will you cash this for me?
chôo-ay bpai **kêun ngern**
hâi nòy dâi mái?
ช่วยไปขึ้นเงินให้หน่อยได้ไหม

cash desk dtó jài ngern
โต๊ะจ่ายเงิน

cash dispenser bor-ri-gahn
ngern dòo-un
บริการเงินด่วน

cassette móo-un tâyp kah-set
ม้วนเทปคาสเซ็ท

cassette recorder krêu-ung lên
tâyp kah-set
เครื่องเล่นเทปคาสเซ็ท

castle bprah-sàht
ปราสาท

casualty department pa-nàirk
oo-bùt-dti-hàyt chòok
chěrn
แผนกอุบัติเหตุฉุกเฉิน

cat mair-o
แมว

catch (verb) jùp
จับ

where do we catch the bus
to ...? rao kêun rót may
bpai ... têe nǎi?
เราขึ้นรถเมล์ไป ... ที่ไหน

Catholic (adj) káirt-oh-lík
แคทอลิก

cauliflower dòrk ga-lùm-
bplee
ดอกกะหล่ำปลี

cave tûm
ถ้ำ

ceiling pay-dahn
เพดาน

cemetery bpàh cháh
ป่าช้า

centigrade* sen-dti-gràyd
เซ็นติเกรด

centimetre* sen-dti-mét
เซ็นติเมตร

central glahng
กลาง

centre sǒon glahng
ศูนย์กลาง

how do we get to the city
centre? bpai sǒon glahng
meu-ung yung-ngai?
ไปศูนย์กลางเมืองอย่างไร

certainly nâir-norn
แน่นอน

certainly not! mâi ròrk!
ไม่หรอก

chair gâo êe
เก้าอี้

champagne chairm-bpayn
แชมเปญ

change (noun: money) sàyt sa-
dtahng
เศษสตางค์

change (verb: money) bplèe-un
เปลี่ยน
can I change this for ...? kŏr
lâirk âi nêe bpen ... dâi mái?
ขอแลกไอ้นี่เป็น ... ได้ไหม
I don't have any change pŏm
(chún) mâi mee **báirnk yôy
yôy**
ผม(ฉัน)ไม่มีแบงค์ย่อยๆ
can you give me change for a
100 baht note? kŏr dtàirk bai
la róy nòy, dâi mái?
ขอแตกใบละร้อยหน่อยได้ไหม

•••••• DIALOGUE ••••••

do we have to change (trains)?
dtôrng **bplèe-un** rót fai rĕu
bplào?
yes, change at Bang Krathum/no it's
a direct train dtôrng, dtôrng
bplèe-un têe bahng gra-toom/
mâi dtôrng, bpen rót dtrong

changed: to get changed bplèe-
un sêu-a
เปลี่ยนเสื้อ
charge (noun) kâh
ค่า
(verb) kít kâh
คิดค่า
charge card see credit card
cheap tòok
ถูก
do you have anything cheaper?
mee a-rai tòok gwàh rĕu

bplào?
มีอะไรถูกกว่าหรือเปล่า
check (verb) chék doo
เช็คดู
could you check the ..., please?
chôo-ay chék doo ... nòy, dâi
mái?
ช่วยเช็คดู ... หน่อยได้ไหม
check (US: noun) chék
เช็ค
(US: bill) bin
บิล
see cheque and bill
check book sa-mòot chék
สมุดเช็ค
check-in dtròo-ut chûng núm-
nùk
ตรวจชั่งน้ำหนัก
check in: where do we have to
check in? rao dtôrng 'check
in' têe năi?
เราต้อง 'check in' ที่ไหน
cheek (on face) gâirm
แก้ม
cheerio! wùt dee hâ!
วัสดีฮ่ะ
cheese ner-ee kăirng
เนยแข็ง
chemist's ráhn kăi yah
ร้านขายยา
see pharmacy
cheque chék
เช็ค
do you take cheques? jai bpen

chék, dâi mái?
จ่ายเป็นเช็คได้ไหม

The safest and most economical way to carry your money is in traveller's cheques. Sterling and dollar cheques issued by American Express or Visa are accepted by banks, exchange booths and upmarket hotels in every sizeable town, and most places also deal in a variety of other currencies. Everyone offers better rates for cheques than for cash and they generally charge a minimal commission per cheque – though kiosks and hotels in isolated places may charge extra.

---

cheque book sa-mòot chék
สมุดเช็ค

cheque card bùt chék
บัตรเช็ค

cherry cher-rêe
เชอรี่

chess màhk róok
หมากรุก

chest nâh òk
หน้าอก

chewing gum màhk fa-rùng
หมากฝรั่ง

Chiangmai? chee-ung mài
เชียงใหม่

chicken gài
ไก่

chickenpox ee-sòok ee-săi
อีสุกอีใส

child dèk
เด็ก

child minder kon lée-ung doo dèk
คนเลี้ยงดูเด็ก

children's pool sà wâi náhm dèk
สระว่ายน้ำเด็ก

chilli prík
พริก

chin kahng
คาง

Chinese (adj) jeen
จีน

chips mun fa-rùng tôrt
มันฝรั่งทอด

chocolate chork-goh-lairt
ช๊อกโกเลต

choose lêu-uk
เลือก

chopsticks dta-gèe-up
ตะเกียบ

Christian name chêu
ชื่อ

Christmas krít-sa-maht
คริสต์มาส

church bòht
โบส

cigar si-gah
ซิการ์

cigarette boo-rèe
บุหรี่

cigarette lighter fai cháirk
ไฟแช็ค

cinema rohng nǔng
โรงหนัง

Cinemas in Bangkok will often have four or five showings of a film in one day. Tickets can be booked in advance from the box office in the foyer. In the capital it is often possible to catch the latest American and European films with English soundtracks and Thai subtitles. The national anthem is played at the beginning and end of each showing; everyone stands to attention during this.

circle wong glom
วงกลม

city meu-ung
เมือง

city centre jai glahng meu-ung
ใจกลางเมือง

clean (adj) sa-àht
สะอาด

can you clean these for me?
tum kwahm sa-àht nêe hâi nòy dâi mái?
ทำความสะอาดนี้ให้หน่อยได้ไหม

cleaning solution (for contact lenses)

núm yah tum kwahm sa-àht
น้ำยาทำความสะอาด

cleansing lotion núm yah tum kwahm sa-àht
น้ำยาทำความสะอาด

clear chút
ชัด

(obvious) hěn dâi chút
เห็นได้ชัด

clever cha-làht
ฉลาด

cliff nâh pǎh
หน้าผา

clinic klee-ník
คลีนิค

cloakroom têe fàhk kǒrng
ที่ฝากของ

clock nah-li-gah
นาฬิกา

close (verb) bpìt
ปิด

• • • • • • DIALOGUE • • • • • •

what time do you close? kOOn bpìt gèe mohng?

we close at 8 p.m. on weekdays and 6 p.m. on Saturdays rao bpìt way-lah sǒrng tôOm ra-wàhng wun jun wun sòOk láir hòk mohng wun sǎo

do you close for lunch? bpìt way-lah ah-hǎhn glahng wun rěu bplào?

yes, between 1 and 3.30 p.m. krúp ra-wàhng way-lah bài mohng těung sǎhm mohng krêung

closed bpìt
ปิด

cloth (fabric) pâh
ผ้า

  (for cleaning etc) pâh kêe réw
  ผ้าขี้ริ้ว

clothes sêu-a pâh
เสื้อผ้า

clothes line rao dtàhk pâh
ราวตากผ้า

clothes peg mái nèep pâh
ไม้หนีบผา

> ### clothing
> The Western liberalism em-
> braced by the Thai sex industry
> is very unrepresentative of the
> general Thai attitude to the body.
> Clothing – or the lack of it – is
> what bothers Thais most about
> tourist behaviour. Stuffy and
> sweaty as it sounds, you need to
> dress modestly at all times, keep-
> ing shorts and singlets for the
> real tourist resorts, and be espe-
> cially diligent about covering up
> in rural areas. Baring your flesh
> on beaches is very much a West-
> ern practice: when Thais go
> swimming they often do so fully
> clothed, and they find topless
> and nude bathing extremely un-
> palatable. It's not illegal, but it
> won't win you many friends.

cloud mâyk kréum
เมฆครึ้ม

cloudy mâyk kréum
เมฆครึ้ม

clutch klút
คลัทช์

coach (bus) rót too-a
รถทัวร์

  (on train) dtôo rót fai
  ตู้รถไฟ

coach station sa-tăhn-nee rót
may
สถานีรถเมล์

coach trip rót num têe-o
รถนำเที่ยว

coast chai ta-lay
ชายทะเล

  on the coast chai ta-lay
  ชายทะเล

coat (long coat) sêu-a kloom
เสื้อคลุม

  (jacket) sêu-a nôrk
  เสื้อนอก

coathanger mái kwăirn
sêu-a
ไม้แขวนเสื้อ

cockroach ma-lairng sàhp
แมลงสาบ

cocoa goh-gôh
โกโก้

coconut ma-práo
มะพร้าว

coconut milk núm ma-práo
น้ำมะพร้าว

code (for phoning) ra-hùt
รหัส
what's the (dialling) code for
Chiangmai? ra-hùt chee-ung
mài ber a-rai?
รหัสเชียงใหม่เบอร์อะไร
coffee gah-fair
กาแฟ
two coffees, please kŏr gah-
fair sŏrng tôo-ay
ขอกาแฟสองถ้วย
coffee shop kòrp-fèe chórp
คอฟฟี่ช๊อบ

Although coffee shops do sell
coffee, the term covers a range
of establishments: some of the
more upmarket ones are in ef-
fect restaurants and others are
places where you can go for a
quick beer and a bowl of noodles. Many are open 24 hours.

coin ngern rĕe-un
เงินเหรียญ
Coke® koh-lâh
โคล่า
cold (adj) năo
หนาว
I'm cold pŏm (chún) **năo**
ผม(ฉัน)หนาว
I have a cold pŏm (chún)
bpen wùt
ผม(ฉัน)เป็นหวัด

collapse: he's collapsed káo
mòt sa-dtì
เขาหมดสติ
collar kor bpòk sêu-a
คอปกเสื้อ
collect gèp
เก็บ
I've come to collect ... pŏm
(chún) mah gèp ...
ผม(ฉัน)มาเก็บ ...
collect call toh-ra-sùp gèp
ngern bplai tahng
โทรศัพท์เก็บเงินปลายทาง
college wít-ta-yah-lai
วิทยาลัย
colour sĕe
สี
do you have this in other
colours? mee sĕe èun mái?
มีสีอื่นไหม
colour film feem sĕe
ฟิล์มสี
comb (noun) wĕe
หวี
come mah
มา

•••••• DIALOGUE ••••••

where do you come from? koon
mah jàhk năi krúp (ká)?
I come from Edinburgh pŏm (chún)
mah jàhk Edinburgh

come back glùp mah
กลับมา

I'll come back tomorrow
prôong née glùp mah
พรุ่งนี้กลับมา

come in chern kâo mah
เชิญเข้ามา

comfortable sa-dòo-uk
สะดวก

compact disc pàirn see dee
แผ่นซีดี

company (business) bor-ri-sùt
บริษัท

compartment (on train) hôrng
pôo doy-ee săhn
ห้องผู้โดยสาร

compass kĕm-tít
เข็มทิศ

complain bòn
บ่น

complaint rêu-ung rórng ree-un
เรื่องร้องเรียน

I have a complaint pŏm
(chún) mee rêu-ung rórng
ree-un
ผม(ฉัน)มีเรื่องร้องเรียน

completely túng mòt
ทั้งหมด

computer korm-pew-dter
คอมพิวเตอร์

concert gahn sa-dairng don-
dtree
การแสดงดนตรี

concussion sa-mŏrng tòok gra-
tóp gra-teu-un
สมองถูกกระทบกระเทือน

conditioner (for hair) kreem nôo-
ut pŏm
ครีมนวดผม

condom tŏong yahng
ถุงยาง

conference gahn bpra-chOOm
การประชุม

confirm rúp-rorng
รับรอง

congratulations! kŏr sa-dairng
kwahm yin dee!
ขอแสดงความยินดี

connecting flight têe-o bin dtòr
เที่ยวบินต่อ

connection dtòr
ต่อ

conscious mee sa-dtì
มีสติ

constipation tórng pòok
ท้องผูก

consulate sa-tăhn gong-sŏOn
สถานกงสุล

contact (verb) dtìt dtòr
ติดต่อ

contact lenses korn-táirk layn
คอนแทคเลนซ์

contraceptive krêu-ung kOOm
gum-nèrt
เครื่องคุมกำเนิด

convenient sa-dòo-uk
สะดวก

that's not convenient nûn mâi
kôy sa-dòo-uk
นั่นไม่ค่อยสะดวก

cook (verb) tum ah-hǎhn
ทำอาหาร

not cooked dìp dìp
ดิบๆ

cooker dtao
เตา

cookie kóok-gêe
คุกกี้

cooking utensils krêu-ung chái
nai kroo-a
เครื่องใช้ในครัว

cool yen
เย็น

cork jòok kòo-ut
จุกขวด

corkscrew têe bpèrt kòo-ut
ที่เปิดขวด

corner: on the corner têe
moom
ที่มุม

in the corner yòo dtrong hǒo-
a mum
อยู่ตรงหัวมุม

correct (right) tòok
ถูก

corridor tahng dern
ทางเดิน

cosmetics krêu-ung sǔm-ahng
เครื่องสำอาง

cost (noun) rah-kah
ราคา

how much does it cost? rah-
kah tâo-rài?
ราคาเท่าไร

cot bplay
เปล

cotton fâi
ผ้าย

cotton wool sǔm-lee
สำลี

couch (sofa) têe nûng rúp kàirk
ที่นั่งรับแขก

cough ai
ไอ

cough medicine yah gâir ai
ยาแก้ไอ

could: could you ...? koon ... dâi
mái?
คุณ ... ได้ไหม

could I have ...? kǒr ... dâi
mái?
ขอ ... ได้ไหม

I couldn't ... pǒm (chún) ...
mâi dâi
ผม(ฉัน) ... ไม่ได้

country (nation) bpra-tâyt
ประเทศ

countryside chon-na-bòt
ชนบท

couple (two people) kôo
คู่

a couple of ... sǒrng sǎhm ...
สองสาม ...

courier múk-koo-tâyt
มัคคุเทศก์

course (main course etc) chóot ah-
hǎhn
ชุดอาหาร

of course nâir-norn
แน่นอน

of course not mâi ròrk
ไม่หรอก

cousin lôok pêe lôok nórng
ลูกพี่ลูกน้อง

cow woo-a
วัว

crab bpoo
ปู

crash (noun) rót chon
รถชน

I've had a crash pŏm (chún)
gèrt rót chon
ผม(ฉัน)เกิดรถชน

crazy bâh
บ้า

cream kreem
ครีม

credit card bùt kray-dìt
บัตรเครดิต

can I pay by credit card? jài
doy-ee bùt kray-dìt dâi mái?
จ่ายโดยบัตรเครดิตได้ไหม

Visa, Access/Mastercard, American Express and Diners Club credit cards and charge cards are accepted at top hotels as well as in some posh restaurants, department stores, tourist shops and travel agents, but surcharging of up to 5 per cent is rife, and theft and forgery are →

major industries – always demand the carbon copies and destroy them immediately, and never leave cards in baggage storage. The most useful cards are Visa and Access/Mastercard, because with these you can also withdraw cash on your bank account from 650 cashpoints/ATMs around the country – most provincial capitals have at least one cashpoint/ATM.

•••••• DIALOGUE ••••••

can I pay by credit card? jài doy-ee
bùt kray-dìt dâi mái?

which card do you want to use? ja
chái bùt a-rai krúp?

Access/Visa

yes, sir dâi krúp

what's the number? ber a-rai
krúp?

and the expiry date? láir-o bùt mòt
ah-yóo mêu-rai?

crisps mun fa-rùng tôrt
มันฝรั่งทอด

crockery tôo-ay chahm
ถ้วยชาม

crossing (by sea) kâhm ta-lay
ข้ามทะเล

crossroads sèe yâirk
สี่แยก

crowd fŏong kon
ฝูงคน

crowded kon nâirn
คนแน่น

crown (on tooth) lèe-um fun
เหลี่ยมฟัน

cruise lôrng reu-a
ลองเรือ

crutches mái yun rúk ráir
ไม้ยันรักแร้

cry (verb) rórng hâi
ร้องไห้

cucumber dtairng gwah
แตงกวา

cup tôo-ay
ถ้วย

a cup of ..., please kŏr ... tôo-ay nèung
ขอ ... ถ้วยหนึ่ง

cupboard dtôo
ตู้

cure (verb) gâir
แก้

curly pŏm yìk
ผมหยิก

current (electrical) gra-săir fai fáh
กระแสไฟฟ้า

(in water) gra-săir náhm
กระแสน้ำ

curtains mâhn
ม่าน

cushion mŏrn
หมอน

custom bpra-pay-nee
ประเพณี

Customs sŏon-la-gah-gorn
ศุลกากร

Thai embassies and consulates can provide up-to-date information on Customs regulations. Rules governing the export of antiques are particularly strict and permission from the Department of Fine Arts (through Bangkok's National Museum) may have to be obtained.

cut (noun) dtùt
ตัด

(verb) roy bàht
รอยบาด

I've cut myself pŏm (chún) mee roy bàht
ผม(ฉัน)มีรอยบาด

cutlery chórn sôrm
ช้อนส้อม

cycling gahn tèep jùk-ra-yahn
การถีบจักรยาน

cyclist kon tèep jùk-ra-yahn
คนถีบจักรยาน

D

dad pôr
พ่อ

daily bpra-jum wun
ประจำวัน

damage (verb) kwahm sĕe-a hăi
ความเสียหาย

damaged sĕe-a láir-o
เสียแล้ว

I'm sorry, I've damaged this
kŏr-tôht pŏm (chún) tum hâi
sĕe-a
ขอโทษผม(ฉัน)ทำให้เสีย

damn! chìp-hăi!
ฉิบหาย

damp (adj) chéun
ชื้น

dance (noun) ra-bum
ระบำ

(verb) dtên rum
เต้นรำ

would you like to dance? yàhk
dtên rum mái?
อยากเต้นรำไหม

dangerous un-dta-rai
อันตราย

Danish den-mahk
เดนมาร์ก

dark (adj: colour) gàir
แก่

(hair) dum
ดำ

it's getting dark mêut láir-o
มืดแล้ว

date*: what's the date today?
wun née wun têe tâo-rài?
วันนี้วันที่เท่าไร

let's make a date for next
Monday nút póp gun wun

jun nâh
นัดพบกันวันจันทร์หน้า

Thais use both the Western
Gregorian calendar and the
Buddhist calendar – Buddha is
said to have attained enlightenment in the year 543 BC, so Thai
dates start from that point: thus
1996 AD becomes 2539 BE
(Buddhist Era).

dates (fruit) in-ta-pa-lŭm
อินทผลัม

daughter lôok săo
ลูกสาว

daughter-in-law lôok sa-pái
ลูกสไภ้

dawn (noun) rôong
รุ่ง

at dawn rôong cháo
รุ่งเช้า

day wun
วัน

the day after tomorrow wun
ma-reun née
วันมะรืนนี้

the day before wun gòrn
วันก่อน

the day before yesterday wun
seun née
วันชืนนี้

every day tóok wun
ทุกวัน

all day túng wun
ทั้งวัน

in two days' time èek sǒrng
wun
อีกสองวัน

day trip bpai glùp wun
dee-o
ไปกลับวันเดียว

dead dtai
ตาย

deaf hǒo nòo-uk
หูหนวก

deal (business) tóo-ra-gìt
ธุรกิจ

it's a deal dtòk long láir-o
ตกลงแล้ว

death gahn dtai
การตาย

decaffeinated coffee gah-fair
mâi mee kah-fay-in
กาแฟไม่มีคาเฟอีน

December tun-wah-kom
ธันวาคม

decide dtùt sǐn jai
ตัดสินใจ

we haven't decided yet rao
yung mâi dâi dtùt sǐn jai
เรายังไม่ได้ตัดสินใจ

decision gahn dtùt sǐn jai
การตัดสินใจ

deck (on ship) dàht fáh
ดาดฟ้า

deckchair gâo êe pâh bai
เก้าอี้ผ้าใบ

deep léuk
ลึก

definitely nâir-norn
แน่นอน

definitely not! mâi ròrk!
ไม่หรอก

degree (qualification) bpa-rin-yah
ปริญญา

delay (noun) kwahm chúk cháh
ความชักช้า

deliberately doy-ee jay-dta-nah
โดยเจตนา

delicatessen ráhn kǎi ah-hǎhn
sǔm-rèt rôop
ร้านขายอาหารสำเร็จรูป

delicious a-ròy
อร่อย

deliver sòng
ส่ง

delivery (of mail) gahn sòng jòt-
mǎi
การส่งจดหมาย

Denmark bpra-tâyt den-mahk
ประเทศเดนมาร์ก

dentist mǒr fun
หมอฟัน

•••••• DIALOGUE ••••••

it's this one here un nêe ná
this one? un née, châi mái?
no that one mâi châi, un nún
here? un nêe, châi mái?
yes châi

dentures chóot fun tee-um
ชุดฟันเทียม

deodorant yah dùp glìn dtoo-a
ยาดับกลิ่นตัว

department pa-nàirk
แผนก

department store hâhng
ห้าง

departure kăh òrk
ขาออก

departure lounge hôrng pôo
doy-ee săhn kăh òrk
ห้องผู้โดยสารขาออก

depend: it depends láir-o dtàir
แล้วแต่

it depends on ... láir-o dtàir ...
แล้วแต่ ...

deposit (as security) ngern fàhk
เงินฝาก

(as part payment) kâh mút-jum
ค่ามัดจำ

description kum ùt-ti-bai
คำอธิบาย

dessert kŏrng wăhn
ของหวาน

destination jòot-măi bplai
tahng
จุดหมายปลายทาง

develop (film) láhng
ล้าง

•••••• DIALOGUE ••••••

could you develop these films?
láhng feem née dâi mái?
yes, certainly dâi krúp
when will they be ready? sèt mêu-
rai?

tomorrow afternoon prôong née
bài

how much is the four-hour service?
bor-ri-gahn sèe chôo-a mohng
tâo-rài?

diabetic (noun) bpen rôhk bao
wăhn
เป็นโรคเบาหวาน

dial (verb) mŏon
หมุน

dialling code ra-hùt toh-ra-sùp
รหัสโทรศัพท์

If you're dialling from abroad,
the international code for Thailand is 66. When calling abroad
from Thailand, dial 001 and
then the relevant country code:

Australia 61	Ireland 353
New Zealand 64	USA 1
Canada 1	UK 44

diamond pét
เพชร

diaper pâh ôrm
ผ้าอ้อม

diarrhoea tórng sĕe-a
ท้องเสีย

do you have something for
diarrhoea? mee yah gâir
tórng sĕe-a mái?
มียาแก้ท้องเสียไหม

diary sa-mòot bun-téuk bpra-

jum wun
สมุดบันทึกประจำวัน

dictionary pót-ja-nah-nóo-grom
พจนานุกรม

didn't* mâi dâi ...
ไม่ได้ ...
see not

die dtai
ตาย

diesel núm mun rót dee-sen
น้ำมันรถดีเซล

diet ah-hǎhn pi-sày t
อาหารพิเศษ
I'm on a diet pǒm (chún)
gum-lung lót núm nùk
ผม(ฉัน)กำลังลดน้ำหนัก
I have to follow a special diet
pǒm (chún) dtôrng tahn ah-
hǎhn pi-sày t
ผม(ฉัน)ต้องทานอาหารพิเศษ

difference kwahm dtàirk
dtàhng
ความแตกต่าง
what's the difference? dtàirk
dtàhng gun yung-ngai?
แตกต่างกันอย่างไร

different dtàhng
ต่าง
this one is different un née
dtàhng gun
อันนี้ต่างกัน
a different table/room **èek**
dtó/hôrng nèung
อีกโต๊ะ/ห้องหนึ่ง

difficult yâhk
ยาก

difficulty bpun-hǎh
ปัญหา

dinghy reu-a bòt
เรือบด

dining room hôrng rúp-bpra-
tahn ah-hǎhn
ห้องรับประทานอาหาร

dinner (evening meal) ah-hǎhn
yen
อาหารเย็น
to have dinner tahn ah-hǎhn
yen
ทานอาหารเย็น

direct (adj) dtrong
ตรง
is there a direct train? mee rót
fai dtrong bpai mái?
มีรถไฟตรงไปไหม

direction tahng
ทาง
which direction is it? yòo
tahng nǎi?
อยู่ทางไหน
is it in this direction? bpai
tahng née, châi mái?
ไปทางนี้ใช่ไหม

directory enquiries bor-ri-gahn
sòrp tǎhm ber toh-ra-sùp
บริการสอบถามเบอร์โทรศัพท์

For international directory
enquiries dial 100.

dirt kêe fóon
ขี้ฝุ่น

dirty sòk-ga-bpròk
สกปรก

disabled pí-gahn
พิการ

disappear hǎi bpai
หายไป

it's disappeared mun hǎi bpai
nǎi gôr mâi róo
มันหายไปไหนก็ไม่รู้

disappointed pìt wǔng
ผิดหวัง

disappointing mâi dee tâo têe
kít wái
ไม่ดีเท่าที่คิดไว้

disaster hǎi-ya-ná
หายนะ

disco dit-sa-gôh
ดิสโก้

discount lót rah-kah
ลดราคา

is there a discount? lót rah-
kah nòy dâi mái?
ลดราคาหน่อยได้ไหม

disease rôhk
โรค

disgusting nâh glèe-ut
น่าเกลียด

dish (meal) gùp kâo
กับข้าว

(bowl) chahm
ชาม

dishcloth pâh chét jahn
ผ้าเช็ดจาน

disinfectant yah kâh chéu-a
rôhk
ยาฆ่าเชื้อโรค

disk (for computer) jahn bun-
téuk
จานบันทึก

disposable diapers/nappies pâh
ôrm sǔm-rèt rôop chái krúng
dee-o
ผ้าอ้อมสำเร็จรูปใช้ครั้งเดียว

distance ra-yá tahng
ระยะทาง

in the distance yòo nai ra-yá
glai
อยู่ในระยะไกล

district kàyt
เขต

disturb róp-goo-un
รบกวน

diversion (detour) bplèe-un sên
tahng dern
เปลี่ยนเส้นทางเดิน

diving board têe gra-dòht náhm
ที่กระโดดน้ำ

divorced yàh gun láir-o
หย่ากันแล้ว

dizzy: I feel dizzy pǒm (chún)
wee-un hǒo-a
ผม(ฉัน)เวียนหัว

do (verb) tum
ทำ

what shall we do? rao ja tum
yung-ngai?
เราจะทำอย่างไร

how do you do it? tum yung-

ngai?
ทำอย่างไร
will you do it for me? chôo-ay tum hâi nòy, dâi mái?
ช่วยทำให้หน่อยได้ไหม

•••••• DIALOGUES ••••••

how do you do? sa-wùt dee krúp (kâ)

nice to meet you yin dee têe dâi róo-jùk gun

what do you do? (work) kOOn tum ngahn a-rai krúp (ká)?

I'm a teacher, and you? bpen kroo, láir-o kOOn lâ?

I'm a student bpen núk sèuk-sǎh
what are you doing this evening? yen née bpai nǎi?

we're going out for a drink, do you want to join us? rao bpai gin lâo, bpai dôo-ay gun mái?

do you want fish sauce? sài núm bplah mái?

I do, but she doesn't mâi sài dtàir káo gôr sài

doctor mǒr
หมอ

we need a doctor rao dtôrng gahn hǎh mǒr
เราต้องการหาหมอ

please call a doctor chôo-ay rêe-uk mǒr
ช่วยเรียกหมอ

Hospital cleanliness and efficiency varies, but generally hygiene and health care standards are good and the ratio of medical staff to patients considerably higher than in most parts of the West. Most doctors speak English. All provincial capitals have at least one hospital: ask at your hotel for advice on and possibly transport to the nearest or most suitable. In the event of a major health crisis, get someone to contact your embassy or insurance company – it may be best to get yourself flown home. If you do have to undergo hospital treatment you'll have to pay, so taking out travel insurance is definitely worth it.

•••••• DIALOGUE ••••••

where does it hurt? jèp dtrong nǎi?
right here dtrong née
does that hurt now? yung jèp yòo rěu bplào?
yes jèp
take this to the pharmacy ao née bpai ráhn kǎi yah

document àyk-ga-sǎhn
เอกสาร
dog mǎh
หมา

doll dtóok-ga-dtah
ตุ๊กตา

domestic flight têe-o bin pai nai
เที่ยวบินภายใน

don't!* yàh!
อย่า

don't do that! yàh tum yàhng
nún!
อย่าทำอย่างนั้น

door bpra-dtoo
ประตู

doorman kon fâo bpra-dtoo
คนเฝ้าประตู

double kôo
คู่

double bed dtee-ung yày
เตียงใหญ่

double room hôrng kôo
ห้องคู่

doughnut doh-nút
โดนัท

down: down here yòo têe nêe
อยู่ที่นี่

put it down over there wahng
bpai têe nôhn
วางไปที่โน่น

it's down there on the right
ler-ee bpai kâhng nâh tahng
dâhn kwǎh meu
เลยไปข้างหน้าทางด้านขวามือ

it's further down the road bpai
dtahm ta-nǒn kâhng nâh
ไปตามถนนข้างหน้า

downmarket (restaurant etc) rah-

kah tòok
ราคาถูก

downstairs kâhng lâhng
ข้างล่าง

dozen lǒh
โหล

half a dozen krêung lǒh
ครึ่งโหล

drain (in sink, in street) tôr ra-bai
ท่อระบาย

draughty: it's draughty mee lom
yen kâo
มีลมเย็นเข้า

draw wâht
วาด

drawer lín-chúk
ลิ้นชัก

drawing rôop wâht
รูปวาด

dreadful yâir
แย่

dream (noun) kwahm fǔn
ความฝัน

dress (noun) sêu-a chóot
เสื้อชุด

dressed: to get dressed dtàirng
dtoo-a
แต่งตัว

dressing (for cut) pâh pun plǎir
ผ้าพันแผล

salad dressing núm (râht) sa-
lùt
น้ำ(ราด)สลัด

dressing gown sêu-a kloom

chóot norn
เสื้อคลุมชุดนอน
drink (noun) krêu-ung dèum
เครื่องดื่ม
(verb) dèum
ดื่ม
a cold drink krêu-ung dèum
yen yen
เครื่องดื่มเย็นๆ
can I get you a drink? kOOn ja
dèum a-rai mái?
คุณจะดื่มอะไรไหม
what would you like (to drink)?
kOOn ja dèum a-rai?
คุณจะดื่มอะไร
no thanks, I don't drink mâi
krúp (kâ) pǒm (chún) mâi
dèum
ไม่ครับ(ค่ะ)ผม(ฉัน)ไม่ดื่ม
I'll just have a drink of water
kǒr náhm bplào tâo-nún
ขอน้ำเปล่าเท่านั้น
see bar
drinking water náhm dèum
น้ำดื่ม
is this drinking water? náhm
née gin dâi mái?
น้ำนี้กินได้ไหม

Thais don't drink water straight
from the tap, and nor should
you: plastic bottles of drinking
water are sold countrywide, even
→

in the smallest villages. Cheap
restaurants and hotels generally
serve free jugs of boiled water
which should be fine to drink,
though not as foolproof as the
bottles.

drive (verb) kùp
ขับ
we drove here rao kùp rót
mah
เราขับรถมา
I'll drive you home pǒm
(chún) kùp rót bpai sòng
ผม(ฉัน)ขับรถไปส่ง
driver kon kùp
คนขับ

driving
Take a look at the general standard of driving (dangerously reck-
less) and state of the roads
(poor) before deciding to rent a
car or motorbike, and then take
time to get used to the more
eccentric conventions. Of these,
perhaps the most notable is the
fact that a major road doesn't
necessarily have right of way
over a minor, but that the bigger vehicle always has right of
way. The published rules of the
road state that everyone drives
→

on the left (which they do) and that they should keep to the speed limit of 60kmh within built-up areas and 80kmh outside them (which they don't). Theoretically, foreigners need an international driver's licence to rent any kind of vehicle, but some companies accept national licences, and the smaller operations (especially bike rentals) may not ask for any kind of proof. If you decide to rent a car go to an international company or a rental company recommended by TAT (Tourist Authority of Thailand), and make sure you get insurance from them. If appropriate, consider the safer option of hiring a driver along with the car, which you can often do for the same price on day rentals.
see **rent**

---

driving licence bai kùp kèe
ใบขับขี่

drop: just a drop, please (of drink)
nít dee-o tâo-nún
นิดเดียวเท่านั้น

drug yah
ยา

drugs (narcotics) yah-sàyp-
dtìt
ยาเสพติด

Only an idiot would try to take drugs through Thai Customs. On no account agree to take a package through Customs that you haven't inspected yourself. Drug smuggling carries a maximum penalty of death and will almost certainly get you from five to twenty years in a Thai prison. Don't expect special treatment as a foreigner.

---

drunk (adj) mao
เมา

drunken driving kùp rót ka-nà
mao
ขับรถขณะเมา

dry (adj) hâirng
แห้ง

dry-cleaner ráhn súk
hâirng
ร้านซักแห้ง

duck bpèt
เป็ด

due: he was due to arrive
yesterday káo koo-un ja mah
mêu-a wahn née
เขาควรจะมาเมื่อวานนี้
when is the train due? rót fai
mah gèe mohng?
รถไฟมากี่โมง

dull (pain) mâi rOOn rairng
ไม่รุนแรง

(weather) mêut moo-a
มืดมัว

dummy (baby's) hŏo-a nom lòrk
หัวนมหลอก

during nai ra-wàhng
ในระหว่าง

dust fòon
ฝุ่น

dustbin tŭng ka-yà
ถังขยะ

dusty mee fòon yér
มีฝุ่นเยอะ

Dutch horl-lairn
ฮอลแลนด์

duty-free (goods) mâi dtôrng
sĕe-a pah-sĕe
ไม่ต้องเสียภาษี

duty-free shop ráhn káh sĭn-
káh bplòrt pah-sĕe ah-
gorn
ร้านค้าสินค้าปลอดภาษีอากร

E

each (every) tóok
ทุก

how much are they each? un
la tâo-rài?
อันละเท่าไร

ear hŏo
หู

earache: I have earache pŏm

(chún) bpòo-ut hŏo
ผม(ฉัน)ปวดหู

early ray-o
เร็ว

early in the morning cháo
dtròo
เช้าตรู่

I called by earlier pŏm (chún)
mah hăh mêu-a gòrn née
ผม(ฉัน)มาหาเมื่อก่อนนี้

earrings dtôOm hŏo
ตุ้มหู

east dta-wun òrk
ตะวันออก

in the east tahng dta-wun òrk
ทางตะวันออก

Easter ee-sa-dtêr
อีสเตอร์

easy ngâi
ง่าย

eat gin kâo
กินข้าว

we've already eaten, thanks
rao gin kâo láir-o
เรากินข้าวแล้ว

---

eating habits

Thais normally eat three meals
a day. Typically, each meal will
consist of rice with a number of
side dishes, such as curry, fried
meat and vegetables and fish.
Thais use a spoon and fork
$\rightarrow$

(although chopsticks are used in the thousands of Chinese noodle shops) and the meal is a constant 'dipping-in' process, taking a spoonful or two at a time from the side dishes.

eau de toilette **núm òp**
น้ำอบ

egg **kài**
ไข่

egg noodles **ba-mèe**
บะหมี่

either: either ... or ... **... rěu ... ... หรือ ...**

either of them **un nǎi gôr dâi**
อันไหนก็ได้

elastic (noun) **sǎi yahng yêut**
สายยางยืด

elastic band **yahng rút**
ยางรัด

elbow **kôr sòrk**
ข้อศอก

electric **fai fáh**
ไฟฟ้า

electrical appliances **krêu-ung fai fáh**
เครื่องไฟฟ้า

electrician **châhng fai fáh**
ช่างไฟฟ้า

electricity **fai fáh**
ไฟฟ้า
see **voltage**

elephant **cháhng**
ช้าง

elevator **líf**
ลิฟท์

else: something else **a-rai èek**
อะไรอีก

somewhere else **têe èun**
ที่อื่น

•••••• DIALOGUE ••••••

would you like anything else? **ao a-rai èek mái?**

no, nothing else, thanks **mâi krúp (kâ), kòrp-koon**

embassy **sa-tǎhn tôot**
สถานทูต

emergency **chòok chěrn**
ฉุกเฉิน

this is an emergency! **bpen pah-wá chòok chěrn!**
เป็นภาวะฉุกเฉิน

emergency exit **tahng òrk chòok chěrn**
ทางออกฉุกเฉิน

empty **wâhng**
ว่าง

end (noun) **jòp**
จบ

(verb) **sîn sòot**
สิ้นสุด, **jòp**
จบ

at the end of the soi **sòot soy**
สุดซอย

when does it end? **jòp mêu-**

ENGLISH ◆ THAI | En

rài?
จบเมื่อไร

engaged (toilet, telephone) mâi
wâhng
ไม่ว่าง

(to be married) mûn
หมั้น

engine (car) krêu-ung yon
เครื่องยนต์

England bpra-tâyt ung-grìt
ประเทศอังกฤษ

English (adj) ung-grìt
อังกฤษ

(language) pah-săh ung-grìt
ภาษาอังกฤษ

I'm English pŏm (chún) bpen
kon ung-grìt
ผม(ฉัน)เป็นคนอังกฤษ

do you speak English? kOOn
pôot pah-săh ung-grìt bpen
mái?
คุณพูดภาษาอังกฤษเป็นไหม

enjoy: to enjoy oneself mee sa-
nòok
มีสนุก

•••••• DIALOGUE ••••••

how did you like the film?
nǔng sa-nòok mái?

I enjoyed it very much, did you
enjoy it? sa-nòok mâhk, kOOn
kít wâh sa-nòok mái?

enjoyable sa-nòok dee
สนุกดี

enlargement (of photo) pâhp ka-
yăi
ภาพขยาย

enormous yài bêr-rêr
ใหญ่เบ้อเร่อ

enough por
พอ

there's not enough mâi por
ไม่พอ

it's not big enough yài mâi
por
ใหญ่ไม่พอ

that's enough por láir-o
พอแล้ว

entrance (noun) tahng kâo
ทางเข้า

envelope sorng jòt-măi
ซองจดหมาย

epileptic bpen rôhk lom bâh
mŏo
เป็นโรคลมบ้าหมู

equipment òop-bpa-gorn
อุปกรณ์

error têe pìt
ที่ผิด

especially doy-ee cha-pòr
โดยเฉพาะ

essential jum-bpen
จำเป็น

it is essential that ... jum-bpen
têe ...
จำเป็นที่ ...

Europe yoo-rohp
ยุโรป

European (adj) yoo-rohp
ยุโรป

even máir dtàir
แม้แต่

even if ... máir wâh ...
แม้ว่า ...

evening (early evening) dtorn yen
ตอนเย็น

(late evening) dtorn glahng keun
ตอนกลางคืน

this evening (early evening) yen née
เย็นนี้,

(late evening) keun née
คืนนี้

in the evening (early evening) dtorn yen
ตอนเย็น

(late evening) dtorn glahng keun
ตอนกลางคืน

evening meal ah-hǎhn yen
อาหารเย็น

eventually nai têe sòot
ในที่สุด

ever ker-ee
เคย

•••••• DIALOGUE ••••••

have you ever been to Phuket?
koon ker-ee bpai poo-gèt mái?

yes, I was there two years ago ker-ee, ker-ee bpai mêu-a sǒrng bpee gòrn

every tóok
ทุก

every day tóok wun
ทุกวัน

everyone tóok kon
ทุกคน

everything tóok yàhng
ทุกอย่าง

everywhere tôo-a bpai
ทั่วไป

exactly! châi láir-o!
ใช่แล้ว

exam gahn sòrp
การสอบ

example dtoo-a yàhng
ตัวอย่าง

for example chên ...
เช่น ...

excellent yêe-um
เยี่ยม

excellent! yêe-um ler-ee!
เยี่ยมเลย

except yók wáyn
ยกเว้น

excess baggage núm nùk gern
น้ำหนักเกิน

exchange rate ùt-dtrah lâirk bplèe-un
อัตราแลกเปลี่ยน

exciting nâh dtèun dtên
น่าตื่นเต้น

excuse me (to get past, to say sorry) kǒr-tôht
ขอโทษ

(to get attention) kOOn krúp
(kâ)
คุณครับ (คะ)

(to say pardon?) a-rai ná?
อะไรนะ

exhaust (pipe) tôr ai sĕe-a
ท่อไอเสีย

exhausted (tired) nèu-ay
เหนื่อย

exhibition ní-tá-sa-gahn
นิทรรศการ

exit tahng òrk
ทางออก

where's the nearest exit?
tahng òrk glâi têe sòot yòo
têe nǎi?
ทางออกใกล้ที่สุดอยู่ที่ไหน

expect kâht
คาด

expensive pairng
แพง

experienced mee bpra-sòp-ba-
gahn
มีประสบการณ์

explain ùt-ti-bai
อธิบาย

can you explain that? chôo-ay
ùt-ti-bai hâi nòy, dâi mái?
ช่วยอธิบายให้หน่อยได้ไหม

express (mail) bprai-sa-nee
dòo-un
ไปรษณีย์ด่วน

(train) rót fai dòo-un
รถไฟด่วน

extension (telephone) dtòr
ต่อ

extension 341, please kŏr
dtòr ber sǎhm sèe nèung
ขอต่อเบอร์สามเสี่เหนึ่ง

extension lead sǎi pôo-ung
สายพ่วง

extra: can we have an extra one?
kŏr èek un nèung
ขออีกอันหนึ่ง

do you charge extra for that?
kít dtàhng hàhk rĕu bplào?
คิดต่างหากหรือเปล่า

extraordinary bplàirk mâhk
แปลกมาก

extremely mâhk lĕu-a gern
มากเหลือเกิน

eye dtah
ตา

will you keep an eye on my
suitcase for me? chôo-ay
fâo gra-bpǎo hâi nòy, dâi
mái?
ช่วยเฝ้ากระเป๋าให้หน่อยได้ไหม

eyebrow pencil din-sŏr kĕe-un
kéw
ดินสอเขียนคิ้ว

eye drops yah yòrt dtah
ยาหยอดตา

eyeglasses (US) wâirn dtah
แว่นตา

eyeliner têe kĕe-un kòrp dtah
ที่เขียนขอบตา

eye make-up remover núm yah

láhng têe kĕe-un kòrp dtah
น้ำยาล้างที่เขียนขอบตา

eye shadow kreem tah nŭng
dtah
ครีมทาหนังตา

F

face nâh
หน้า

factory rohng ngahn
โรงงาน

Fahrenheit* fah-ren-háit
ฟาเรนไฮท์

faint (verb) bpen lom
เป็นลม

she's fainted káo bpen
lom
เขาเป็นลม

I feel faint pŏm (chún) róo-
sèuk bpen lom
ผม(ฉัน)รู้สึกเป็นลม

fair (funfair) ngahn òrk ráhn
งานออกร้าน

(trade) ngahn sa-dairng sĭn-
káh
งานแสดงสินค้า

(adj) yóot-dti-tum
ยุติธรรม

fairly kôrn-kâhng
ค่อนข้าง

fake kŏrng bplorm
ของปลอม

fall (US) réu-doo bai-mái

rôo-ung
ฤดูใบไม้ร่วง

in the fall dtorn réu-doo bai-
mái rôo-ung
ตอนฤดูใบไม้ร่วง

fall (verb) hòk lóm
หกล้ม

she's had a fall káo hòk lóm
เขาหกล้ม

false mâi jing
ไม่จริง

family krôrp-kroo-a
ครอบครัว

famous mee chêu sĕe-ung
มีชื่อเสียง

fan (electrical) pút lom
พัดลม

(handheld) pút
พัด

(sports) kon chôrp doo gee-
lah
คนชอบดูกีฬา

fan belt săi pahn
สายพาน

fantastic yêe-um yôrt
เยี่ยมยอด

far glai
ไกล

•••••• DIALOGUE ••••••

is it far from here? yòo glai mái?
no, not very far mâi glai
well how far? gèe gi-loh-met?
it's about 20 kilometres bpra-mahn
yêe-sìp gi-loh-met

fare kâh doy-ee săhn
ค่าโดยสาร

farm fahm
ฟาร์ม

fashionable tun sa-măi
ทันสมัย

fast ray-o
เร็ว

fat (person) ôo-un
อ้วน

(on meat) mun
มัน

father pôr
พ่อ

father-in-law (of a man) pôr dtah
พ่อตา

(of a woman) pôr pŏo-a
พ่อผัว

faucet górk náhm
ก๊อกน้ำ

fault kwahm pìt
ความผิด

sorry, it was my fault kŏr-tôht
kwahm pìt kŏrng pŏm
(chún)
ขอโทษ ความผิดของผม(ฉัน)

it's not my fault mâi châi
kwahm pìt kŏrng pŏm
(chún)
ไม่ใช่ความผิดของผม(ฉัน)

faulty pìt
ผิด

favourite bpròht
โปรด

fax (machine) krêu-ung toh-ra-
săhn
เครื่องโทรสาร

(verb: person) sòng toh-ra-săhn
bpai hâi
ส่งโทรสารไปให้

(document) bun-téuk toh-ra-
săhn, fáirks
บันทึกโทรสาร, แฟกซ์

February gOOm-pah-pun
กุมภาพันธ์

feel róo-sèuk
รู้สึก

I feel hot pŏm (chún) róo-
sèuk rórn
ผม(ฉัน)รู้สึกร้อน

I feel unwell pŏm (chún) róo-
sèuk mâi sa-bai
ผม(ฉัน)รู้สึกไม่สบาย

I feel like going for a walk pŏm
(chún) yàhk ja bpai dern lên
ผม(ฉัน)อยากจะไปเดินเล่น

how are you feeling? kOOn róo-
sèuk bpen yung-ngai bâlıng?
คุณรู้สึกเป็นอย่างไรบาง

I'm feeling better pŏm (chún)
róo-sèuk kôy yung chôo-a
ผม(ฉัน)รู้สึกค่อยยังชั่ว

felt-tip (pen) bpàhk-gah may-jik
ปากกาเมจิก

fence róo-a
รั้ว

fender gun chon
กันชน

ferry reu-a kâhm fâhk
เรือข้ามฟาก

Regular ferries connect all major islands with the mainland, and for the vast majority of crossings you simply buy your ticket on board. Boats generally operate a reduced service during the monsoon season – from May till September along the east coast and Andaman coast and from November through April on the Gulf coast – while the more remote spots become inaccessible in these periods. Wherever there's a decent public waterway, there'll be a longtailed boat ready to ferry you along it. Longtailed boats carry from ten to twenty passengers: in Bangkok most follow fixed routes, but elsewhere most are for rent.

festival ngahn
งาน
fetch rúp
รับ
I'll fetch him pǒm (chún) ja bpai rúp káo
ผม(ฉัน)จะไปรับเขา
will you come and fetch me later? mah rúp pǒm (chún)

tee lǔng dâi mái?
มารับผม(ฉัน)ทีหลังได้ไหม
feverish bpen kâi
เป็นไข้
few: a few sǒrng sǎhm
สองสาม
a few days sǒrng sǎhm wun
สองสามวัน
fiancé(e) kôo mûn
คู่หมั้น
field sa-nǎhm
สนาม
fight (noun) gahn chók dtòy
การชกต่อย
fill dterm
เติม
fill in gròrk
กรอก
do I have to fill this in? dtôrng gròrk un née rěu bplào?
ต้องกรอกอันนี้หรือเปล่า
fill up tum hâi dtem
ทำให้เต็ม
fill it up, please dterm núm mun hâi dtem
เติมน้ำมันให้เต็ม
filling (in tooth) òot fun
อุดฟัน
film (movie) nǔng
หนัง
(for camera) feem
ฟิล์ม

•••••• D I A L O G U E ••••••

do you have this kind of film? mee
feem bàirp née mái?

yes, how many exposures? mee, ao
gèe rôop?

36 sǎhm sìp

film processing láhng feem
ล้างฟิล์ม

filthy sòk-ga-bpròk
สกปรก

find (verb) jer
เจอ

I can't find it pǒm (chún) hǎh
mâi jer
ผม(ฉัน)หาไม่เจอ

I've found it pǒm (chún) jer
láir-o
ผม(ฉัน)เจอแล้ว

find out hǎh rai la-êe-ut
หารายละเอียด

could you find out for me?
chôo-ay hǎh rai la-êe-ut hâi
nòy dâi mái?
ช่วยหารายละเอียดให้หน่อย
ได้ไหม

fine (weather) dee
ดี

(punishment) kâh bprùp
ค่าปรับ

•••••• D I A L O G U E S ••••••

how are you? bpen yung-ngai
bâhng?

I'm fine, thanks sa-bai dee kòrp-
koon mâhk

is that OK? oh kay mái?

that's fine thanks dee láir-o kòrp-
koon

finger néw meu
นิ้วมือ

finish (verb) jòp
จบ

I haven't finished yet pǒm
(chún) yung mâi **sèt**
ผม(ฉัน)ยังไม่เสร็จ

when does it finish? **jòp** gèe
mohng?
จบกี่โมง

fire: fire! fai mâi!
ไฟไหม้

can we light a fire here? gòr
fai dtrong née dâi mái?
ก่อไฟตรงนี้ได้ไหม

fire alarm sǔn-yahn fay mâi
สัญญาณไฟไหม้

fire brigade gorng dtum-ròo-ut
dùp plerng
กองตำรวจดับเพลิง
see police

fire escape bun-dai sǔm-rùp
něe fai
บรรไดสำหรับหนีไฟ

fire extinguisher krêu-ung dùp
plerng
เครื่องดับเพลิง

first râirk
แรก

I was first pǒm (chún) bpen

kon râirk
ผม(ฉัน)เป็นคนแรก

at first tee râirk
ทีแรก

the first time krúng râirk
ครั้งแรก

first on the left lée-o sái tée
tahng yâirk kâhng nâh
เลี้ยวซ้ายที่ทางแยกข้างหน้า

first aid gahn bpa-tǒm pa-yah-
bahn
การปฐมพยาบาล

first-aid kit chóot bpa-thǒm pa-
yah-bahn
ชุดปฐมพยาบาล

first class (travel etc) chún nèung
ชั้นหนึ่ง

first floor chún sǒrng
ชั้นสอง

(US) chún nèung
ชั้นหนึ่ง

first name chêu
ชื่อ

fish (noun) bplah
ปลา

fisherman kon jùp bplah
คนจับปลา

fishing gahn jùp bplah
การจับปลา

fishing boat reu-a bpra-mong
เรือประมง

fishing village mòo bâhn bpra-
mong
หมู่บ้านประมง

fishmonger's ráhn kǎi bplah
ร้านขายปลา

fit (attack) ah-gahn bpen lom
อาการเป็นลม

fit: it doesn't fit me sài mâi dâi
ใส่ไม่ได้

fitting room hôrng lorng sêu-a
pâh
ห้องลองเสื้อผ้า

fix (verb: arrange) jùt
จัด

can you fix this? (repair) un née
gâir dâi mái?
อันนี้แก้ได้ไหม

fizzy sâh
ซ่า

flag tong
ธง

flannel (facecloth) pâh chét nâh
ผ้าเช็ดหน้า

flash (for camera) fláirt
แฟลช

flat (noun: apartment) fláirt
แฟลต

(adj) bairn
แบน

I've got a flat tyre yahng bairn
ยางแบน

flavour rót
รส

flea mùt
หมัด

flight têe-o bin
เที่ยวบิน

flight number têe-o bin măi-
lâyk
เที่ยวบินหมายเลข

flippers rorng táo ma-nóot gòp
รองเท้ามนุษย์กบ

floating market dta-làht náhm
ตลาดน้ำ

flood núm tôo-um
น้ำท่วม

floor (of room) péun
พื้น
(storey) chún
ชั้น
on the floor yòo bon péun
อยู่บนพื้น

florist ráhn kăi dòrk-mái
ร้านขายดอกไม้

flour bpâirng săh-lee
แป้งสาลี

flower dòrk-mái
ดอกไม้

flu kâi wùt
ไข้หวัด

fluent: John speaks fluent Thai
John pôot pah-săh tai dâi
khlôrng
จอห์นพูดภาษาไทยได้คล่อง

fly (noun) ma-lairng wun
แมลงวัน
(verb) bin
บิน
can we fly there? bpai krêu-
ung bin dâi mái?
ไปเครื่องบินได้ไหม

fly in bin kâo mah
บินเข้ามา

fly out bin òrk bpai
บินออกไป

fog mòrk long
หมอกลง

foggy: it's foggy mòrk long
หมอกลง

folk dancing gahn fórn rum
péun meu-ung
การฟ้อนรำพื้นเมือง

folk music don-dtree péun
meu-ung
ดนตรีพื้นเมือง

follow dtahm
ตาม
follow me dtahm pŏm (chún)
mah
ตามผม(ฉัน)มา

food ah-hăhn
อาหาร

food poisoning ah-hăhn bpen pít
อาหารเป็นพิษ

food shop/store ráhn kăi kŏrng
chum
ร้านขายของชำ

foot* (of person) táo
เท้า
on foot dern bpai
เดินไป

football (game) fóot-born
ฟุตบอล
(ball) lôok fóot-born
ลูกฟุตบอล

football match gahn kàirng kǔn
fóot-born
การแข่งขันฟุตบอล

for: do you have something for ...?
(headache/diarrhoea etc) mee a-
rai gâir ... mái?
มีอะไรแก้ ... ไหม

•••••• DIALOGUES ••••••

who's the fried rice for? kâo pùt
sǔm-rùp krai?
that's for me sǔm-rùp pǒm
and this one? láir-o nêe lâ?
that's for her sǔm-rùp káo

where do I get the bus for
Bangsaen? kêun rót bpai bahng-
sǎirn têe-nǎi?
the bus for Bangsaen leaves from
the central market rót bpai bahng-
sǎirn òrk jàhk dta-làht glahng

how long have you been here for?
koon yòo têe nêe nahn tâo-rài?
I've been here for two days, how
about you? yòo sǒrng wun, láir-o
koon lâ?
I've been here for a week pǒm
(chún) yòo têe nêe ah-tít nèung
láir-o

forehead nâh pàhk
หน้าผาก
foreign dtàhng bpra-tâyt
ต่างประเทศ
foreigner chao dtàhng bpra-

tâyt
ชาวต่างประเทศ
forest bpàh
ป่า
forget leum
ลืม
I forget, I've forgotten pǒm
(chún) leum láir-o
ผม(ฉัน)ลืมแล้ว
fork sôrm
ส้อม
(in road) tahng yâirk
ทางแยก
form (document) bàirp form
แบบฟอร์ม
formal (dress) bpen tahng gahn
เป็นทางการ
fortnight sǒrng ah-tít
สองอาทิตย์
fortunately chôhk dee
โชคดี
forward: could you forward my
mail? chôo-ay sòng jòt-mǎi
dtòr bpai hâi dôo-ay
ช่วยส่งจดหมายต่อไปให้ด้วย
forwarding address têe yòo
sǔm-rùp sòng jòt-mǎi bpai
hâi
ที่อยู่สำหรับส่งจดหมายไปให้
foundation cream kreem rorng
péun
ครีมรองพื้น
fountain núm póo
น้ำพุ

foyer (of hotel) hôrng tŏhng
glahng sŭm-rùp rúp kàirk
ห้องโถงกลางสำหรับรับแขก
(of theatre) bor-ri-wayn nûng
púk ror
บริเวณนั่งพักรอ

fracture (noun) gra-dòok hùk
กระดูกหัก

France bpra-tâyt fa-rùng-sàyt
ประเทศฝรั่งเศส

free ì-sa-rá
อิสระ
(no charge) free
ฟรี
is it free (of charge)? free rěu
bplào?
ฟรีหรือเปล่า

freeway tahng dòo-un
ทางด่วน

freezer dtôo châir kăirng
ตู้แช่แข็ง

French (adj) fa-rùng-sàyt
ฝรั่งเศส
(language) pah-săh fa-rùng-
sàyt
ภาษาฝรั่งเศส

French fries mun fa-rùng tôrt
มันฝรั่งทอด

frequent bòy bòy
บ่อย ๆ
how frequent is the bus to
Pattaya? mee rót bpai pút-ta-
yah bòy kâir năi?
มีรถไปพัทยาบ่อยแค่ไหน

fresh (weather, breeze) sòt chêun
สดชื่น
(fruit etc) sòt
สด

fresh orange núm sôm kún
น้ำส้มคั้น

Friday wun sòok
วันศุกร์

fridge dtôo yen
ตู้เย็น

fried pùt
ผัด

fried egg kài dao
ไข่ดาว

fried noodles (Thai-style) pùt tai
ผัดไทย
(Chinese-style) pùt see éw
ผัดซีอิ๊ว

fried rice kâo pùt
ข้าวผัด

friend pêu-un
เพื่อน

friendly bpen pêu-un
เป็นเพื่อน

frog gòp
กบ

from jàhk
จาก
when does the next train from
Ubon arrive? rót fai jàhk oo-
bon têe-o nâh mah tĕung gèe
mohng?
รถไฟจากอุบลเที่ยวหน้ามา
ถึงกี่โมง

from Monday to Friday **dtûng
dtàir** wun jun jon těung wun
sòok

ตั้งแต่วันจันทร์จนถึงวันศุกร์

from next Thursday **dtûng
dtàir** wun pa-réu-hùt

ตั้งแต่วันพฤหัส

•••••• DIALOGUE ••••••

where are you from? koon **mah
jàhk** năi?

I'm from Slough pŏm (chún) mah
jàhk Slough

front nâh
หน้า

in front kâhng nâh
ข้างหน้า

in front of the hotel kâhng nâh
rohng rairm
ข้างหน้าโรงแรม

at the front kâhng nâh
ข้างหน้า

frozen châir kăirng
แช่แข็ง

frozen food ah-hăhn châir
kăirng
อาหารแช่แข็ง

fruit pŏn-la-mái
ผลไม้

fruit juice núm pŏn-la-mái
น้ำผลไม้

fry (deep-fry) tôrt
ทอด

(stir-fry) pùt
ผัด

frying pan ga-tá
กะทะ

full dtem
เต็ม

it's full of ... dtem bpai
dôo-ay ...
เต็มไปด้วย ...

I'm full pŏm (chún) ìm láir-o
ผม(ฉัน)อิ่มแล้ว

full board gin yòo prórm
กินอยู่พร้อม

fun: it was fun sa-nòok dee
สนุกดี

funeral ngahn sòp
งานศพ

funny (strange) bplàirk
แปลก

(amusing) dta-lòk
ตลก

furniture krêu-ung reu-un
เครื่องเรือน

further ler-ee bpai
เลยไป

it's further down the road bpai
dtahm ta-nŏn kâhng nâh
ไปตามถนนข้างหน้า

•••••• DIALOGUE ••••••

how much further is it to Hua Hin?
bpai hŏo-a hĭn èek glai mái?

about 5 kilometres bpra-mahn hâh
gi-loh-met

fuse few
ฟิวส์

the lights have fused few kàht
ฟิวส์ขาด

fuse box glòrng few
กล่องฟิวส์

fuse wire săi few
สายฟิวส์

future a-nah-kót
อนาคต

in future nai a-nah-kót
ในอนาคต

G

game (cards etc) gaym
เกม

(match) gahn lên
การเล่น

(meat) néu-a sùt bpàh
เนื้อสัตว์ป่า

garage (for fuel) púm núm mun
ปั๊มน้ำมัน

(for repairs) òo sôrm rót
อู่ซ่อมรถ

(for parking) rohng rót
โรงรถ

see petrol

garbage (waste) ka-yà
ขยะ

garden sŏo-un
สวน

garlic gra-tee-um
กระเทียม

gas gáirt
แก๊ส

(US) núm mun
น้ำมัน

see petrol

gas cylinder (camping gas) tŭng gáirt
ถังแก๊ส

gasoline núm mun
น้ำมัน

see petrol

gas station bpúm núm mun
ปั๊มน้ำมัน

gate bpra-dtoo
ประตู

(at airport) chôrng kâo
ช่องเข้า

gay gra-ter-ee
กระเทย

gay bar bah sŭm-rùp gra-ter-ee
บาร์สำหรับกระเทย

gearbox glòrng gee-a
กล่องเกียร์

gear lever kun gee-a
คันเกียร์

gears gee-a
เกียร์

general (adj) tôo-a bpai
ทั่วไป

gents (toilet) boo-ròot
บุรุษ

genuine (antique etc) táir
แท้

German (adj) yer-ra-mun
เยอรมัน
(language) pah-săh yer-ra-mun
ภาษาเยอรมัน
German measles rôhk hùt yer-ra-mun
โรคหัดเยอรมัน
Germany bpra-tâyt yer-ra-mun
ประเทศเยอรมัน
get (fetch) dâi
ได้
will you get me another one, please? kŏr ao èek un nèung dâi mái?
ขอเอาอีกอันหนึ่งได้ไหม
how do I get to ...? bpai ... yung-ngai?
ไป ... อย่างไร
do you know where I can get them? sâhp mái wâh ja séu dâi têe năi?
ทราบไหมว่าจะซื้อได้ที่ไหน
get back (return) glùp
กลับ
get in (arrive) tĕung
ถึง
get off long
ลง
where do I get off? pŏm (chún) long têe năi?
ผม(ฉัน)ลงที่ไหน
get on (to train etc) kêun
ขึ้น

get out (of car etc) long
ลง
get up (in the morning) dtèun
ตื่น
gift kŏrng kwŭn
ของขวัญ
gin lâo yin
เหล้ายิน
a gin and tonic, please kŏr yin toh-nik
ขอยินโทนิค
girl pôo-yĭng
ผู้หญิง
girlfriend fairn
แฟน
give hâi
ให้
can you give me some change? kŏr lâirk sàyt sa-dtahng dâi mái?
ขอแลกเศษสตางค์ได้ไหม
I gave it to him pŏm (chún) hâi káo bpai láir-o
ผม(ฉัน)ให้เขาไปแล้ว
will you give this to ...? chôo-ay ao née bpai hâi ... nòy, dâi mái?
ช่วยเอานี้ไปให้ ... หน่อยได้ไหม

•••••• DIALOGUE ••••••

how much do you want for this? nêe kít tâo-rài?
200 baht sŏrng róy bàht
I'll give you 150 baht pŏm (chún) ja hâi koon róy hâh sìp bàht

give back keun
คืน

glad yin dee
ยินดี

glass gâir-o
แก้ว

glasses (spectacles) wâirn dtah
แว่นตา

gloves tŏong meu
ถุงมือ

glue (noun) gao
กาว

go bpai
ไป

we'd like to go to the waterfalls
rao yàhk ja bpai têe-o núm
dtòk
เราอยากจะไปเที่ยวน้ำตก

where are you going? koon
bpai năi?
คุณไปไหน

where does this bus go? rót
may săi née bpai năi?
รถเมล์สายนี้ไปไหน

let's go! bpai tèr!
ไปเถอะ

she's gone (left) káo bpai
láir-o
เขาไปแล้ว

where has he gone? káo bpai
năi?
เขาไปไหน

I went there last week pŏm
(chún) bpai têe nûn mêu-a

ah-tít têe láir-o
ผม(ฉัน)ไปที่นั่นเมื่ออาทิตย์ที่แล้ว

go away bpai
ไป

go away! bpai hâi pón!
ไปให้พ้น

go back (return) glùp
กลับ

go down (the stairs etc) long bpai
ลงไป

go in (enter) kâo bpai
เข้าไป

go out (in the evening) têe-o bpai
ไปเที่ยว

do you want to go out tonight?
keun née yàhk bpai têe-o
mái?
คืนนี้อยากไปเที่ยวไหม

go through pàhn bpai
ผ่านไป

go up (the stairs etc) kêun bpai
ขึ้นไป

goat páir
แพะ

God pra-jâo
พระเจ้า

goggles wâirn dtah dum
náhm
แว่นตาดำน้ำ

gold torng
ทอง

Golden Triangle săhm lèe-um
torng kum
สามเหลี่ยมทองคำ

goldsmith châhng torng
ช่างทอง

golf górp
กอล์ฟ

golf course sa-nǎhm górp
สนามกอล์ฟ

good dee
ดี

good! dee láir-o!
ดีแล้ว

goodbye lah gòrn ná
ลาก่อนนะ

good evening sa-wùt dee krúp
(kâ)
สวัสดีครับ(ค่ะ)

good morning sa-wùt dee krúp
(kâ)
สวัสดีครับ(ค่ะ)

good night sa-wùt dee krúp (kâ)
สวัสดีครับ(ค่ะ)

goose hàhn
ห่าน

got: we've got to leave rao
dtôrng bpai
เราต้องไป

have you got any ...? mee ...
mái?
มี ... ไหม

government rút-ta-bahn
รัฐบาล

gradually tee la nòy
ทีละหน่อย

grammar wai-yah-gorn
ไวยากรณ์

gram(me) grum
กรัม

granddaughter lǎhn sǎo
หลานสาว

grandfather (maternal) dtah
ตา

(paternal) bpòo
ปู่

grandmother (maternal) yai
ยาย

(paternal) yâh
ย่า

grandson lǎhn chai
หลานชาย

grapefruit sôm oh
ส้มโอ

grapes a-ngòon
องุ่น

grass yâh
หญ้า

grateful róo-sèuk kòrp-koon
รู้สึกขอบคุณ

great (excellent) yôrt
ยอด

that's great! yôrt!
ยอด

Great Britain bpra-tâyt ung-grìt
ประเทศอังกฤษ

Greece bpra-tâyt greet
ประเทศกรีซ

greedy dta-glà
ตะกละ

green sěe kěe-o
สีเขียว

greengrocer's ráhn kǎi pùk
ร้านขายผัก

---

greeting people
Thais very rarely shake hands, using instead the **wai** – a prayer-like gesture made with raised hands – to greet and say good-bye and to acknowledge respect, gratitude or apology. The wai changes according to the relative status of the two people involved: Thais can instantane-ously assess which wai to use, but as a foreigner your safest bet is to go for the 'stranger's' wai, which requires that your hands be raised close to your chest and your fingertips placed just below your chin. If someone makes a wai at you, you should definitely wai back, but it's generally wise not to initiate.

---

grey sěe tao
สีเทา

grill (noun) dtao bpîng
เตาปิ้ง

grilled yâhng
ย่าง

grocer's ráhn kǎi kǒrng chum
ร้านขายของชำ

ground péun din
พื้นดิน

on the ground bon péun din
บนพื้นดิน

ground floor chún nèung
ชั้นหนึ่ง

group glòom
กลุ่ม

guarantee (noun) bai rúp-rorng
ใบรับรอง

is it guaranteed? mee bai rúp bpra-gun mái?
มีใบรับประกันไหม

guest kàirk
แขก

guesthouse gáyt háot
เกส์ตเฮาส์

Any place calling itself a guest-house – which could be anything from a bamboo hut to a three-storey concrete block – is almost certain to provide cheap, basic accommodation specifically aimed at Western travellers, usually consisting of a sparse double room with a fan and (usually shared) bathroom. You'll find them in all major tourist centres, on beaches, where they're also called bunga-lows, and even in the most un-likely remote spots.
see **hotel**

---

guide (noun: person) múk-koo-

tâyt
มัคคุเทศก์

guidebook kôo meu num têe-o
คู่มือนำเที่ยว

guided tour rai-gahn num têe-o
รายการนำเที่ยว

guitar gee-dtah
กีตาร์

Gulf of Thailand ào tai
อ่าวไทย

gum (in mouth) ngèu-uk
เงือก

gun (pistol) bpeun pók
ปืนพก

(rifle) bpeun yao
ปืนยาว

gym rohng yim
โรงยิม

H

hair pŏm
ผม

hairbrush bprairng pŏm
แปรงผม

haircut dtùt pŏm
ตัดผม

hairdresser's (men's) ráhn
dtàirng pŏm chai
ร้านแดงผมชาย

(women's) ráhn tum pŏm sa-
dtree
ร้านทำผมสตรี

hairdryer krêu-ung bpào

pŏm
เครื่องเป่าผม

hair gel kreem sài pŏm
ครีมใส่ผม

hairgrips gìp nèep pŏm
กิบหนีบผม

hair spray sa-bpray chèet pŏm
สเปรย์ฉีดผม

half* krêung
ครึ่ง

half an hour krêung chôo-a
mohng
ครึ่งชั่วโมง

half a litre krêung lít
ครึ่งลิตร

about half that bpra-mahn
krêung nèung
ประมาณครึ่งหนึ่ง

half-price krêung rah-kah
ครึ่งราคา

ham mŏo hairm
หมูแฮม

hamburger hairm-ber-gêr
แฮมเบอร์เกอร์

hammer (noun) kórn
ม้อน

hand meu
มือ

---

holding hands

Public displays of physical affec-
tion in Thailand are much more
acceptable between friends of
the same sex than between →

lovers of opposite sexes. Holding hands and hugging is as common among male friends as with females, so if you're given fairly intimate caresses by a Thai acquaintance of the same sex, don't assume you're being propositioned.

handbag gra-bpǎo tĕu
กระเป๋าถือ

handbrake brayk meu
เบรคมือ

handkerchief pâh chét nâh
ผ้าเช็ดหน้า

handle (on door, suitcase) dâhm
ด้าม

hand luggage gra-bpǎo tĕu
กระเป๋าถือ

hang-gliding gahn hŏhn rôrn
การโหนร่อน

hangover bpòo-ut hǒo-a
ปวดหัว

I've got a hangover pǒm
(chún) bpòo-ut hǒo-a

happen gèrt kêun
เกิดขึ้น

what's happening? gèrt a-rai
kêun?
เกิดอะไรขึ้น

what has happened? mee a-
rai gèrt kêun?
มีอะไรเกิดขึ้น

happy dee jai
ดีใจ

I'm not happy about this rêu-
ung née pǒm (chún) mâi sa-
bai jai
เรื่องนี้ผม(ฉัน)ไม่สบายใจ

harbour tâh reu-a
ท่าเรือ

hard kǎirng
แข็ง

(difficult) yâhk
ยาก

hard-boiled egg kài dtôm
kǎirng
ไข่ต้มแข็ง

hardly mâi kôy ...
ไม่ค่อย ...

hardly ever mâi kôy ...
ไม่ค่อย ...

hardware shop ráhn kǎi krêu-
ung lèk
ร้านขายเครื่องเหล็ก

hat mòo-uk
หมวก

hate (verb) glèe-ut
เกลียด

have* mee
มี

can I have a ...? kǒr ... nòy
ขอ ... หน่อย

do you have ...? mee ...
mái?
มี ... ไหม

what'll you have? (drink) kOOn

ja dèum a-rai?
คุณจะดื่มอะไร

I have to leave now pŏm
(chún) **dtôrng** bpai dĕe-o
née
ผม(ฉัน)ต้องไปเดี๋ยวนี้

do I have to ...? pŏm (chún)
dtôrng ... rĕu bplào?
ผม(ฉัน)ต้อง ... หรือเปล่า

can we have some ...? kŏr ...
nòy dâi mái?
ขอ ... หน่อยได้ไหม

hayfever rôhk hèut
โรคหืด

he* káo
เขา

head hŏo-a
หัว

headache bpòo-ut hŏo-a
ปวดหัว

headlights fai nâh rót
ไฟหน้ารถ

headphones hŏo fung
หูฟัง

healthy (person) mee sÒOk-ka-
pâhp dee
มีสุขภาพดี

(food) bpen bpra-yòht gàir
râhng-gai
เป็นประโยชน์แก่ร่างกาย

hear dâi yin
ได้ยิน

can you hear me? dâi yin mái?

I can't hear you, could you repeat
that? pŏm (chún) mâi dâi yin,
pôot èek tee dâi mái?

hearing aid krêu-ung chôo-ay
fung
เครื่องช่วยฟัง

heart hŏo-a jai
หัวใจ

heart attack hŏo-a jai wai
หัวใจไว

heat kwahm rórn
ความร้อน

heating krêu-ung tum kwahm
rórn
เครื่องทำความร้อน

heavy nùk
หนัก

heel (of foot) sôn táo
ส้นเท้า

(of shoe) sôn rorng táo
สนรองเท้า

could you heel these? bplèe-
un sôn mài hâi nòy, dâi mái?
เปลี่ยนส้นใหม่ให้หน่อยได้ไหม

height kwahm sŏong
ความสูง

helicopter hay-li-korp-dter
เฮลิคอปเตอร์

hello sa-wùt dee
สวัสดี

(answer on phone) hun-loh
ฮันโล

helmet (for motorbike) mòo-uk
gun chon
หมวกกันชน

help (noun) kwahm chôo-ay
lĕu-a
ความช่วยเหลือ

(verb) chôo-ay
ช่วย

help! chôo-ay dôo-ay!
ช่วยด้วย

can you help me? chôo-ay
pŏm (chún) nòy, dâi mái?
ช่วยผม(ฉัน)หน่อยได้ไหม

thank you very much for your
help kòrp-kOOn têe dâi chôo-
ay lĕu-a
ขอบคุณที่ได้ช่วยเหลือ

helpful bpen bpra-yòht
mâhk
เป็นประโยชน์มาก

hepatitis dtùp ùk-sàyp
ตับอักเสบ

her*: I haven't seen her pŏm
(chún) mâi dâi hĕn káo
ผม(ฉัน)ไม่ได้เห็นเขา

to her gàir káo
แก่เขา

with her gùp káo
กับเขา

for her sŭm-rùp káo
สำหรับเขา

that's her nûn káo
นั่นเขา

that's her towel bpen pâh

chét dtoo-a kŏrng káo
เป็นผ้าเช็ดตัวของเขา

herbs (for cooking) krêu-ung
tâyt
เครื่องเทศ

(medicinal) sa-mŏon prai
สมุนไพร

here têe-nêe
ที่นี่

here is/are ... nêe ...
นี่ ...

here you are (offering) nêe ngai
นี่ไง

hers* kŏrng káo
ของเขา

that's hers nûn kŏrng káo
นั่นของเขา

hey! háy!
เฮ

hi! (hello) bpai nǎi?
ไปไหน

hide (verb) sôrn
ซ่อน

high sŏong
สูง

highchair gâo êe sŏong
เก้าอี้สูง

highway tahng dòo-un
ทางด่วน

hill kǎo
เขา

him*: I haven't seen him pŏm
(chún) mâi dâi hĕn káo
ผม(ฉัน)ไม่ได้เห็นเขา

to him gàir káo
แก่เขา

with him gùp káo
กับเขา

for him sŭm-rùp káo
สำหรับเขา

that's him nûn káo
นั่นเขา

hip sa-pôhk
สะโพก

hire châo
เช่า

for hire hâi châo
ให้เช่า

where can I hire a bike? (bicycle)
châo jùk-ra-yahn dâi têe nǎi?
เช่าจักรยานได้ที่ไหน

see rent

his*: it's his car bpen rót kǒrng
káo
เป็นรถของเขา

that's his nûn kǒrng káo
นี่นของเขา

hit (verb) dtee
ตี

hitch-hike bòhk rót
โบกรถ

hobby ngahn a-di-râyk
งานอดิเรก

hold (verb) tĕu
ถือ

hole roo
รู

holiday wun yòot
วันหยุด

on holiday yòot púk pòrn
หยุดพักผ่อน

Holland bpra-tâyt hor-lairn
ประเทศฮอลแลนด์

home bâhn
บ้าน

at home (in my house etc) têe
bâhn
ที่บ้าน

(in my country) nai bpra-tâyt
pǒm (chún)
ในประเทศผม(ฉัน)

we go home tomorrow (to
country) rao glùp bâhn
prôong née
เรากลับบ้านพรุ่งนี้

honest sêu dtrong
ซื่อตรง

honey núm pêung
น้ำผึ้ง

honeymoon hun-nee-moon
ฮันนีมูน

hood (US: car) gra-bprohng rót
กระโปรงรถ

hope wǔng
หวัง

I hope so wǔng wâh yung
ngún
หวังว่าอย่างนั้น

I hope not wǔng wâh kong
mâi
หวังว่าคงไม่

hopefully wǔng wâh ...
หวังว่า ...

horn (of car) dtrair
แตร

horrible nâh glèe-ut
น่าเกลียด

horse máh
ม้า

horse riding kèe máh
ขี่ม้า

hospital rohng pa-yah-bahn
โรงพยาบาล

hospitality gahn dtôrn rúp kùp
sôo
การตอนรับขับสู้

thank you for your hospitality
kòrp-koon têe dtôrn rúp kùp
sôo
ขอบคุณที่ตอนรับขับสู้

hostess (in bar) pôo-yǐng bah
ผู้หญิงบาร์

hot rórn
ร้อน

(spicy) pèt
เผ็ด

I'm hot pǒm (chún) rórn
ผม(ฉัน)ร้อน

it's hot today wun née ah-
gàht rórn jung ler-ee
วันนี้อากาศร้อนจังเลย

hotel rohng rairm
โรงแรม

Few Thais use guesthouses, opting instead for hotels. Beds in
single rooms (**hôrng dèe-o**) are
→

large enough for a couple, and
it's quite acceptable for two people to ask and pay for a single.
Usually run by Chinese-Thais,
you'll find three- or four-storey
budget hotels in every sizeable
town, often near the bus station.
They are generally clean
and usually come with an
en-suite bathroom, fan (or air-
conditioning) and boiled water,
which makes them good value
in terms of facilities. Moderate
hotels are sometimes good
value, offering many of the trim-
mings of a top-end hotel (TV,
fridge, air-conditioning, pool)
but none of the prestige.
Many of Thailand's upmarket
hotels belong to international
chains, maintaining top-quality
standards in Bangkok and
major resorts at rates far lower
than you'd pay for luxury accommodation in the West. Some of
the best home-grown upmarket
hotels are up to B1000 cheaper
for equally fine service, rooms
equipped with TV, minibar and
balcony, and full use of the
hotel sports facilities and swimming pools.

hotel room hôrng nai rohng
  rairm
  ห้องในโรงแรม
hour chôo-a mohng
  ชั่วโมง
house bâhn
  บ้าน
how? yung-ngai?
  อย่างไร
how many? gèe?
  กี่
how do you do? sa-wùt dee
  krúp (kâ)
  สวัสดีครับ(ค่ะ)

•••••• D I A L O G U E S ••••••

how are you? bpen yung-ngai
  bâhng?
fine, thanks, and you? sa-bai dee
  krúp (kâ) láir-o koon lâ?

how much is it? tâo-rài?
50 baht hâh sìp baht
I'll take it ao

humid chéun
  ชื้น
hungry hěw kâo
  หิวข้าว
  are you hungry? hěw kâo mái?
  หิวข้าวไหม
hurry (verb) rêep
  รีบ
  I'm in a hurry pǒm (chún)
  dtôrng rêep
  ผม(ฉัน)ต้องรีบ

there's no hurry mâi dtôrng
  rêep
  ไม่ต้องรีบ
hurry up! ray-o ray-o
  kâo!
  เร็ว ๆ เข้า
hurt (verb) jèp
  เจ็บ
it really hurts jèp jing
  jing
  เจ็บจริง ๆ
husband sǎh-mee
  สามี

I

I* (male) pǒm
  ผม
  (female) chún; dee-chún
  ฉัน; ดิฉัน
ice núm kǎirng
  น้ำแข็ง
  with ice sài núm kǎirng
  ใส่น้ำแข็ง
  no ice, thanks mâi sài núm
  kǎirng
  ไม่ใส่น้ำแข็ง
ice cream ait-greem
  ไอศกรีม
ice-cream cone groo-ay sài ait-
  greem
  กรวยใส่ไอศกรีม
iced coffee gah-fair yen
  กาแฟเย็น

ice lolly ait-greem tâirng
ไอศกรีมแท่ง

idea kwahm kít
ความคิด

idiot kon bâh
คนบ้า

if tâh
ถ้า

ignition fai krêu-ung yon
ไฟเครื่องยนต์

ill mâi sa-bai
ไม่สบาย

I feel ill pǒm (chún) mâi sa-
bai
ผม(ฉัน)ไม่สบาย

illness kwahm jèp
bpòo-ay
ความเจ็บป่วย

imitation (leather etc) tee-um
เทียม

immediately tun-tee
ทันที

important sǔm-kun
สำคัญ

it's very important sǔm-kun
mâhk
สำคัญมาก

it's not important mâi sǔm-
kun
ไม่สำคัญ

impossible bpen bpai mâi
dâi
เป็นไปไม่ได้

impressive nâh têung
น่าทึ่ง

improve dee kêun
ดีขึ้น

I want to improve my Thai
pǒm (chún) yàhk ja pôot
pah-sǎh tai hâi dee kêun
ผม(ฉัน)อยากจะพูดภาษา
ไทยให้ดีขึ้น

in: it's in the centre nai jai
glahng meu-ung
ในใจกลางเมือง

in my car nai rót pǒm (chún)
ในรถผม(ฉัน)

in Chiangmai têe chee-ung-
mài
ที่เชียงใหม่

in two days from now èek
sǒrng wun dtòr jàhk née
อีกสองวันต่อจากนี้

in five minutes èek hâh nah-
tee
อีกห้านาที

in May deu-un préut-sa-pah-
kom
เดือนพฤษภาคม

in English bpen pah-sǎh ung-
grìt
เป็นภาษาอังกฤษ

in Thai bpen pah-sǎh tai
เป็นภาษาไทย

is he in? káo yòo mái?
เขาอยู่ไหม

inch* néw
นิ้ว

include roo-um
รวม

does that include meals? roo-um ah-hǎhn dôo-ay rĕu bplào?
รวมอาหารด้วยหรือเปล่า

is that included? roo-um yòo dôo-ay rĕu bplào?
รวมอยู่ด้วยหรือเปล่า

inconvenient mâi sa-dòo-uk
ไม่สะดวก

incredible mâi nâh chêu-a
ไม่น่าเชื่อ

India bpra-tâyt in-dee-a
ประเทศอินเดีย

Indian (adj) kàirk
แขก

indicator (on car) fai lée-o
ไฟเลี้ยว

indigestion ah-hǎhn mâi yôy
อาหารไม่ย่อย

Indonesia bpra-tâyt in-doh-nee-see-a
ประเทศอินโดนีเซีย

indoors kâhng nai
ข้างใน

inexpensive mâi pairng, tòok
ไม่แพง, ถูก

infection ah-gahn ùk-sàyp
อาการอักเสบ

infectious rôhk dtìt dtòr
โรคติดต่อ

inflammation ah-gahn bpòo-ut boo-um
อาการปวดบวม

informal bpen gun ayng
เป็นกันเอง

information kào-sǎhn
ข่าวสาร

do you have any information about ...? mee rai la-èe-ut gèe-o gùp ... mái?
มีรายละเอียดเกี่ยวกับ ... ไหม

information desk têe sòrp tǎhm
ที่สอบถาม

injection chèet yah
ฉีดยา

injured bàht jèp
บาดเจ็บ

she's been injured káo bàht jèp
เขาบาดเจ็บ

inner tube (for tyre) yahng nai
ยางใน

innocent bor-ri-sòot
บริสุทธ์

insect ma-lairng
แมลง

insect bite ma-lairng gùt
แมลงกัด

do you have anything for insect bites? mee yah tah gâir ma-lairng gùt mái?
มียาทาแก้แมลงกัดไหม

insect repellent yah gun ma-lairng
ยากันแมลง

inside kâhng nai
ข้างใน

inside the hotel kâhng nai rohng rairm
ข้างในโรงแรม

let's sit inside bpai nûng kâhng nai tèr
ไปนั่งข้างในเถอะ

insist ka-yún ka-yor
คะยั้นคะยอ

I insist pǒm (chún) ka-yún ka-yor
ผม(ฉัน)คะยั้นคะยอ

insomnia norn mâi lùp
นอนไม่หลับ

instant coffee gah-fair pǒng
กาแฟผง

instead tairn
แทน

give me that one instead ao un nún tairn
เอาอันนั้นแทน

instead of ... tairn têe ja ...
แทนที่ ...

insulin in-soo-lin
อินซูลิน

insurance gahn bpra-gun pai
การประกันภัย

intelligent cha-làht
ฉลาด

interested: I'm interested in ...
pǒm (chún) sǒn jai ...
ผม(ฉัน)สนใจ ...

interesting nâh sǒn jai
น่าสนใจ

that's very interesting nâh sǒn
jai mâhk
น่าสนใจมาก

international sǎh-gon
สากล

interpret bplair
แปล

interpreter lâhm
ล่าม

intersection sèe yâirk
สี่แยก

interval (at theatre) púk krêung
พักครึ่ง

into nai
ใน

I'm not into ... pǒm (chún) mâi chôrp ...
ผม(ฉัน)ไม่ชอบ ...

introduce náir-num
แนะนำ

may I introduce ...? pǒm (chún) kǒr náir-num hâi róo-jùk gùp
ผม(ฉัน)ขอแนะนำให้รู้จักกับ ...

invitation kum chern
คำเชิญ

invite chern choo-un
เชิญชวน

Ireland ai-lairn
ไอร์แลนด์

iron (for ironing) dtao rêet
เตารีด

can you iron these for me?
chôo-ay rêet hâi nòy dâi mái?
ช่วยรีดให้หน่อยได้ไหม

is* bpen
เป็น

island gòr
เกาะ

it mun
มัน

it is ... bpen ...
เป็น ...

is it ...? ... châi mái?
... ใช่ไหม

where is it? yòo têe nǎi?
อยู่ที่ไหน

it's him káo nûn làir
เขานั่นแหละ

it was ... bpen ...
เป็น ...

Italy bpra-tâyt ì-dtah-lee
ประเทศอิตาลี

itch: it itches kun
คัน

J

jack (for car) mâir rairng
แม่แรง

jacket sêu-a nôrk
เสื้อนอก

jam yairm
แยม

jammed: it's jammed mun dtìt
nâirn
มันติดแน่น

January mók-ga-rah-kom
มกราคม

Japan yêe-bpòon
ญี่ปุ่น

Japanese yêe-bpòon
ญี่ปุ่น

jar (noun) hǎi
ไห

jaw kǎh-gun-grai
ขากรรไกร

jazz jáirt
แจ๊ส

jealous hěung
หึง

jeans yeen
ยีนส์

jellyfish mairng ga-prOOn
แมงกะพรุน

jersey sêu-a sa-wét-dtêr
เสื้อสเวตเตอร์

jetty tâh reu-a
ท่าเรือ

jeweller's ráhn kǎi krêu-ung
pét ploy
ร้านขายเครื่องเพชรพลอย

jewellery pét ploy
เพชรพลอย

Jewish yew
ยิว

job ngahn
งาน

jogging jórk-gîng
จ๊อกกิ้ง

to go jogging bpai jórk-gîng
ไปจ๊อกกิ้ง

joke dta-lòk
ตลก

journey gahn dern tahng
การเดินทาง

have a good journey! dern
tahng dôo-ay dee ná!
เดินทางด้วยดีนะ

jug yêu-uk
เหยือก

a jug of water yêu-uk náhm
เหยือกน้ำ

juice náhm pǒn-la-mái
น้ำผลไม้

July ga-rúk-ga-dah-kom
กรกฎาคม

jump (verb) gra-dòht
กระโดด

jumper sêu-a sa-wét-dtêr
เสื้อสเวตเตอร์

junction tahng yâirk
ทางแยก

June mí-too-nah-yon
มิถุนายน

jungle bpàh
ป่า

just (only) tâo-nún
เท่านั้น

just two sǒrng un tâo-nún
สองอันเท่านั้น

just for me sǔm-rùp pǒm
(chún) kon dee-o
สำหรับผม(ฉัน)คนเดียว

just here dtrong née
ตรงนี้

not just now mâi ao děe-o née
ไม่เอาเดี๋ยวนี้

we've just arrived rao pêrng
mah mêu-a gêe née ayng
เราเพิ่งมาเมื่อกี้นี้เอง

K

keep gèp
เก็บ

keep the change mâi dtôrng
torn
ไม่ต้องทอน

can I keep it? pǒm (chún)
gèp wái dâi mái?
ผม(ฉัน)เก็บไว้ได้ไหม

please keep it ao wái ler-ee
เอาไว้เลย

ketchup sórt ma-kěu-a tâyt
ซอสมะเขือเทศ

kettle gah náhm
กาน้ำ

key goon-jair
กุญแจ

the key for room 201, please
kǒr goon-jair hôrng sǒrng
sǒon sèe
ขอกุญแจห้องสองศูนย์สี่

keyring hòo-ung goon-jair
ห่วงกุญแจ

kidneys (in body) dtai
ไต

(food) krêu-ung nai
เครื่องใน

kill kâh
ฆ่า
kilo* gi-loh
กิโล
kilometre* gi-loh-mét
กิโลเมตร
how many kilometres is it
to ...? bpai ... gèe
gi-loh?
ไป ... กี่กิโล
kind (generous) jai dee
ใจดี
that's very kind kOOn jai dee
mâhk
คุณใจดีมาก

• • • • • • DIALOGUE • • • • • •

which kind do you want? ao bàirp
nǎi?
I want this/that kind ao bàirp née/
nún

king nai lǒo-ung
ในหลวง
kiosk dtôo
ตู้
kiss jòop
จูบ
kitchen hôrng kroo-a
ห้องครัว
knee hǒo-a kào
หัวเข่า
knickers gahng gayng nai sa-
dtree
กางเกงในสตรี

knife mêet
มีด
knock (verb) kór
เคาะ
knock down (road accident) rót
chon
รถชน
he's been knocked down káo
tòok rót chon
เขาถูกรถชน
knock over (object, pedestrian)
chon lóm
ชนล้ม
know (somebody) róo-jùk
รู้จัก
(something) róo; sâhp
รู้; ทราบ
(a place) róo-jùk
รู้จัก
I don't know pǒm (chún) mâi
róo/sâhp
ผม(ฉัน)ไม่รู้/ทราบ
I didn't know that pǒm (chún)
mâi róo/sâhp mah gòrn
ผม(ฉัน)ไม่รู้/ทราบมาก่อน
do you know where I can
find ...? sâhp mái wâh ja hǎh
... dâi têe nǎi?
ทราบไหมว่าจะหา ... ได้ที่ไหน

L

label bpâi
ป้าย

ladies' (room) sa-dtree
สตรี

ladies' wear krêu-ung dtàirng
gai sa-dtree
เครื่องแต่งกายสตรี

lady pôo-yǐng
ผู้หญิง

lager lah-ger
ลาเกอร์
see beer

lake ta-lay sàhp
ทะเลสาบ

lamb (meat) néu-a gàir
เนื้อแกะ

lamp kohm fai fáh
โคมไฟฟ้า

lane (motorway) chôrng
ช่อง
(small road) soy
ซอย

language pah-sǎh
ภาษา

language course bàirp ree-un
pah-sǎh
แบบเรียนภาษา

Laos bpra-tâyt lao
ประเทศลาว

large yài
ใหญ่

last sòot tái
สุดท้าย

last week mêu-a ah-tít gòrn
เมื่ออาทิตย์ก่อน

last Friday mêu-a wun sòok
gòrn
เมื่อวันศุกร์ก่อน

last night mêu-a keun née
เมื่อคืนนี้

what time is the last train to
Ubon? rót fai bpai OO-bon
têe-o sòot tái òrk gèe
mohng?
รถไฟไปอุบลเที่ยวสุดท้าย
ออกกี่โมง

late cháh
ช้า

sorry I'm late kǒr-tôht têe
mah cháh
ขอโทษที่มาช้า

the train was late rót fai mah
těung cháh
รถไฟมาถึงช้า

we must go – we'll be late rao
dtôrng bpai děe-o ja mâi tun
เราต้องไป เดี๋ยวจะไม่ทัน

it's getting late dèuk láir-o
ดึกแล้ว

later tee lǔng
ทีหลัง

I'll come back later děe-o ja
glùp mah
เดี๋ยวจะกลับมา

see you later děe-o jer gun èek
เดี๋ยวเจอกันอีก

later on tee lǔng
ทีหลัง

latest yàhng cháh têe sòot
อย่างช้าที่สุด
by Wednesday at the latest wun
póot yàhng cháh têe sòot
วันพุธอย่างช้าที่สุด

laugh (verb) hǒo-a rór
หัวเราะ

laundry (clothes) sêu-a pâh
เสื้อผ้า
(place) ráhn súk pâh
ร้านซักผ้า

lavatory hôrng náhm
ห้องน้ำ

law gòt-mǎi
กฎหมาย

lawn sa-nǎhm yâh
สนามหญ้า

lawyer ta-nai kwahm
ทนายความ

laxative yah tài
ยาถ่าย

lazy kêe gèe-ut
ขี้เกียจ

lead (electrical) sǎi fai fáh
สายไฟฟ้า
(verb) num
นำ
where does this lead to? nêe
bpai těung nǎi?
นี่ไปถึงไหน

leaf bai mái
ใบไม้

leaflet bai bplew
ใบปลิว

leak rôo-a
รั่ว
the roof leaks lǔng-kah rôo-a
หลังคารั่ว

learn ree-un
เรียน

least: not in the least mâi ler-ee
ไม่เลย
at least yàhng nóy têe sòot
อย่างน้อยที่สุด

leather nǔng
หนัง

leave (verb: behind) tíng wái
ทิ้งไว้
(go away) jàhk bpai
จากไป
I am leaving tomorrow pǒm
(chún) **bpai** prôong née
ผม(ฉัน)ไปพรุ่งนี้
he left yesterday káo **bpai**
mêu-a wahn née
เขาไปเมื่อวานนี้
may I leave this here? kǒr
fàhk wái têe nêe dâi mái?
ขอฝากไว้ที่นี่ได้ไหม
I left my coat in the bar pǒm
(chún) **tíng** sêu-a wái têe bah
ผม(ฉัน)ทิ้งเสื้อไว้ที่บาร์
when does the bus for
Bangsaen leave? rót bpai
bahng-sǎirn **òrk** gèe mohng?
รถไปบางแสนออกกี่โมง

left sái
ซ้าย

on the left tahng sái
ทางซ้าย

to the left tahng sái
ทางซ้าย

turn left lée-o sái
เลี้ยวซ้าย

there's none left mâi mee **lěu-
a yòo**
ไม่มีเหลืออยู่

left-handed ta-nùt meu sái
ถนัดมือซ้าย

left luggage (office) têe fàhk
gra-bpǎo
ที่ฝากกระเป๋า

leg kǎh
ขา

lemon ma-nao
มะนาว

lemonade núm ma-nao
น้ำมะนาว

lemon tea núm chah sài ma-
nao
น้ำชาใส่มะนาว

lend: will you lend me your ... ?
kǒr yeum ... nòy, dâi mái?
ขอยืม ... หน่อยได้ไหม

lens (of camera) layn
เลนส์

lesbian 'lesbian'
เล็สเบียน

less nóy gwàh
นอยกว่า

less than ... nóy gwàh ...
นอยกว่า ...

less expensive tòok gwàh
ถูกกว่า

lesson bòt ree-un
บทเรียน

let (allow) hâi
ให้

will you let me know? chôo-ay
bòrk hâi pǒm (chún) sâhp
dôo-ay
ช่วยบอกให้ผม(ฉัน)ทราบด้วย

I'll let you know pǒm (chún)
ja bòrk hâi sâhp
ผม(ฉัน)จะบอกให้ทราบ

let's go for something to eat
bpai tahn kâo mái?
ไปทานข้าวไหม

let off: will you let me off
at ...? kǒr long têe ... dâi
mái?
ขอลงที่ ... ได้ไหม

letter jòt-mǎi
จดหมาย

do you have any letters for me?
mee jòt-mǎi mah těung pǒm
(chún) mái?
มีจดหมายมาถึงผม(ฉัน)ไหม

letterbox dtôo jòt-mǎi
ตู้จดหมาย

lettuce pùk-gàht
ผักกาด

lever (noun) kun yók
คันยก

library hǒr sa-mòot
หอสมุด

licence bai un-nóo-yâht
ใบอนุญาต

lid fǎh
ฝา

lie (verb: tell untruth) goh-hòk
โกหก

lie down norn
นอน

life chee-wít
ชีวิต

lifebelt choo chêep
ชูชีพ

life jacket sêu-a choo chêep
เสื้อชูชีพ

lift (in building) líf
ลิฟท์

could you give me a lift? chôo-
ay bpai sòng nòy, dâi mái?
ช่วยไปส่งหน่อยได้ไหม

would you like a lift? bpai
sòng hâi ao mái?
ไปส่งให้เอาไหม

light (noun) fai
ไฟ

(not heavy) bao
เบา

do you have a light? (for
cigarette) mee fai mái?
มีไฟไหม

light green sěe kěe-o òrn
สีเขียวอ่อน

light bulb lòrt fai fáh
หลอดไฟฟ้า

I need a new light bulb pǒm

(chún) dtôrng-gahn lòrt fai
fáh
ผม(ฉัน)ต้องการหลอดไฟฟ้า

lighter (cigarette) fai cháirk
ไฟแช็ก

lightning fáh lâirp
ฟ้าแลบ

like (verb) chôrp
ชอบ

I like it pǒm (chún) chôrp
ผม(ฉัน)ชอบ

I like going for walks pǒm
(chún) chôrp bpai dern lên
ผม(ฉัน)ชอบไปเดินเล่น

I like you pǒm (chún) chôrp
koon
ผม(ฉัน)ชอบคุณ

I don't like it pǒm (chún) mâi
chôrp
ผม(ฉัน)ไม่ชอบ

do you like ...? koon chôrp ...
mái?
คุณชอบ ...ไหม

I'd like a beer pǒm (chún) ao
bee-a kòo-ut nèung
ผม(ฉัน)เอาเบียร์ขวดหนึ่ง

I'd like to go swimming pǒm
(chún) yàhk bpai wâi náhm
ผม(ฉัน)อยากไปว่ายน้ำ

would you like a drink? koon
dèum a-rai mái?
คุณดื่มอะไรไหม

would you like to go for a
walk? koon yàhk bpai

dern lên mái?
คุณอยากไปเดินเล่นไหม

what's it like? bpen **yung
ngai?**
เป็นอย่างไร

I want one like this ao **bàirp
née**
เอาแบบนี้

lime ma-nao kwai
มะนาวควาย

line (on paper) sên
เส้น

(phone) săi
สาย

could you give me an outside
line? chôo-ay dtòr săi kâhng
nôrk hâi nòy, dâi mái?
ช่วยต่อสายข้างนอกให้หน่อย
ได้ไหม

lips rim fěe bpàhk
ริมฝีปาก

lip salve kêe pêung tah rim fěe
bpàhk
ขี้ผึ้งทาริมฝีปาก

lipstick líp sa-dtík
ลิปสติก

listen fung
ฟัง

litre* lít
ลิตร

little lék
เล็ก

just a little, thanks **nít dee-o**
nít dee-o tâo-nún
นิดเดียวเท่านั้น

a little milk nom nít nòy
นมนิดหน่อย

a little bit more èek nít **nèung**
อีกนิดหนึ่ง

live (verb) mee chee-wít yòo
มีชีวิตอยู่

we live together rao yòo dôo-
ay gun
เราอยู่ด้วยกัน

• • • • • • DIALOGUE • • • • • •

where do you live? koon yòo têe
năi?

I live in London pǒm (chún) yòo
têe lorn-dorn

lively (person, town) mee chee-wít
chee-wah
มีชีวิตชีวา

liver (in body, food) dtùp
ตับ

loaf bporn
ปอนด์

lobby (in hotel) pa-nàirk dtôrn
rúp
แผนกต้อนรับ

lobster gôong yài
กุ้งใหญ่

local tǎir-o née
แถวนี้

can you recommend a local
restaurant? chôo-ay náir-num
ráhn ah-hǎhn tǎir-o née hâi
nòy dâi mái?
ช่วยแนะนำร้านอาหารแถวนี้
ให้หน่อยได้ไหม

lock (noun) gOOn-jair
กุญแจ
(verb) sài gOOn-jair
ใส่กุญแจ
it's locked sài gOOn-jair
láir-o
ใส่กุญแจแล้ว

lock out: I've locked myself out
bpìt gOOn-jair láir-o kâo
hôrng mâi dâi
ปิดกุญแจแล้วเข้าห้องไม่ได้

locker (for luggage etc) dtôo
ตู้

lollipop om-yím
อมยิ้ม

London lorn-dorn
ลอนดอน

long yao
ยาว
how long will it take to fix it?
chái way-lah sôrm **nahn** tâo-
rài?
ใช้เวลาซ่อมนานเท่าไร
how long does it take? chái
way-lah **nahn** tâo-rài?
ใช้เวลานานเท่าไร
a long time nahn
นาน
one day/two days longer èek
wun sŏrng wun
อีกวันสองวัน

long-distance call toh tahng glai
โทรทางไกล

long-tailed boat reu-a hăhng

yao
เรือหางยาว

look: I'm just looking, thanks
pŏm (chún) chom doo tâo-
nún
ผม(ฉัน)ชมดูเท่านั้น
you don't look well kOOn tâh
tahng mâi sa-bai
คุณท่าทางไม่สบาย
look out! ra-wung ná!
ระวังนะ
can I have a look? kŏr doo
nòy, dâi mái?
ขอดูหน่อยได้ไหม

look after doo lair
ดูแล

look at doo
ดู

look for hăh
หา
I'm looking for ... pŏm (chún)
gum-lung hăh ...
ผม(ฉัน)กำลังหา ...

loose (handle etc) lòot
หลุด

lorry rót bun-tóok
รถบรรทุก

lose hăi
หาย
I've lost my way pŏm (chún)
lŏng tahng
ผม(ฉัน)หลงทาง
I'm lost, I want to get to ... pŏm
(chún) lŏng tahng, dtôrng-

gahn bpai ...
ผม(ฉัน)หลงทาง ต้องการไป ...

I've lost my bag gra-bpǎo
pǒm (chún) hǎi
กระเป๋าผม(ฉัน)หาย

lost property (office) têe jâirng
kǒrng hǎi
ที่แจ้งของหาย

lot: a lot, lots mâhk
มาก

not a lot mâi mâhk
ไม่มาก

a lot of people kon mâhk
คนมาก

a lot bigger yài mâhk gwàh
ใหญ่มากกว่า

I like it a lot pǒm (chún)
chôrp mâhk
ผม(ฉัน)ชอบมาก

lotion yah tah
ยาทา

loud dung
ดัง

lounge (in house, hotel) hôrng
nûng lên
ห้องนั่งเล่น

(in airport) hôrng púk pôo
doy-ee sǎhn
ห้องพักผู้โดยสาร

love (noun) kwahm rúk
ความรัก

(verb) rúk
รัก

I love Thailand pǒm (chún)

rúk meu-ung tai
ผม(ฉัน)รักเมืองไทย

lovely sǒo-ay
สวย

low (prices, bridge) dtùm
ต่ำ

luck chôhk
โชค

good luck! chôhk dee!
โชคดี

luggage gra-bpǎo
กระเป๋า

luggage trolley rót kěn
รถเข็น

lump (on body) néu-a ngôrk
เนื้องอก

lunch ah-hǎhn glahng wun
อาหารกลางวัน

lungs bpòrt
ปอด

luxurious (hotel, furnishings) rǒo-
rǎh
หรูหรา

luxury kǒrng fôom feu-ay
ของฟุ่มเฟือย

M

machine krêu-ung
เครื่อง

mad (insane) bâh
บ้า

(angry) gròht
โกรธ

magazine nít-ta-ya-sǎhn
นิตยสาร

maid (in hotel) yǐng rúp
chái
หญิงรับใช้

maiden name nahm sa-gOOn
derm
นามสกุลเดิม

mail (noun) jòt-mǎi
จดหมาย

(verb) sòng jòt-mǎi
ส่งจดหมาย

is there any mail for me? mee
jòt-mǎi sǔm-rùp pǒm (chún)
mái?
มีจดหมายสำหรับผม(ฉัน)ไหม
see post office

mailbox dtôo jòt-mǎi
ตู้จดหมาย

main sǔm-kun
สำคัญ

main post office bprai-sa-nee
glahng
ไปรษณีย์กลาง

main road ta-nǒn yài
ถนนใหญ่

mains switch (for electricity) sa-
wít sǎi fai yài
สวิชสายไฟใหญ่

make (brand name) yêe hôr
ยี่ห้อ

(verb) tum
ทำ

I make it 500 baht pǒm
(chún) kít wâh hâh róy bàht
ผม(ฉัน)คิดว่าห้าร้อยบาท

what is it made of? tum dôo-
ay a-rai?
ทำด้วยอะไร

make-up krêu-ung sǔm-ahng
เครื่องสำอาง

malaria kâi jùp sùn, mah-lay-
ree-a
ไข้จับสั่น, มาเลเรีย

malaria tablets yah gâir mah-
lay-ree-a
ยาแก้มาเลเรีย

Malay (adj) ma-lah-yoo
มลายู

Malaysia bpra-tâyt mah-lay-
see-a
ประเทศมาเลเซีย

man pôo-chai
ผู้ชาย

manager pôo-jùt-gahn
ผู้จัดการ

can I see the manager? kǒr
póp pôo-jùt-gahn nòy
ขอพบผู้จัดการหน่อย

mango ma-môo-ung
มะม่วง

---

manners

According to ancient Hindu
belief the head is the most sacred part of the body and the
feet the most unclean. This
belief, imported into Thailand,
→

means that it's very rude to touch another person's head or to point your feet either at a human being or at a sacred image. When sitting on a temple floor for example, you should tuck your legs beneath you rather than stretch them out towards the Buddha. These hierarchies also forbid people from wearing shoes (which are even more unclean than feet) inside temples and most private homes. By extension, Thais take offence when they see someone sitting on the 'head', or prow, of a boat.

The left hand is used for washing after defecating, so Thais never use it to put food in their mouth, pass things or shake hands – as a foreigner though, you'll be assumed to have different customs, so left-handers shouldn't worry unduly.

many mâhk
มาก
not many mâi mâhk
ไม่มาก
map păirn-têe
แผนที่

Bangkok bookshops are the best source of maps – but the general standard of maps is low.

March mee-nah-kom
มีนาคม
margarine ner-ee tee-um
เนยเทียม
market dta-làht
ตลาด

Smaller markets selling only foodstuffs, cheap household goods and toiletries can still be found even in the centre of Bangkok. They are usually at their busiest at about 7 a.m. as housewives and maids do the day's shopping. Bangkok's biggest market is at Chatuchak Park near the Northern Bus Station; held on Saturday and Sunday, it sells virtually everything, including tapes, books, furniture, 'antiques', plants, pets, electrical goods, as well as every conceivable kind of foodstuff.

marmalade yairm
แยม
married: I'm married pŏm
(chún) dtàirng ngahn láir-o
ผม(ฉัน)แต่งงานแล้ว

are you married? kOOn dtàirng
ngahn láir-o rěu yung?
คุณแต่งงานแล้วหรือยัง

mascara mair-sa-kah-rah
แมสคารา

massage nôo-ut
นวด

match (football etc) gahn kàirng
kǔn
การแข่งขัน

matches mái kèet
ไม้ขีด

material (fabric) pâh
ผ้า

matter: it doesn't matter mâi
bpen rai
ไม่เป็นไร

what's the matter? bpen
a-rai?
เป็นอะไร

mattress têe norn
ที่นอน

May préut-sa-pah-kom
พฤษภาคม

may: may I have another one?
kǒr èek un nèung dâi mái?
ขออีกอันหนึ่งได้ไหม

may I come in? kâo mah dâi
mái?
เข้ามาได้ไหม

may I see it? kǒr doo nòy dâi
mái?
ขอดูหน่อยได้ไหม

may I sit here? nûng têe nêe

dâi mái?
นั่งที่นี่ได้ไหม

maybe bahng tee
บางที

mayonnaise núm sa-lùt
น้ำสลัด

me* (male) pǒm
ผม

(female) dee-chún, chún
ดิฉัน, ฉัน

that's for me nûn sǔm-rùp
pǒm (chún)
นั่นสำหรับผม(ฉัน)

send it to me sòng mah hâi
pǒm (chún)
ส่งมาให้ผม(ฉัน)

me too pǒm (chún) gôr měu-
un gun
ผม(ฉัน)ก็เหมือนกัน

meal ah-hǎhn
อาหาร

•••••• DIALOGUE ••••••

did you enjoy your meal? ah-hǎhn
a-ròy mái?

it was excellent, thank you a-ròy
mâhk

mean (verb) mǎi kwahm
หมายความ

what do you mean? kOOn mǎi
kwahm wâh a-rai?
คุณหมายความว่าอะไร

•••••• DIALOGUE ••••••

what does this word mean? kum
née **bplàir wâh** a-rai?
it means ... in English pah-săh ung-
grìt **bplair wâh** ...

measles rôhk hùt
โรคหัด

meat néu-a
เนื้อ

mechanic châhng krêu-ung
ช่างเครื่อง

medicine yah
ยา

medium (adj: size) glahng
กลาง

medium-rare (steak) sòok sòok
dìp dìp
สุกๆดิบๆ

medium-sized ka-nàht glahng
ขนาดกลาง

meet (verb) póp
พบ

nice to meet you yin dee têe
dâi róo-jùk gun
ยินดีที่ได้รู้จักกัน

where shall I meet you? póp
gun têe nǎi?
พบกันที่ไหน

meeting bpra-choom
ประชุม

meeting place têe nút póp
ที่นัดพบ

melon dtairng tai
แตงไทย

men pôo-chai
ผู้ชาย

mend sôrm
ซ่อม

could you mend this for me?
koon sôrm hâi dâi mái?
คุณซ่อมให้ได้ไหม

men's room boo-ròot
บุรุษ

menswear krêu-ung dtàirng
gai boo-ròot
เครื่องแต่งกายบุรุษ

mention (verb) glào tĕung
กล่าวถึง

don't mention it mâi bpen rai
ไม่เป็นไร

menu may-noo
เมนู

may I see the menu, please?
kŏr doo may-noo nòy krúp
(kâ)
ขอดูเมนูหน่อยครับ(ค่ะ)

see **Menu Reader** page 232

message kào
ข่าว

are there any messages for me?
mee krai sùng a-rai wái rĕu
bplào?
มีใครสั่งอะไรไว้หรือเปล่า

I want to leave a message for ...
pŏm (chún) yàhk ja fàhk
bòrk a-rai hâi ...
ผม(ฉัน)อยากจะฝากบอก
อะไรให้ ...

metal (noun) loh-hà
โลหะ

metre* mét
เมตร

midday têe-ung wun
เที่ยงวัน

at midday têe-ung wun
เที่ยงวัน

middle: in the middle yòo
dtrong glahng
อยู่ตรงกลาง

in the middle of the night
dtorn glahng keun
ตอนกลางคืน

the middle one un glahng
อันกลาง

midnight têe-ung keun
เที่ยงคืน

at midnight têe-ung keun
เที่ยงคืน

might: I might ... bahng tee pŏm
(chún) àht ja ...
บางทีผม(ฉัน)อาจจะ ...

I might not ... bahng tee pŏm
(chún) àht ja mâi ...
บางทีผม(ฉัน)อาจจะไม่ ...

I might want to stay another
day bahng tee pŏm (chún)
àht ja yòo èek wun nèung
บางทีผม(ฉัน)อาจจะอยู่อีกวันหนึ่ง

migraine bpòo-ut hŏo-a kâhng
dee-o
ปวดหัวข้างเดียว

mild (taste) mâi pèt
ไม่เผ็ด

mile* mai
ไมล์

milk nom
นม

millimetre* min-li-mét
มิลลิเมตร

minced meat néu-a sùp
เนื้อสับ

mind: never mind mâi bpen rai
ไม่เป็นไร

I've changed my mind pŏm
(chún) bplèe-un jai láir-o
ผม(ฉัน)เปลี่ยนใจแล้ว

•••••• DIALOGUE ••••••

do you mind if I open the window?
kŏr bpèrt nâh-dtàhng nòy, dâi
mái?

no, I don't mind dâi

mine*: it's mine kŏrng pŏm
(chún)
ของผม(ฉัน)

mineral water núm râir
น้ำแร่

minute nah-tee
นาที

in a minute èek bpra-dĕe-o
อีกประเดี๋ยว

just a minute dĕe-o, dĕe-o
เดี๋ยว ๆ

mirror gra-jòk ngao
กระจกเงา

Miss nahng-săo
นางสาว

miss: I missed the bus pŏm

(chún) dtòk rót may
ผม(ฉัน)ตกรถเมล์

missing hǎi bpai
หายไป

one of my ... is missing kǒng
pǒm (chún) hǎi bpai ...
ของผม(ฉัน)หายไป ...

there's a suitcase missing mee
gra-bpǎo hǎi bpai
มีกระเป๋าหายไป

mist mòrk
หมอก

mistake (noun) kwahm pìt
ความผิด

I think there's a mistake pǒm
(chún) kít wâh mee kǒr pìt
lék nòy
ผม(ฉัน)คิดว่ามีข้อผิดเล็กหน่อย

sorry, I've made a mistake kǒr-
tôht, pǒm (chún) tum pìt
ขอโทษผม(ฉัน)ทำผิด

misunderstanding kwahm kâo
jai pìt
ความเข้าใจผิด

mix-up: sorry, there's been a mix-
up kǒr-tôht, mee kwahm kâo
jai pìt
ขอโทษ มีความเข้าใจผิด

mobile phone toh-ra-sùp rái sái
โทรศัพท์ไร้สาย

modern tun sa-mǎi
ทันสมัย

moisturizer kreem bum-roong
pěw
ครีมบำรุงผิว

moment: I won't be a moment
ror děe-o
รอเดี๋ยว

monastery wút
วัด

Monday wun jun
วันจันทร์

money ngern
เงิน

monk prá
พระ

Monks come only just beneath
the monarchy in the social
hierarchy, and they too are
addressed and discussed in a
special respectful language. If
there's a monk around, he'll
always get a seat on the bus,
usually the back one. Theoretically, monks are forbidden to
have any close contact with
women which means that females shouldn't sit or stand next
to a monk, or even brush against
his robes. If a woman has to pass
something to a monk, she has
to put the object down so that
he can then pick it up – rather
than hand it over directly.

monsoon mor-ra-sǒom
มรสุม

month deu-un
เดือน

monument a-nóo-săh-wa-ree
อนุสาวรีย์

moon prá-jun
พระจันทร์

moped rót mor-dter-sai
รถมอร์เตอร์ไซค์

more* èek
อีก

can I have some more water, please? kŏr náhm èek nòy krúp (kâ)
ขอน้ำอีกหน่อยครับ(ค่ะ)

more expensive/interesting pairng/nâh sŏn jai gwàh
แพง/น่าสนใจกว่า

more than 50 hâh sìp gwàh
ห้าสิบกว่า

more than that mâhk gwàh nún
มากกว่านั้น

a lot more èek mâhk
อีกมาก

•••••• DIALOGUE ••••••

would you like some more? ao èek mái?

no, no more for me, thanks por láir-o, kòrp-kOOn krúp (kâ)

how about you? láir-o, kOOn lâ?

I don't want any more, thanks por láir-o krúp (kâ)

morning dtorn cháo
ตอนเช้า

this morning cháo née
เช้านี้

in the morning dtorn cháo
ตอนเช้า

mosquito yOOng
ยุง

Malarial mosquitoes are active from dusk until dawn and during this time you should smother yourself and your clothes in mosquito repellent: this is stocked in shops, guest-houses and department stores all over Thailand. At night you should either sleep under a mosquito net or in a room with screens across the windows. Many hotels in tourist areas provide screens or a net – and the latter can be bought very cheaply in Bangkok. The first signs of malaria are remarkably similar to flu: if you suspect anything go to a hospital or clinic immediately. Mosquito coils – also widely available in Thailand – also help keep the insects at bay.

mosquito net móong
มุ้ง

mosquito repellent yah gun yOOng
ยากันยุง

most: I like this one most of all

pŏm (chún) chôrp un née
mâhk têe sòot
ผม(ฉัน)ชอบอันนี้มากที่สุด

most of the time **sòo-un mâhk**
ส่วนมาก

most tourists nûk tôrng têe-o
sòo-un mâhk
นักท่องเที่ยวส่วนมาก

mostly sòo-un mâhk
ส่วนมาก

mother mâir
แม่

mother-in-law (of a man) mâir yai
แม่ยาย

(of a woman) mâir pŏo-a
แม่ผัว

motorbike rót mor-dter-sai
รถมอร์เตอร์ไซค์

motorboat reu-a yon
เรือยนตร์

motorway tahng dòo-un
ทางด่วน

mountain poo-kăo
ภูเขา

in the mountains nai poo-kăo
ในภูเขา

mouse nŏo
หนู

moustache nòo-ut
หนวด

mouth bpàhk
ปาก

mouth ulcer plăir nai bpàhk
แผลในปาก

move: he's moved to another
room káo **yái** bpai yòo èek
hôrng nèung
เขาย้ายไปอยู่อีกห้องหนึ่ง

could you move your car?
chôo-ay **lêu-un** rót kŏrng
koon, dâi mái?
ช่วยเลื่อนรถของคุณได้ไหม

could you move up a little?
chít nai nòy dâi mái?
ชิดในหน่อยได้ไหม

where has it moved to? (shop,
restaurant etc) **yái** bpai yòo têe
năi?
ย้ายไปอยู่ที่ไหน

movie nŭng
หนัง

movie theater rohng nŭng
โรงหนัง

Mr nai
นาย

Mrs nahng
นาง

much mâhk
มาก

much better/worse dee/yâir
mâhk gwàh
ดี/แย่มากกว่า

much hotter rórn mâhk gwàh
ร้อนมากกว่า

not much mâi mâhk
ไม่มาก

not very much mâi kôy mâhk
ไม่ค่อยมาก

I don't want very much pǒm
(chún) mâi ao mâhk
ผม(ฉัน)ไม่เอามาก

mud klohn
โคลน

mug: I've been mugged pǒm
(chún) tòok jêe
ผม(ฉัน)ถูกจี้

mum mâir
แม่

mumps kahng toom
คางทูม

museum pí-pít-ta-pun
พิพิธภัณฑ์

National museums tend to stick
to government office hours and
are open Monday to Friday from
8.30 a.m. to noon and from 1 to
4.30 p.m.; some close on Mon-
days and Tuesdays rather than
at weekends.

mushrooms hèt
เห็ด

music don-dtree
ดนตรี

musician núk don-dtree
นักดนตรี

Muslim (adj) ì-sa-lahm
อิสลาม

mussels hǒy mairng pôo
หอยแมงภู่

must*: I must pǒm (chún)

dtông
ผม(ฉัน)ต้อง

I mustn't drink alcohol pǒm
(chún) dtông mâi gin lâo
ผม(ฉัน)ต้องไม่กินเหล้า

mustard núm jîm mut-sa-
dtàht
น้ำจิ้มมัสตาด

my* kǒrng pǒm (chún)
ของผม(ฉัน)

myself: I'll do it myself pǒm
(chún) ja tum ayng
ผม(ฉัน)จะทำเอง

by myself dôo-ay dton ayng
ด้วยตนเอง

N

nail (finger) lép meu
เล็บมือ
(metal) dta-bpoo
ตะปู

nailbrush bprairng kùt lép
แปรงขัดเล็บ

nail varnish yah tah lép
ยาทาเล็บ

name chêu
ชื่อ

my name's ... pǒm chêu ...
ผมชื่อจอห์น ...

what's your name? koon chêu
a-rai?
คุณชื่ออะไร

what is the name of this street?

nêe ta-nŏn a-rai?
นี่ถนนอะไร

First names are more important in Thailand than family names. Do not mistake this use of first names for informality. When addressing people of similar age or older, regardless of their sex, you should use the polite term 'koon' in front of their first name.

napkin pâh chét bpàhk
ผ้าเช็ดปาก

nappy pâh ôrm
ผ้าอ้อม

narrow (street) kâirp
แคบ

nasty nâh too-râyt
น่าทุเรศ

national hàirng châht
แห่งชาติ

national anthem
You should be prepared to stand when the national anthem is played at the beginning of every cinema programme, and to stop in your tracks if you hear the national anthem being played over a town's public address system – many small towns do this twice a day at 8 a.m. and 6 p.m.

nationality sŭn-châht
สัญชาติ

natural tum-ma-châht
ธรรมชาติ

nausea ah-gahn klêun hěe-un
อาการคลื่นเหียน

navy (blue) sěe fáh gàir
สีฟ้าแก่

near glâi
ใกล้

is it near the city centre? yòo glâi meu-ung mái?
อยู่ใกล้เมืองไหม

do you go near the museum? koon pàhn bpai glâi glâi pít-ta-pun mái?
คุณผ่านไปใกล้ๆ พิพิธภัณฑ์ไหม

where is the nearest ...? ... glâi têe sòot yòo têe nǎi?
... ใกล้ที่สุดอยู่ที่ไหน

nearby yòo glâi
อยู่ใกล้

nearly gèu-up
เกือบ

necessary jum-bpen
จำเป็น

neck kor
คอ

necklace sôy kor
สร้อยคอ

necktie nék-tai
เน็คไท

need: I need ... pŏm (chún)

dtôrng-gahn ...
ผม(ฉัน)ต้องการ ...
do I need to pay? dtôrng jài
rěu bplào?
ต้องจ่ายหรือเปล่า
needle kěm
เข็ม
negative (film) feem nay-gah-
dteef
ฟิล์มเนกาตีฟ
nephew lǎhn chai
หลานชาย
net (in sport) dtah-kài
ตาข่าย
never mâi ker-ee
ไม่เคย

•••••• DIALOGUE ••••••

have you ever been to Hua Hin?
koon ker-ee bpai hǒo-a hǐn mái?
no, never, I've never been there mâi
ker-ee, pǒm (chún) mâi ker-ee
bpai

new mài
ใหม่
news (radio, TV etc) kào
ข่าว
newsagent's ráhn kǎi núng-sěu
pim
ร้านขายหนังสือพิมพ์
newspaper núng-sěu pim
หนังสือพิมพ์
newspaper kiosk dtôo núng-
sěu pim
ตู้หนังสือพิมพ์

New Year bpee mài
ปีใหม่
Happy New Year! sa-wùt dee
bpee mài!
สวัสดีปีใหม่

The traditional Thai New Year
festival is called Songkran and
occurs in the middle of April.
January 1st is, however, recog-
nized as the beginning of the
calendar year in Thailand,
although the year is calculated
according to Buddhist Era,
which is 543 years ahead of the
AD year.

New Year's Eve wun sîn bpee
วันสิ้นปี
New Zealand bpra-tâyt new
see-láirn
ประเทศนิวซีแลนด์
New Zealander: I'm a New
Zealander pǒm (chún) bpen
kon new see-láirn
ผม(ฉัน)เป็นคนนิวซีแลนด์
next nâh
หน้า
the next turning/street on the
left lée-o sái têe tahng yâirk/
ta-nǒn kâhng nâh
เลี้ยวซ้ายที่ทางแยก/
ถนนข้างหน้า
at the next stop bpâi nâh
ป้ายหน้า

next week ah-tít nâh
อาทิตย์หน้า

next to dtìt gùp
ติดกับ

nice (food) a-ròy
อร่อย

(looks, view etc) sŏo-ay
สวย

(person) dee
ดี

niece lăhn săo
หลานสาว

night glahng keun
กลางคืน

at night dtorn glahng keun
ตอนกลางคืน

good night sa-wùt dee
สวัสดี

•••••• DIALOGUE ••••••

do you have a single room for one
night? mee hórng sŭm-rùp keun
dee-o mái?

yes, madam mee krúp

how much is it per night? keun la
tâo-rài?

it's 1,000 baht for one night keun
la pun bàht

thank you, I'll take it kòrp-kOOn ao
hôrng née

nightclub náit klúp
ไนท์คลับ

nightdress chóot norn
ชุดนอน

no* mâi
ไม่

I've no change mâi mee sàyt
sa-dtahng
ไม่มีเศษสตางค์

there's no ... left mâi mee ...
lěu-a yòo
ไม่มี ... เหลืออยู่

no way! mâi mee tahng!
ไม่มีทาง

oh no! (upset) dtai jing!
ตายจริง

nobody mâi mee krai
ไม่มีใคร

there's nobody there mâi mee
krai yòo
ไม่มีใครอยู่

noise sěe-ung
เสียง

noisy: it's too noisy nòo-uk hŏo
หนวกหู

non-alcoholic mâi mee un-gor-
horl
ไม่มีอัลกอฮอล

nonsmoking hâhm sòop boo-
rèe
ห้ามสูบบุหรี่

noodles gŏo-ay dtěe-o
ก๋วยเตี๋ยว

noodle shop ráhn gŏo-ay
dtěe-o
ร้านก๋วยเตี๋ยว

noon têe-ung wun
เที่ยงวัน

at noon   têe-ung wun
เที่ยงวัน

no-one   mâi mee krai
ไม่มีใคร

nor: nor do I   pǒm (chún) gôr
mâi měu-un gun
ผม(ฉัน)ก็ไม่เหมือนกัน

normal   tum-ma-dah
ธรรมดา

north   něu-a
เหนือ

in the north   nai pâhk něu-a
ในภาคเหนือ

to the north   tahng něu-a
ทางเหนือ

north of Bangkok   tahng něu-a
kǒrng grooong-tâyp
ทางเหนือของกรุงเทพฯ

northeast   dta-wun òrk chěe-
ung něu-a
ตะวันออกเฉียงเหนือ

Northern Ireland   ai-lairn něu-a
ไอร์แลนด์เหนือ

northwest   dta-wun dtòk chěe-
ung něu-a
ตะวันตกเฉียงเหนือ

Norway   bpra-tâyt nor-way
ประเทศนอรเว

nose   ja-mòok
จมูก

nosebleed   lêu-ut gum-dao ǒrk
เลือดกำเดาออก

not*   mâi
ไม่

no thanks, I'm not hungry   mâi
krúp (kâ) pǒm (chún) mâi
hěw
ไม่ครับ (ค่ะ) ผม(ฉัน)ไม่หิว

I don't want any, thank you
pǒm (chún) mâi ao kòrp-
koon
ผม(ฉัน)ไม่เอาขอบคุณ

it's not necessary   mâi jum-
bpen
ไม่จำเป็น

I didn't know that   pǒm (chún)
mâi sâhp rêu-ung nún
ผม(ฉัน)ไม่ทราบเรื่องนั้น

not that one – this one   mâi
châi un nún – un nêe
ไม่ใช่อันนั้นอันนี้

note (banknote)   bai báirng
ใบแบ๊งค์

notebook   sa-mòot
สมุด

notepaper (for letters)   gra-dàht
kěe-un jòt-măi
กระดาษเขียนจดหมาย

nothing   mâi mee a-rai
ไม่มีอะไร

nothing for me, thanks   mâi ao
a-rai krúp (kâ) kòrp-koon
ไม่เอาอะไรครับ(ค่ะ)ขอบคุณ

nothing else   mâi mee a-rai
èek
ไม่มีอะไรอีก

novel   na-wa-ni-yai
นวนิยาย

November préut-sa-ji-gah-yon
พฤศจิกายน

now dĕe-o née
เดี๋ยวนี้

number mǎi-lâyk
หมายเลข

I've got the wrong number toh
pìt **ber**
โทรผิดเบอร์

what is your phone number?
ber toh-ra-sùp kŏrng kOOn
lâyk a-rai?
เบอร์โทรศัพท์ของคุณเลขอะไร

number plate bpâi ta-bee-un
rót
ป้ายทะเบียนรถ

nurse (woman) nahng pa-yah-
bahn
นางพยาบาล

nut (for bolt) glee-o
เกลียว

nuts tòo-a
ถั่ว

O

occupied (line etc) mâi wâhng
ไม่ว่าง

o'clock* mohng
โมง

October dtOO-lah-kom
ตุลาคม

odd (strange) bplàirk
แปลก

of* kŏrng
ของ

off (lights) bpìt
ปิด

it's just off Sukhumwit Road
yòo tăir-o ta-nŏn sOO-kŏOm-
wít
อยู่แถวถนนสุขุมวิท

we're off tomorrow (leaving)
rao bpai prôOng née
เราไปพรุ่งนี้

offensive nâh rung-gèe-ut
น่ารังเกียจ

office (place of work) sǔm-núk
ngahn
สำนักงาน

officer (said to policeman) nai
dtum-ròo-ut
นายตำรวจ

often bòy bòy
บ่อย ๆ

not often mâi bòy
ไม่บ่อย

how often are the buses? rót
mah bòy kâir nǎi?
รถมาบ่อยแค่ไหน

oil núm mun
น้ำมัน

(motor) núm mun krêu-ung
น้ำมันเครื่อง

ointment yah tah
ยาทา

OK oh-kay
โอเค

are you OK? kOOn oh-kay mái?

คุณโอเคไหม

is that OK with you? kOOn oh-kay mái?

คุณโอเคไหม

is it OK to ...? ... dâi mái?

... ได้ไหม

that's OK thanks (it doesn't matter) mâi bpen rai

ไม่เป็นไร

I'm OK (nothing for me, I've got enough) pŏm (chún) por láir-o

ผม(ฉัน)พอแล้ว

(I feel OK) pŏm (chún) oh kay

ผม(ฉัน)โอเค

is this train OK for ...? rót fai née bpai ... châi mái?

รถไฟนี้ไป ... ใช่ไหม

old (person) gàir

แก

(thing) gào

เก่า

•••••• DIALOGUE ••••••

how old are you? kOOn **ah-yóo** tâo-rài?

I'm 25 pŏm (chún) ah-yóo yêe-sìp hâh bpee

and you? láir-o kOOn lâ?

old-fashioned láh sa-măi

ล้าสมัย

old town (old part of town) meu-ung gào

เมืองเก่า

olive oil núm mun ma-gòrk

น้ำมันมะกอก

olives ma-gòrk

มะกอก

omelette kài jee-o

ไข่เจียว

on* bon

บน

on the beach têe chai hàht

ที่ชายหาด

on the street bon ta-nŏn

บนถนน

is it on this road? yòo ta-nŏn née rěu bplào?

อยู่ถนนนี้หรือเปล่า

on the plane bon krêu-ung bin

บนเครื่องบิน

on Saturday wun sâo

วันเสาร์

on television nai tee wee

ในทีวี

I haven't got it on me pŏm (chún) mâi dâi ao mah dôo-ay

ผม(ฉัน)ไม่ได้เอามาด้วย

this one's on me (drink) pŏm (chún) lée-ung

ผม(ฉัน)เลี้ยง

the light wasn't on fai mâi bpèrt yòo

ไฟไม่เปิดอยู่

what's on tonight? keun née mee a-rai?
คืนนี้มีอะไร

once (one time) krúng nèung
ครั้งหนึ่ง

at once (immediately) tun-tee
ทันที

one* nèung
หนึ่ง

the white one un sěe kǎo
อันสีขาว

one-way ticket dtǒo-a bpai
ตั๋วไป

onion hǒo-a hǒrm
หัวหอม

only tâo-nún
เท่านั้น

only one un dee-o tâo-nún
อันเดียวเท่านั้น

it's only 6 o'clock pee-ung hòk mohng tâo-nún
เพียงหกโมงเท่านั้น

I've only just got here pǒm (chún) pêung mah dǎe-o née ayng
ผม(ฉัน)เพิ่งมาเดี๋ยวนี้เอง

on/off switch sa-wít bpèrt/bpìt
สวิชเปิด/ปิด

open (adj, verb) bpèrt
เปิด

when do you open? bpèrt gèe mohng?
เปิดกี่โมง

I can't get it open bpèrt mâi dâi
เปิดไม่ได้

in the open air glahng jâirng
กลางแจ้ง

opening times way-lah bpìt-bpèrt
เวลาปิดเปิด

open ticket dtǒo-a mâi jum-gùt way-lah
ตั๋วไม่จำกัดเวลา

operation (medical) gahn pàh dtùt
การผ่าตัด

operator (telephone) pa-núk ngahn toh-ra-sùp
พนักงานโทรศัพท์

opposite: the opposite direction tahng dtrong kâhm
ทางตรงข้าม

the bar opposite bah dtrong kâhm
บาร์ตรงข้าม

opposite my hotel dtrong kâhm rohng rairm
ตรงข้ามโรงแรม

optician jùk-sòo pâirt
จักษุแพทย์

or rěu
หรือ

orange (fruit) sôm
ส้ม

(colour) sěe sôm
สีส้ม

orange juice núm sôm
น้ำส้ม

orchestra wong don-dtree
วงดนตรี

order: can we order now? (in restaurant) kŏr sùng dĕe-o née dâi mái?
ขอสั่งเดี๋ยวนี้ได้ไหม

I've already ordered, thanks pŏm (chún) sùng láir-o
ผม(ฉัน)สั่งแล้ว

I didn't order this pŏm (chún) mái dâi sùng
ผม(ฉัน)ไม่ได้สั่ง

out of order sĕe-a
เสีย

ordinary tum-ma-dah
ธรรมดา

other èun
อื่น

the other one (person) èek kon nèung
อีกคนหนึ่ง

(thing) èek un nèung
อีกอันหนึ่ง

the other day (recently) mêu-a mái gèe wun
เมื่อไม่กี่วัน

I'm waiting for the others (other people) pŏm (chún) ror kon èun
ผม(ฉัน)รอคนอื่น

do you have any others? mee yàhng èun mái?
มีอย่างอื่นไหม

otherwise mí-cha-nún
มิฉะนั้น

our* kŏrng rao
ของเรา

ours* kŏrng rao
ของเรา

out: he's out (not at home) káo mâi yòo
เขาไม่อยู่

three kilometres out of town nôrk meu-ung bpai săhm gi-loh
นอกเมืองไปสามกิโล

outdoors glahng jâirng
กลางแจ้ง

outside kâhng nôrk
ข้างนอก

can we sit outside? nûng kâhng nôrk dâi mái?
นั่งข้างนอกได้ไหม

oven dtao
เตา

over: over here têe nêe
ที่นี่

over there têe nôhn
ที่โน่น

over 500 hâh róy gwàh
ห้าร้อยกว่า

it's over (finished) jòp láir-o
จบแล้ว

overcharge: you've overcharged me kOOn kít ngern mâhk bpai
คุณคิดเงินมากไป

overcoat sêu-a nôrk
เสื้อนอก

overnight (travel) dern tahng
glahng keun
เดินทางกลางคืน

overtake sairng
แซง

owe: how much do I owe you?
pŏm (chún) bpen nêe kOOn
tâo-rài?
ผม(ฉัน)เป็นหนี้คุณเท่าไร

own: my own ... **kŏrng** pŏm
(chún) **ayng** ...
ของผม(ฉัน)เอง ...

are you on your own? kOOn
mah **kon dee-o** rĕu bplào?
คุณมาคนเดียวหรือเปล่า?

I'm on my own pŏm (chún)
mah **kon dee-o**
ผม(ฉัน)มาคนเดียว

owner jâo-kŏrng
เจ้าของ

oyster hŏy nahng rom
หอยนางรม

P

pack (verb) jùt gra-bpăo
จัดกระเป๋า

a pack of ... hòr ...
ห่อ ...

package (parcel) hòr
ห่อ

packed lunch ah-hăhn glahng
wun glòrng
อาหารกลางวันกล่อง

packet: a packet of cigarettes
sorng bOO-rèe
ซองบุหรี่

paddy field nah
นา

page (of book) nâh
หน้า

could you page Mr ...? chôo-ay
hăh ber toh-ra-sùp kOOn ...
hâi dôo-ay
ช่วยหาเบอร์โทรศัพท์คุณ ...
ให้ด้วย

pagoda jay-dee
เจดีย์

pain kwahm jèp bpòo-ut
ความเจ็บปวด

I have a pain here jèp dtrong
née
เจ็บตรงนี้

painful jèp bpòo-ut
เจ็บปวด

painkillers yah ra-ngúp bpòo-ut
ยาระงับปวด

paint (noun) sĕe
สี

painting (picture) pâhp kĕe-un
ภาพเขียน

pair: a pair of ... ... kôo nèung
... คู่หนึ่ง

Pakistani (adj) kon bpah-gee-
sa-tăhn
คนปากีสถาน

palace wung
วัง

pale sĕe òrn
สีอ่อน

pale blue sĕe fáh òrn
สีฟ้าอ่อน

pan (frying pan) gra-tá
กระทะ

panties gahng gayng nai sa-
dtree
กางเกงในสตรี

pants (underwear: men's) gahng
gayng nai
กางเกงใน

(women's) gahng gayng nai sa-
dtree
กางเกงในสตรี

(US: trousers) gahng-gayng
กางเกง

pantyhose tŏong yai boo-a
ถุงใยบัว

paper gra-dàht
กระดาษ

(newspaper) núng-sĕu-pim
หนังสือพิมพ์

a piece of paper gra-dàht
pàirn nèung
กระดาษแผ่นหนึ่ง

paper handkerchiefs gra-dàht
chét nâh
กระดาษเช็ดหน้า

parcel hòr
ห่อ

pardon (me)? (didn't understand,
hear) a-rai ná krúp (ká)?
อะไรนะครับ(คะ)

parents pôr mâir
พ่อแม่

parents-in-law (wife's parents) pôr
dtah mâir yai
พ่อตาแม่ยาย

(husband's parents) pôr pŏo-a
mâir pŏo-a
พ่อผัวแม่ผัว

park (noun) sŏo-un săh-tah-ra-
ná
สวนสาธารณะ

(verb) jòrt
จอด

can I park here? jòrt têe nêe
dâi mái?
จอดที่นี่ได้ไหม

parking lot têe jòrt rót
ที่จอดรถ

part (noun) sòo-un
ส่วน

partner (boyfriend, girlfriend etc) fairn
แฟน

party (group) glòom kon
กลุ่มคน

(celebration) ngahn lée-ung
งานเลี้ยง

pass (in mountains) chôrng kăo
ช่องเขา

passenger pôo doy-ee săhn
ผู้โดยสาร

passport núng-sĕu dern tahng
หนังสือเดินทาง

past*: in the past mêu-a gòrn
เมื่อก่อน

just past the post office ler-ee
bprai-sa-nee bpai èek nít
nèung

เลยไปรษณีย์ไปอีกนิดหนึ่ง

path tahng
ทาง

pattern bàirp
แบบ

pavement bàht wít-tĕe
บาทวิถี

on the pavement bon bàht
wít-tĕe
บนบาทวิถี

pay (verb) jài
จ่าย

can I pay, please? kŏr bin nòy
ขอบิลหน่อย

it's already paid for jài láir-o
จ่ายแล้ว

•••••• DIALOGUE ••••••

who's paying? krai bpen kon jài
ngern?

I'll pay pŏm (chún) ayng

no, you paid last time, I'll pay kOOn
jài dtorn krúng gòrn láir-o ná
pŏm (chún) jài ayng

pay phone toh-ra-sùp săh-tah-
ra-ná
โทรศัพท์สาธารณะ

peaceful (quiet) ngêe-up
เงียบ

peach lôok pêech
ลูกพีช

peanuts tòo-a
ถั่ว

pear lôok pair
ลูกแพร์

peculiar (taste, custom) bplàirk
แปลก

pedestrian crossing tahng máh-
lai
ทางม้าลาย

pedestrian precinct têe hâhm
rót kâo
ที่ห้ามรถเข้า

peg (for washing) mái nèep pâh
ไม้หนีบผ้า

pen bpàhk-gah
ปากกา

pencil din-sŏr
ดินสอ

penfriend pêu-un tahng jòt-măi
เพื่อนทางจดหมาย

penicillin yah pen-ni-seen-lin
ยาเพนนิซีลลิน

penknife mêet púp
มีดพับ

people kon
คน

the other people in the hotel
kon èun nai rohng rairm
คนอื่นในโรงแรม

too many people kon mâhk
bpai
คนมากไป

pepper (spice) prík tai
พริกไทย

(vegetable) prík yòo-uk
พริกหยวก

per: per night keun la ...
คืนละ ...

how much per day? wun la
tâo-rài?
วันละเท่าไร

per cent bper-sen
เปอร์เซ็นต์

perfect yôrt yêe-um
ยอดเยี่ยม

perfume núm hŏrm
น้ำหอม

perhaps bahng tee
บางที

perhaps not bahng tee mâi
บางทีไม่

period (of time) chôo-a rá-yá
ชั่วระยะ

(menstruation) bpra-jum deu-
un
ประจำเดือน

perm dùt pŏm
ดัดผม

permit (noun) bai un-nóo-yâht
ใบอนุญาต

person kon
คน

personal stereo work-mairn
วอล์กแมน

petrol núm mun
น้ำมัน

Núm mun is the general word for oil but it is also the colloquial word for petrol. If you ask for núm mun in a petrol station you'll get petrol; if you want oil, you should ask for **núm mun krêu-ung**. Petrol is cheapest at the big petrol stations found in every town; most small villages have roadside huts where the fuel is pumped out of a large barrel. In most petrol stations, star symbols on the pumps are sufficient to indicate the grade of petrol; four-star/premium is sometimes called **pi-sàyt** (literally: special) while three-star/regular is **tum-ma-dah** (ordinary). Thais use the English word 'diesel' although it is normally pronounced **dee-sen**. Unleaded petrol is **núm mun rái sähn dta-gòo-a**.

petrol can gra-bpŏrng núm
mun
กระป๋องน้ำมัน

petrol station bpúm núm
mun
ปั๊มน้ำมัน

pharmacy hâhng kǎi yah
ห้างขายยา

There's no need to bring huge supplies of non-prescription medicines with you as Thai pharmacies (open daily from 8.30 a.m. to 8 p.m.) are well-stocked with local and international brands of medicines, and are much cheaper than in the West. All pharmacies, whatever size the town, are run by highly-trained English-speaking pharmacists and they are usually the best people to talk to if your symptoms aren't bad enough to warrant seeing a doctor.

phone toh-ra-sùp
โทรศัพท์

Every so often phone lines get jammed and a whole town becomes incommunicado for a few hours, but generally the phone system works well. Payphones generally come in two colours: red for local calls and blue for long-distance calls within Thailand. Red phones take the medium-sized one-baht coins and will give you three minutes per B1. The blue ones aren't very common outside Bangkok, so in smaller towns you usually →

have to go to a private long-distance telephone office, generally located near the post office, which will make the connection for you.

The cheapest way of making an international call is to use the government telephone centre. Nearly always located within or adjacent to the town's main post office, and open daily from about 7 a.m. to 11 p.m. (open 24 hours in Bangkok), the government phone centres allot you a booth and leave you to do the dialling (in Bangkok) or call via the operator for you (in other towns). If you can't get to one of the official places, try the slightly more expensive private international call offices in tourist areas, or the even pricier services offered by the posher hotels.

phone book sa-mòot mǎi-lâyk toh-ra-sùp
สมุดหมายเลขโทรศัพท์
phone box dtôo toh-ra-sùp
ตู้โทรศัพท์
phonecard bùt toh-ra-sùp
บัตรโทรศัพท์
phone number ber toh-ra-sùp
เบอร์โทรศัพท์

photo rôop tài
รูปถ่าย
excuse me, could you take a
photo of us? kǒr-tôht krúp
(kâ), chôo-ay tài rôop rao
hâi nòy dâi mái?
ขอโทษครับ(ค่ะ)ช่วยถ่ายรูปเราให้
หน่อยได้ไหม

phrasebook kôo meu sǒn-ta-
nah
คู่มือสนทนา

Phuket poo-gèt
ภูเก็ต

piano bpee-a-noh
เปียโน

pickpocket ka-moy-ee lóo-ung
gra-bpǎo
ขโมยล้วงกระเป๋า

pick up: will you be there to pick
me up? ja bpai rúp pǒm
(chún) mái?
จะไปรับผม(ฉัน)ไหม

picnic (noun) bpìk-ník
ปิคนิค

picture (painting, photo) rôop
รูป

pie pai
ไพ

piece chín
ชิ้น
a piece of … … chín
nèung
… ชิ้นหนึ่ง

pill (contraceptive pill) yah koom
gum-nèrt
ยาคุมกำเนิด
I'm on the pill chún chái yah
koom gum-nèrt
ฉันใช้ยาคุมกำเนิด

pillow mǒrn
หมอน

pillow case bplòrk mǒrn
ปลอกหมอน

pin (noun) kěm mòot
เข็มหมุด

pineapple sùp-bpa-rót
สับปะรด

pineapple juice núm sùp-bpa-
rót
น้ำสับปะรด

pink sěe chom-poo
สีชมพู

pipe (for smoking) glôrng yah sên
กล้องยาเส้น
(for water) tôr
ท่อ

pipe cleaners mái tum kwahm
sà-aht glôrng yah sên
ไม้ทำความสะอาดกล้องยาเส้น

pity: it's a pity nâh sǒng-
sǎhn
น่าสงสาร

pizza pee-sâh
พีซซา

place (noun) sa-tǎhn-têe
สถานที่
at your place têe bâhn koon
ที่บ้านคุณ

at his place têe bâhn káo
ที่บ้านเขา

plain (not patterned) mâi mee lôo-
ut lai
ไม่มีลวดลาย

plane krêu-ung bin
เครื่องบิน

by plane doy-ee krêu-ung
bin
โดยเครื่องบิน

plant dtôn mái
ต้นไม้

plaster cast fèu-uk
เฝือก

plasters plah-sa-dter
พลาสเตอร์

plastic bplah-sa-dtìk
ปลาสติค

(credit cards) bùt kray-dìt
บัตรเครดิต

plastic bag tǒong bplah-sa-dtìk
ถุงปลาสติค

plate jahn
จาน

platform chahn chah-lah
ชานชาลา

which platform is it for
Chiangmai? bpai chee-ung-
mài chahn chah-lah a-rai?
ไปเชียงใหม่ชานชาลาอะไร

play (verb) lên
เล่น

(noun: in theatre) la-korn
ลคร

playground (for children) sa-nǎhm

dèk lên
สนามเด็กเล่น

pleasant sa-nòok
สนุก

please (requesting something) kǒr ...
ขอ ...

(offering) chern krúp (kâ)
เชิญครับ(ค่ะ)

yes please ao krúp (kâ)
เอาครับ(ค่ะ)

could you please ...? chôo-ay
... nòy dâi mái?
ช่วยหน่อย ... ได้ไหม

please don't yàh ler-ee krúp
(kâ)
อย่าเลยครับ(ค่ะ)

pleased: pleased to meet you
yin dee têe dâi róo-jùk
gun
ยินดีที่ได้รู้จักกัน

pleasure: my pleasure (response to
thanks) mâi bpen rai
ไม่เป็นไร

plenty: plenty of ... ... mâhk
... มาก

there's plenty of time mee
way-lah mâhk
มีเวลามาก

that's plenty, thanks por láir-o
kòrp-koon
พอแล้วขอบคุณ

pliers keem bpàhk kêep
คีมปากคีบ

plug (electrical) bplúk
ปลั๊ก

(for car) hŏo-a tee-un
หัวเทียน

(in sink) jòok òot
จุกอุด

plumber châhng bpra-bpah
ช่างประปา

p.m.*

pocket gra-bpăo
กระเป๋า

point: two point five sŏrng jòot
hâh
สองจุดห้า

there's no point mâi mee
bpra-yòht
ไม่มีประโยชน์

points (in car) torng kăo
ทองขาว

poisonous bpen pít
เป็นพิษ

police dtum-ròo-ut
ตำรวจ

call the police! rêe-uk dtum-
ròo-ut mah!
เรียกตำรวจมา

There is a special department
for tourist-related crimes and
complaints called the Tourist
Assistance Centre (TAC), set up
to mediate between tourists, police and accused persons (particularly shopkeepers and tour
agents). In emergencies, always
contact the English-speaking →

tourist police who have offices
within or adjacent to many
regional TAT (Tourist Authority
of Thailand) offices – this is in-
variably more efficient than directly contacting the local
police, ambulance or fire service.

policeman dtum-ròo-ut
ตำรวจ

police station sa-tăh-nee dtum-
ròo-ut
สถานีตำรวจ

policewoman dtum-ròo-ut yĭng
ตำรวจหญิง

polish (noun) yah kùt
ยาขัด

polite sOO-pâhp
สุภาพ

polluted bpen pít
เป็นพิษ

pony máh glàirp
ม้าแกลบ

pool (for swimming) sà wâi náhm
สระว่ายน้ำ

poor (not rich) jon
จน

(quality) mâi ao năi
ไม่เอาไหน

pop music don-dtree pórp
ดนตรีพอพ

pop singer núk rórng
นักร้อง

popular bpen têe nee-yom
เป็นที่นิยม

population bpra-chah-gorn
ประชากร

pork néu-a mŏo
เนื้อหมู

port (for boats) tâh reu-a
ท่าเรือ

porter (in hotel) kon fâo bpra-dtoo
คนเฝ้าประตู

portrait pâhp kĕe-un dtoo-a jing
ภาพเขียนตัวจริง

posh (restaurant, people) rŏo-răh
หรูหรา

possible bpen bpai dâi
เป็นไปได้

is it possible to …? … bpen bpai dâi mái?
… เป็นไปได้ไหม

as … as possible yàhng … têe sòot têe ja … dâi
อย่าง … ที่สุดที่จะ … ได้

post (noun: mail) jòt-măi
จดหมาย

(verb) sòng jòt-măi
ส่งจดหมาย

could you post this for me?
chôo-ay sòng jòt-măi née hâi nòy dâi mái?
ช่วยส่งจดหมายนี้ให้หน่อยได้ไหม

postbox dtôo bprai-sa-nee
ตู้ไปรษณีย์

postcard bpóht-gáht
โปสการ์ด

postcode ra-hùt bprai-sa-nee
รหัสไปรษณีย์

poster bpoh-sa-dter
โปสเตอร์

poste restante 'poste restante'

post office bprai-sa-nee
ไปรษณีย์

Post offices are open Monday to Friday from 8 a.m. to 4 p.m. and on Saturday from 8 a.m. to noon. On weekdays some are closed from noon to 1 p.m. and some may stay open until 6 p.m. Mail takes about seven days to get between Bangkok and Europe or North America, and a little longer in isolated areas. Almost all main post offices across the country operate a poste restante service and will hold letters for two to three months. Mail should be addressed: Name (family name underlined or capitalized), Poste Restante, GPO, Town or City, Thailand. It will be filed by surname, though it's always wise to check under your initial as well. The poste restante at Bangkok GPO is open from Monday to Friday from 8 a.m. to →

---

8 p.m. and until 1 p.m. on Saturdays; others follow regular post office hours.
see **stamp**

potato mun fa-rùng
มันฝรั่ง

potato chips (US) mun fa-rùng tôrt
มันฝรั่งทอด

pots and pans môr kâo môr gairng
หม้อข้าวหม้อแกง

pottery krêu-ung bpûn din pǎo
เครื่องปั้นดินเผา

pound* (money) bporn
ปอนด์

power cut dtùt fai
ตัดไฟ

power point bplúk fai
ปลั๊กไฟ

practise: I want to practise my Thai pǒrm (chún) yàhk ja fèuk pôot pah-sǎh tai
ผม(ฉัน)อยากจะฝึกพูดภาษาไทย

prawns gôong
กุ้ง

prefer: I prefer ... pǒrm (chún) chôrp ... mâhk gwàh
ผม(ฉัน)ชอบ ... มากกว่า

pregnant mee tórng
มีท้อง

prescription (for medicine) bai

sùng yah
ใบสั่งยา

present (gift) kǒrng kwǔn
ของขวัญ

president (of country) bpra-tah-nah-tí-bor-dee
ประธานาธิบดี

pretty sǒo-ay
สวย

it's pretty expensive pairng mĕu-un gun ná
แพงเหมือนกันนะ

price rah-kah
ราคา

priest prá
พระ

prime minister nah-yók rút-ta-mon-dtree
นายกรัฐมนตรี

printed matter sìng dtee pim
สิ่งตีพิมพ์

priority (in driving) sìt pàhn bpai gòrn
สิทธิผ่านไปก่อน

prison kóok
คุก

private sòo-un dtoo-a
ส่วนตัว

private bathroom hôrng náhm sòo-un dtoo-a
ห้องน้ำส่วนตัว

probably kong-ja
คงจะ

ENGLISH ✦ THAI | Pr

133

problem bpun-hǎh
ปัญหา
no problem! mâi mee bpun-
hǎh!
ไม่มีปัญหา

program(me) (noun) bproh-
grairm
โปรแกรม

promise: I promise pǒm (chún)
sǔn-yah
ผม(ฉัน)สัญญา

pronounce: how is this pronounced? nêe òrk sǎe-ung
yung-ngai?
นี่ออกเสียงอย่างไร

properly (repaired, locked etc) tòok
dtôrng
ถูกต้อง

Protestant krít
คริสต์

public convenience sôo-um sǎh-
tah-ra-ná
ส้วมสาธารณะ

public holiday wun yòot râht-
cha-gahn
วันหยุดราชการ

pudding (dessert) kǒrng wǎhn
ของหวาน

pull deung
ดึง

pullover sêu-a sa-wét-dtêr
เสื้อสเวตเตอร์

puncture (noun) yahng dtàirk
ยางแตก

purple sǎe môo-ung
สีม่วง

purse (for money) gra-bpǎo sa-
dtahng
กระเป๋าสตางค์
(US) gra-bpǎo tǔu
กระเป๋าถือ

push plùk
ผลัก

pushchair rót kěn
รถเข็น

put sài
ใส่
where can I put ...? ... sài dâi
têe nǎi?
... ใส่ได้ที่ไหน
could you put us up for the
night? kǒr káhng keun têe
nêe nòy dâi mái?
ขอค้างคืนที่นี่หน่อยได้ไหม

pyjamas sêu-a gahng-gayng
norn
เสื้อกางเกงนอน

Q

quality koon-na-pâhp
คุณภาพ

quarantine (place) dâhn gùk
rôhk
ด่านกักโรค
(period) ra-yá way-lah têe gùk
rôhk wái
ระยะเวลาที่กักโรคไว้

quarter nèung nai sèe
หนึ่งในสี่

quayside: on the quayside têe
tâh reu-a
ที่ท่าเรือ

question kum tǎhm
คำถาม

queue (noun) kew
คิว

quick ray-o
เร็ว

that was quick ray-o jing
เร็วจริง

what's the quickest way there?
bpai tahng nǎi ray-o têe sòot?
ไปทางไหนเร็วที่สุด

fancy a quick drink? yàhk bpai
dèum a-rai mái?
อยากไปดื่มอะไรไหม

quickly ray-o
เร็ว

quiet (place, hotel) ngêe-up
เงียบ

quiet! ngêe-up ngêe-up nòy!
เงียบ ๆ หน่อย

quite (fairly) por sǒm-koo-un
พอสมควร

(very) tee dee-o
ทีเดียว

that's quite right tòok láir-o
ถูกแล้ว

quite a lot mâhk por sǒm-
koo-un
มากพอสมควร

R

rabbit (meat) gra-dtài
กระต่าย

race (for runners, cars) gahn
kàirng kǔn
การแข่งขัน

racket (tennis, squash) mái dtee
ไม้ตี

radiator môr náhm
หม้อน้ำ

radio wít-ta-yóo
วิทยุ

on the radio tahng wít-ta-
yóo
ทางวิทยุ

rail: by rail doy-ee rót fai
โดยรถไฟ

railway tahng rót fai
ทางรถไฟ

rain (noun) fǒn
ฝน

in the rain dtàhk fǒn
ตากฝน

it's raining fǒn dtòk
ฝนตก

raincoat sêu-a fǒn
เสื้อฝน

rape (noun) kòm kěun
ข่มขืน

rare (uncommon) hǎh yâhk
หายาก

(steak) sòok sòok dìp dìp
สุก ๆ ดิบ ๆ

rash (on skin) pèun
ผื่น

rat nǒo
หนู

rate (for changing money) ùt-dtrah
อัตรา

rather: it's rather good kôrn
kâhng dee
ค่อนข้างดี

I'd rather ... pǒm (chún) yàhk
ja ... dee gwàh
ผม(ฉัน)อยากจะ ... ดีกว่า

razor (dry, electric) mêet gohn
มีดโกน

razor blades bai mêet gohn
ใบมีดโกน

read àhn
อ่าน

ready prórm, sèt
พร้อม, เสร็จ

are you ready? sèt láir-o rěu
yung?
เสร็จแล้วหรือยัง

I'm not ready yet pǒm (chún)
yung mâi sèt
ผม(ฉัน)ยังไม่เสร็จ

•••••• DIALOGUE ••••••

when will it be ready? sèt mêu-a
rài?

it should be ready in a couple of days
èek sǒrng sǎhm wun koo-un ja sèt

real jing
จริง

really jing jing
จริง ๆ

I'm really sorry pǒm (chún)
sěe-a jai jing jing
ผม(ฉัน)เสียใจจริง ๆ

that's really great dee jung ler-
ee
ดีจังเลย

really? (doubt) jing lěr?
จริงหรือ

(polite interest) lěr?
หรือ

rear lights fai lǔng rót
ไฟหลังรถ

rearview mirror gra-jòk lǔng
กระจกหลัง

reasonable (price) rah-kah yao
ราคาเยา

receipt bai sèt rúp ngern
ใบเสร็จรับเงิน

recently mêu-a ray-o ray-o née
เมื่อเร็ว ๆ นี้

reception (in hotel) pa-nàirk
dtôrn rúp
แผนกต้อนรับ

(for guests) ngahn lée-ung
dtôrn rúp
งานเลี้ยงต้อนรับ

at reception têe pa-nàirk
dtôrn rúp
ที่แผนกต้อนรับ

reception desk pa-nàirk dtôrn
rúp
แผนกต้อนรับ

receptionist pa-núk ngahn
  dtôrn rúp
  พนักงานต้อนรับ

recognize jum dâi
  จำได้

recommend: could you recommend ...? kOOn náir-num ...
  dâi mái?
  คุณแนะนำ ... ได้ไหม

record (music) pàirn sěe-ung
  แผ่นเสียง

red sěe dairng
  สีแดง

red wine lâo wai dairng
  เหล้าไวน์แดง

refund (noun) keun ngern
  คืนเงิน

  can I have a refund? keun
  ngern hâi dâi mái?
  คืนเงินให้ได้ไหม

region pâhk
  ภาค

registered: by registered mail jòt-
  măi long ta-bee-un
  จดหมายลงทะเบียน

registration number ta-bee-un
  rót
  ทะเบียนรถ

relative (noun) yâht
  ญาติ

religion sàh-sa-năh
  ศาสนา

  see Buddhism and monk

remember: I don't remember

pǒm (chún) jum mâi dâi
ผม(ฉัน)จำไม่ได้

I remember pǒm (chún) jum
dâi
ผม(ฉัน)จำได้

do you remember? jum dâi
mái?
จำได้ไหม

rent (noun: for apartment etc) kâh
châo
ค่าเช่า

(verb: car etc) châo
เช่า

•••••• DIALOGUE ••••••

I'd like to rent a car pǒm (chún)
yàhk ja châo rót
for how long? châo gèe wun?
two days sǒrng wun
this is our range nêe rót kǒrng rao
I'll take the ... ao ...
is that with unlimited mileage? lâirn
dâi doy-ee mâi jum-gùt ra-yá
tahng châi mái?
it is krúp
can I see your licence, please? kǒr
doo bai kùp kèe
and your passport láir-o núng-sěu
dern tahng
is insurance included? roo-um kâh
bpra-gun dôo-ay rěu bplào?
yes, but you pay the first 2,000 baht
krúp dtàir kOOn jài sǒrng pun
bâht râirk ná krúp

can you leave a deposit of 3,000 baht? chôo-ay wahng kâh mút-jum săhm pun bàht dâi mái?

rented car rót châo
รถเช่า

repair (verb) sôrm
ซ่อม

can you repair it? sôrm dâi mái?
ซ่อมได้ไหม

repeat pôot èek tee
พูดอีกที

could you repeat that? pôot èek tee dâi mái?
พูดอีกทีได้ไหม

reservation jorng
จอง

I'd like to make a reservation kŏr jorng
ขอจอง

•••••• DIALOGUE ••••••

I have a reservation pŏm (chún) dâi jorng wái láir-o
yes sir, what name please? krúp kOOn chêu a-rai?

reserve (verb) jorng
จอง

•••••• DIALOGUE ••••••

can I reserve a table for tonight? chún kŏr jorng dtór sǔm-rùp keun née dâi mái?
yes madam, for how many people? dâi krúp mee gèe kon?

for two sŏrng kon
and for what time? láir-o gèe mohng?
for eight o'clock sŏrng tôom
and could I have your name, please? láir-o kOOn chêu a-rai krúp?

rest: I need a rest pŏm (chún) dtôrng púk pòrn
ผม(ฉัน)ต้องพักผ่อน

the rest of the group pôo-uk kon èun
พวกคนอื่น

restaurant ráhn ah-hǎhn
ร้านอาหาร

Throughout the country most cheap Thai restaurants and cafés specialize in one general food type or preparation method – a 'noodle shop' for example will do fried noodles and noodle soups, plus a basic fried rice, but they won't have curries, meat or fish dishes. Similarly, a restaurant displaying whole roast chickens and ducks in its window will offer these sliced or with chillis and sauces and served over rice, but their menu probably won't extend to noodles or fish, while in 'curry shops' your options are limited to the vats of curries stewing →

away in the hot cabinet.

To get a choice of low-cost food, it's sometimes best to head for the local night market, a term for the gatherings of open-air night-time kitchens found in every town. Operating from about 6 p.m. to 6 a.m., they are to be found close to the fruit and vegetable market or bus station. Having decided what you want, you order from the cook and sit down at the nearest table; there's no territorialism about night markets, so it's normal to eat several dishes from separate stalls and rely on the nearest cook to sort out the bill.

For a more relaxing ambience, Bangkok and Chiangmai both have a range of gourmet restaurants specializing in 'royal' Thai cuisine, which differs from standard fare mainly in the quality of the ingredients and the way the food is presented.

---

restaurant car rót sa-bee-ung
รถเสบียง

rest room hôrng náhm
ห้องน้ำ

retired: I'm retired pǒm (chún)
ga-see-un
ผม(ฉัน)เกษียน

return: a return to ... dtǒo-a bpai
glùp ...
ตัวไปกลับ ...

return ticket dtǒo-a bpai
glùp
ตัวไปกลับ
see **ticket**

reverse charge call toh-ra-sùp
gèp ngern bplai tahng
โทรศัพท์เก็บเงินปลายทาง

reverse gear gee-a tǒy lǔng
เกียร์ถอยหลัง

revolting nâh rung-gèe-ut
น่ารังเกียจ

rib sêe krohng
ซี่โครง

rice kâo
ข้าว

rich (person) roo-ay
รวย
(food) mun
มัน

ridiculous nâh hǒo-a rór
น่าหัวเราะ

right (correct) tòok
ถูก
(not left) kwǎh
ขวา
you were right kOOn tòok
láir-o
คุณถูกแล้ว
that's right tòok láir-o
ถูกแล้ว
this can't be right mâi tòok

nâir nâir
ไม่ถูกแน่ๆ

right! ao lá!
เอาละ

is this the right road for ...?
bpai ... tahng ta-nŏn née
tòok mái?
ไป ... ทางถนนนี้ถูกไหม

on the right tahng **kwăh**
ทางขวา

turn right lée-o **kwăh**
เลี้ยวขวา

right-hand drive poo-ung ma-lai
kwăh
พวงมาลัยขวา

ring (on finger) wăirn
แหวน

I'll ring you pŏm (chún) ja toh
bpai tĕung
ผม(ฉัน)จะโทรไปถึง

ring back toh glùp mah
โทรกลับมา

ripe (fruit) sòok
สุก

rip-off: it's a rip-off lòrk
dtôm
หลอกต้ม

rip-off prices rah-kah lòrk
dtôm
ราคาหลอกต้ม

risky sèe-ung
เสี่ยง

river mâir náhm
แม่น้ำ

road (in town, country) ta-nŏn
ถนน

is this the road for ...? nêe ta-
nŏn bpai ... châi mái?
นี่ถนนไป ... ใช่ไหม

down the road yòo glâi glâi
kâir née
อยู่ใกล้ๆแค่นี้

road accident rót chon gun
รถชนกัน

road map păirn-têe ta-nŏn
แผ่นที่ถนน

roadsign krêu-ung măi ja-rah
jorn
เครื่องหมายจราจร

rob: I've been robbed pŏm
(chún) tòok ka-moy-ee
ผม(ฉัน)ถูกขโมย

rock hĭn
หิน

(music) rórk
ร็อค

on the rocks (with ice) sài núm
kăirng
ใส่น้ำแข็ง

roll (bread) ka-nŏm-bpung
ขนมปัง

roof lŭng-kah
หลังคา

roof rack gròrp dtìt lŭng-kah
rót
กรอบติดหลังคารถ

room hôrng
ห้อง

in my room nai hôrng pǒm
(chún)
ในห้องผม(ฉัน)

•••••• DIALOGUE ••••••

do you have any rooms? mee
hôrng wâhng mái?

for how many people? sǔm-rùp
gèe kon?

for one/for two kon dee-o/sǒrng
kon

yes, we have rooms free mee, mee
hôrng wâhng

for how many nights will it be? yòo
gèe keun?

just for one night keun dee-o tâo-
nún

how much is it? keun la tâo-rài?

can I see it? kǒr doo nòy dâi mái?

OK, I'll take it oh-kay, ao

room service bor-ri-gahn rúp
chái nai hôrng púk
บริการรับใช้ในห้องพัก

rope chêu-uk
เชือก

roughly (approximately) bpra-
mahn
ประมาณ

round: it's my round bpen tee
kǒrng pǒm
เป็นที่ของผม

roundabout (for traffic) wong
wee-un
วงเวียน

round trip ticket dtǒo-a bpai
glùp
ตั๋วไปกลับ

route tahng
ทาง

what's the best route? bpai
tahng nǎi dee têe sòot?
ไปทางไหนดีที่สุด

royal family
The royal family is universally
esteemed in Thailand, where
almost every household displays
a picture of King Bhumibol and
Queen Sirikit in a prominent position. When addressing or
speaking about royalty, Thais
use a special language full of
deferentials, called **râht-cha-
sùp** (literally: royal language).
Even a hint of disrespect will
cause deep offence – as the
monarch's head features on all
Thai currency, you should never
step on a coin or banknote because this would be tantamount
to kicking the king in the face.

rubber (material) yahng
ยาง
(eraser) yahng lóp
ยางลบ
rubber band yahng rút
ยางรัด

rubbish (waste) ka-yà
ขยะ

(poor quality goods) mâi ao nǎi
ไม่เอาไหน

rubbish! (nonsense) mâi bpen
rêu-ung!
ไม่เป็นเรื่อง

rucksack bpây lǔng
เป้หลัง

rude mâi sOO-pâhp
ไม่สุภาพ

ruins sâhk sa-lùk hùk
pung
ซากสลักหักพัง

rum lâo rum
เหล้ารัม

rum and Coke® rum airn
kóhk
รัมแอนด์โค้ก

run (verb: person) wîng
วิ่ง

how often do the buses run?
rót may wîng tèe mái?
รถเมล์วิ่งถี่ไหม

I've run out of money pǒm
(chún) mót ngern
ผม(ฉัน)หมดเงิน

S

sad sâo
เศร้า

saddle (for bike) ahn jùk-gra-
yahn
อานจักรยาน

(for horse) ahn máh
อานม้า

safe (not in danger) bplòrt-pai
ปลอดภัย

(not dangerous) mâi un-dta-rai
ไม่อันตราย

safety pin kěm glùt
เข็มกลัด

sail (noun) bai reu-a
ใบเรือ

sailboard (noun) gra-dahn dtôh
lom
กระดานโต้ลม

sailboarding gahn lên gra-dahn
dtôh lom
การเล่นกระดานโต้ลม

salad sa-lùt
สลัด

salad dressing náhm sa-lùt
น้ำสลัด

sale: for sale kǎi
ขาย

salt gleu-a
เกลือ

same: the same měu-un gun
เหมือนกัน

the same as this měu-un
yàhng née
เหมือนอย่างนี้

the same again, please kǒr
yàhng derm
ขออย่างเดิม

it's all the same to me a-rai
gôr dâi
อะไรก็ได้

sand sai
ทราย

sandals rorng táo dtàir
รองเท้าแตะ

sandwich sairn-wít
แซนด์วิช

sanitary napkins, sanitary towels
pâh un-nah-mai
ผ้าอนามัย

Saturday wun săo
วันเสาร์

sauce núm jîm
น้ำจิ้ม

saucepan môr
หม้อ

saucer jahn rorng tôo-ay
จานรองถ้วย

sauna sao-nah
เซานา

sausage sâi gròrk
ไส้กรอก

say (verb) bòrk, pôot
บอก, พูด
  how do you say ... in Thai?
  pah-săh tai ... pôot wâh
  yung-ngai?
  ภาษาไทย ... พูดว่าอย่างไร
  what did he say? káo pôot
  wâh yung-ngai?
  เขาพูดว่าอย่างไร
  she said ... káo bòrk wâh ...
  เขาบอกว่า ...
  could you say that again?
  pôot èek tee dâi mái?
  พูดอีกทีได้ไหม

scarf (for neck) pâh pun kor
ผ้าพันคอ
  (for head) pâh pôhk sĕe-sà
  ผ้าโพกศีรษะ

scenery poo-mi-bpra-tâyt
ภูมิประเทศ

schedule (US) dtah-rahng way-
lah
ตารางเวลา

scheduled flight dtah-rahng têe-
o bin

school rohng ree-un
โรงเรียน

scissors: a pair of scissors dta-
grai
ตะไกร

scooter rót sa-góot-dter
รถสกู๊ตเตอร์

scotch lâo wít-sa-gêe
เหล้าวิสกี้

Scotch tape® sa-górt táyp
สก๊อตเทป

Scotland sa-górt-lairn
สก๊อตแลนด์

Scottish kon sa-górt
คนสก๊อต
  I'm Scottish pŏm (chún) bpen
  kon sa-górt
  ผม(ฉัน)เป็นคนสก๊อต

scrambled eggs kài kŏn
ไข่ขน

scratch (noun) roy kòo-un
รอยขวน

screw (noun) dta-bpoo koo-ung
ตะปูควง

screwdriver kăi koo-ung
ไขควง

sea ̂ta-lay
ทะเล

by the sea chai ta-lay
ชายทะเล

seafood ah-hăhn ta-lay
อาหารทะเล

seafood restaurant pút-ta-kahn
ah-hăhn ta-lay
ภัตตาคารอาหารทแล

seafront chai ta-lay
ชายทะเล

seagull nók nahng noo-un
นกนางนวล

search (verb) hăh
หา

seashell bplèu-uk hŏy
เปลือกหอย

seasick: I feel seasick pŏm
(chún) róo-sèuk mao
klêun
ผม(ฉัน)รู้สึกเมาคลื่น

I get seasick pŏm (chún) mao
klêun ngâi
ผม(ฉัน)เมาคลื่นง่าย

seaside: by the seaside chai ta-
lay
ชายทะเล

seat têe nûng
ที่นั่ง

is this seat taken? têe nêe
wâhng mái?
ที่นี่ว่างไหม

seat belt kĕm kùt ni-ra-pai
เข็มขัดนิรภัย

sea urchin bpling ta-lay
ปลิงทะเล

seaweed săh-rài-ta-lay
สาหร่ายทะเล

secluded dòht dèe-o
โดดเดี่ยว

second (adj) têe sŏrng
ที่สอง

(of time) wí-nah-tee
วินาที

just a second! dĕe-o gòrn!
เดี๋ยวก่อน

second class (travel etc) chún
sŏrng
ชั้นสอง

second floor (UK) chún nèung
ชั้นหนึ่ง

(US) chún sŏrng
ชั้นสอง

see hĕn
เห็น

can I see? kŏr doo nòy, dâi
mái?
ขอดูหน่อยได้ไหม

have you seen ...? hĕn ... rĕu
bplào?
เห็น ... หรือเปล่า

I saw him this morning hĕn
mêu-a cháo née
เห็นเมื่อเช้านี้

see you! jer gun mài ná!
เจอกันไหมนะ

I see (I understand) kâo jai
láir-o
เข้าใจแล้ว

self-service bor-ri-gahn chôo-
ay dtoo-a ayng
บริการช่วยตัวเอง

sell kǎi
ขาย
do you sell ...? mee ... kǎi
mái?
มี ... ขายไหม

Sellotape® sa-górt táyp
สก๊อตเทป

send sòng
ส่ง
I want to send this to England
pǒm (chún) yàhk ja sòng nêe
bpai ung-grìt
ผม(ฉัน)อยากจะส่งนี้ไปอังกฤษ

senior citizen kon cha-rah
คนชรา

separate dtàhng hàhk
ต่างหาก

separated: I'm separated (man)
pǒm yâirk gun gùp pun-ra-
yah
ผมแยกกันกับภรรยา
(woman) chún yâirk gun gùp
sǎh-mee
ฉันแยกกันกับสามี

separately (pay, travel) yâirk gun
แยกกัน

September gun-yah-yon
กันยายน

septic mee chéu-a
มีเชื้อ

serious (person) ao jing ao jung
เอาจริงเอาจัง
(situation) dtreung krêe-ut
(problem, illness) nùk
หนัก

service charge (in restaurant) kâh
bor-ri-gahn
ค่าบริการ

service station bpúm núm mun
ปั๊มน้ำมัน

serviette pâh chét bpàhk
ผ้าเช็ดปาก

set menu ah-hǎhn chóot
อาหารชุด

several lǎi
หลาย

sew yép
เย็บ
could you sew this back on?
chôo-ay yép hâi nòy dâi mái?
ช่วยเย็บให้หน่อยได้ไหม

sex gahn rôo-um bpra-way-nee
การร่วมประเวณี

sexy sek-sêe
เซ็กซี่

shade: in the shade nai rôm
ในร่ม

shake: let's shake hands jùp
meu gun
จับมือกัน

shallow (water) dtêun
ตื้น

shame: what a shame! nâh sĕe-
a dai!
น่าเสียดาย

shampoo (noun) chairm-poo
แชมพู

shampoo and set sà sét
สระเซ็ท

share (verb: room, table etc) bàirng
แบ่ง

sharp (knife) kom
คม

(taste) bprêe-o
เปรี้ยว

(pain) sĕe-o
เสียว

shattered (very tired) nèu-ay
mâhk
เหนื่อยมาก

shaver krêu-ung gohn nòo-ut
เครื่องโกนหนวด

shaving foam kreem gohn nòo-
ut
ครีมโกนหนวด

shaving point bplúk krêu-ung
gohn nòo-ut
ปลั๊กเครื่องโกนหนวด

she* káo
เขา

is she here? káo yòo têe nêe
mái?
เขาอยู่ที่นี่ไหม

sheet (for bed) pâh bpoo têe
norn
ผ้าปูที่นอน

shelf hîng
หิ้ง

shellfish hŏy
หอย

ship reu-a
เรือ

by ship tahng reu-a
ทางเรือ

shirt sêu-a chért
เสื้อเชิ้ต

shit! âi hâh!
ไอ้ห่า

shock: I got an electric shock
from the ... pŏm (chún) tòok
fai chórk têe ...
ผม(ฉัน)ถูกไฟช๊อคที่ ...

shock-absorber chórk
ช๊อค

shocked dtòk jai
ตกใจ

shocking lĕu-a gern jing jing
เหลือเกินจริงๆ

shoe rorng táo
รองเท้า

a pair of shoes rorng táo kôo
nèung
รองเท้าคู่หนึ่ง

shoelaces chêu-uk pòok rorng
táo
เชือกผูกรองเท้า

shoe polish yah kùt rorng
táo
ยาขัดรองเท้า

shoe repairer kon sôrm rorng

táo
คนซ่อมรองเท้า

shop ráhn
ร้าน

> Most shops open at least Monday to Saturday from about 8 a.m. to 8 p.m., while department stores are open daily from around 9.30 a.m. to 9 p.m.

shopping: I'm going shopping
pǒm (chún) bpai séu kǒrng
ผม(ฉัน)ไปซื้อของ

shopping centre sǒon gahn káh
ศูนย์การค้า

shop window nâh gra-jòk
ráhn
หน้ากระจกร้าน

shore chai fùng
ชายฝั่ง

short (person) dtêe-a
เตี้ย

(time) sûn
สั้น

shortcut tahng lút
ทางลัด

shorts gahng-gayng kǎh sûn
กางเกงขาสั้น

(US: underwear) gahng gayng
nai
กางเกงใน

should: what should I do? pǒm
(chún) koo-un ja tum yung-

ngai?
ผม(ฉัน)ควรจะทำอย่างไร

you should ... koon
koo-un ja ...
คุณควรจะ ...

you shouldn't ... koon mâi
koo-un ja ...
คุณไม่ควรจะ ...

he should be back soon děe-o
káo kong glùp mah
เดี๋ยวเขาคงกลับมา

shoulder lài
ไหล่

shout (verb) dta-gohn
ตะโกน

show (in theatre) gahn sa-dairng
การแสดง

could you show me? kǒr doo
nòy
ขอดูหน่อย

shower (rain) fǒn bproy bproy
ฝนปรอยๆ

(in bathroom) fùk boo-a
ฝักบัว

with shower mee fùk boo-a
มีฝักบัว

shower gel kreem àhp náhm
ครีมอาบน้ำ

shut (verb) bpìt
ปิด

when do you shut? koon bpìt
gèe mohng?
คุณปิดกี่โมง

when does it shut? bpìt gèe

mohng?
ปิดกี่โมง

they're shut káo bpìt láir-o
เขาปิดแล้ว

I've shut myself out leum ao
goon-jair òrk mah
ลืมเอากุญแจออกมา

shut up! yòot pôot ná!
หยุดพูดนะ

shutter (on camera) chút-dter
ชัตเตอร์

(on window) bahn glèt nâh-
dtàhng
บานเกล็ดหน้าต่าง

shy ai
อาย

sick (ill) mâi sa-bai
ไม่สบาย

I'm going to be sick (vomit)
róo-sèuk wâh klêun sâi
รู้สึกว่าคลื่นไส้

side kâhng
ข้าง

the other side of the street èek
fâhk nèung kŏrng ta-nŏn
อีกฟากหนึ่งของถนน

sidelights fai kâhng
ไฟข้าง

side salad sa-lùt
สลัด

side street soy
ซอย

sidewalk bàht wít-tĕe
บาทวิถี

sight: the sights of ... sa-tăhn-têe
nâh têe-o nai ...
สถานที่น่าเที่ยวใน ...

sightseeing: we're going
sightseeing rao ja bpai têe-o
เราจะไปเที่ยว

sightseeing tour rai gahn num
têe-o
รายการนำเที่ยว

sign (roadsign etc) bpâi sŭn-yahn
ja-rah-jorn
ป้ายสัญญาณจราจร

signal: he didn't give a signal
(driver, cyclist) káo mâi dâi hâi
sŭn-yahn
เขาไม่ได้ให้สัญญาณ

signature lai sen
ลายเซ็น

signpost dtìt bpâi ja-rah-jorn
ติดป้ายจราจร

silence kwahm ngêe-up
ความเงียบ

silk măi
ไหม

silly ngôh
โง่

silver (noun) ngern
เงิน

silver foil gra-dàht dta-gòo-a
กระดาษตะกั่ว

similar mĕu-un
เหมือน

simple (easy) ngâi
ง่าย

since: since last week **dtûng dtàir** ah-tít gòrn
ตั้งแต่อาทิตย์ก่อน
  since I got here **dtûng dtàir pŏm (chún) mah tĕung**
ตั้งแต่ผม(ฉัน)มาถึง
sing **rórng playng**
ร้องเพลง
singer **núk rórng**
นักร้อง
single: a single to ... **dtŏo-a bpai ...**
ตั๋วไป ...
  I'm single **pŏm (chún) bpen sòht**
ผม(ฉัน)เป็นโสด
single bed **dtee-ung dèe-o**
เตียงเดี่ยว
single room **hôrng dèe-o**
ห้องเดี่ยว
single ticket **dtŏo-a bpai**
ตั๋วไป
sink (in kitchen) **àhng**
อ่าง
sister (older) **pêe sǎo**
พี่สาว
  (younger) **nórng sǎo**
น้องสาว
sister-in-law (older) **pêe sa-pái kŏrng**
พี่สะใภ้ของ
  (younger) **nórng sa-pái kŏrng**
น้องสะใภ้ของ

sit: can I sit here? **kŏr nûng têe nêe, dâi mái?**
ขอนั่งที่นี่ได้ไหม
  is anyone sitting here? **mee kon nûng têe nêe rĕu bplào?**
มีคนนั่งที่นี่หรือเปล่า
sit down **nûng**
นั่ง
  sit down **chern nûng see**
เชิญนั่งซิ
size **ka-nàht**
ขนาด
skin **pĕw**
ผิว
skin-diving **gahn dum náhm léuk**
การดำน้ำลึก
skinny **pŏrm**
ผอม
skirt **gra-bprohng**
กระโปรง
sky **fáh**
ฟ้า
sleep (verb) **norn lùp**
นอนหลับ
  did you sleep well? **lùp dee mái?**
หลับดีไหม
sleeper (on train) **rót norn**
รถนอน
sleeping bag **tŏong norn**
ถุงนอน
sleeping car **rót norn**
รถนอน

sleeping pill yah norn lùp
ยานอนหลับ

sleepy: I'm feeling sleepy pŏm
(chún) ngôo-ung norn
ผม(ฉัน)ง่วงนอน

sleeve kǎirn sêu-a
แขนเสื้อ

slide (photographic) sa-lai
สไลด์

slip (garment) gra-bprohng chún
nai
กระโปรงชั้นใน

slippery lêun
ลื่น

slow cháh
ช้า

slow down! (driving) kùp cháh
cháh nòy!
ขับช้า ๆ หน่อย

(speaking) pôot cháh cháh
nòy!
พูดช้า ๆ หน่อย

slowly cháh
ช้า

very slowly cháh mâhk
ช้ามาก

small lék
เล็ก

smell: it smells (smells bad) měn
เหม็น

smile (verb) yím
ยิ้ม

smoke (noun) kwun
ควัน

do you mind if I smoke? kǒr
sòop boo-rèe dâi mái?
ขอสูบบุหรี่ได้ไหม

I don't smoke pŏm (chún)
mâi sòop boo-rèe
ผม(ฉัน)ไม่สูบบุหรี่

do you smoke? koOn sòop
boo-rèe mái?
คุณสูบบุหรี่ไหม

snake ngoo
งู

sneeze (verb) jahm
จาม

snorkel tôr hǎi jai
ท่อหายใจ

snow (noun) hí-má
หิมะ

so: it's so good dee jung ler-ee
ดีจังเลย

it's so expensive pairng jung
ler-ee
แพงจังเลย

not so much mâi kôy mâhk
ไม่ค่อยมาก

not so bad mâi kôy lay-o
ไม่ค่อยเลว

so am I pŏm (chún) gôr
měu-un gun
ผม(ฉัน)ก็เหมือนกัน

so do I pŏm (chún) gôr měu-
un gun
ผม(ฉัน)ก็เหมือนกัน

so-so rêu-ay rêu-ay
เรื่อย ๆ

soap sa-bòo
สบู่

soap powder pǒng súk fôrk
ผงซักฟอก

sober mâi mao
ไม่เมา

sock tôong táo
ถุงเท้า

socket (electrical) bplúk fai
ปลั๊กไฟ

soda (water) núm soh-dâh
น้ำโซดา

sofa têe nûng rúp kàirk
ที่นั่งรับแขก

soft (material etc) nîm
นิ่ม

soft drink náhm kòo-ut
น้ำขวด

sole (of shoe, of foot) péun rorng
táo
พื้นรองเท้า

could you put new soles on
these? sài péun rórng táo
mài hâi nòy, dâi mái?
ใส่พื้นรองเท้าใหม่ให้หน่อยได้ไหม

some bahng
บาง

some people bahng kon
บางคน

can I have some? kǒr nòy, dâi
mái?
ขอหน่อยได้ไหม

somebody, someone krai
ใคร

something a-rai
อะไร

something to eat kǒrng gin
ของกิน

sometimes bahng tee
บางที

somewhere têe nǎi
ที่ไหน

son lôok chai
ลูกชาย

song playng
เพลง

son-in-law lôok kěr-ee
ลูกเขย

soon děe-o
เดี๋ยว

I'll be back soon děe-o glùp
ná
เดี๋ยวกลับนะ

as soon as possible yàhng
ray-o têe sòot têe ja ray-o dâi
อย่างเร็วที่สุดที่จะเร็วได้

sore: it's sore jèp
เจ็บ

sore throat jèp kor
เจ็บคอ

sorry: (I'm) sorry pǒm (chún)
sěe-a jai
ผม(ฉัน)เสียใจ

sorry? (didn't understand)
a-rai na?
อะไรนะ

sort: what sort of ...? ... bàirp nǎi?
... แบบไหน

soup sóop
ซุป

sour (taste) bprêe-o
เปรี้ยว

south dtâi
ใต้

in the south nai pâhk dtâi
ในภาคใต้

South Africa ah-fri-gah dtâi
อาฟริกาใต้

South China Sea ta-lay jeen dtâi
ทะเลจีนใต้

southeast dta-wun òrk chěe-ung dtâi
ตะวันออกเฉียงใต้

southwest dta-wun dtòk chěe-ung dtâi
ตะวันตกเฉียงใต้

souvenir kǒrng têe ra-léuk
ของที่ระลึก

soy sauce núm see éw
น้ำซีอิ๊ว

Spain bpra-tâyt sa-bpayn
ประเทศสเปน

spanner gOOn-jair bpàhk dtai
กุญแจปากตาย

spare part a-lài
อะไหล่

spare tyre yahng a-lài
ยางอะไหล่

spark plug hǒo-a tee-un
หัวเทียน

speak: do you speak English?
kOOn pôot pah-sǎh ung-grìt

bpen mái?
คุณพูดภาษาอังกฤษเป็นไหม

I don't speak ... pǒm (chún)
pôot ... mâi bpen
ผม(ฉัน)พูด ... ไม่เป็น

can I speak to ...? kǒr pôot
gùp ... nòy, dâi mái?
ขอพูดกับ ... หน่อยได้ไหม

•••••• DIALOGUE ••••••

can I speak to Tongchai? kǒr pôot
gùp kOOn Tong-chai nòy, dâi mái
ká?

who's calling? krai pôot krúp?

it's Patricia chún Patricia pôot kâ

I'm sorry, he's not in, can I take a
message? káo mâi yòo krúp mee
a-rai ja fàhk bòrk mái?

no thanks, I'll call back later mâi
mee kâ ja toh glùp mah dtorn
lǔng

please tell him I called chôo-ay
bòrk káo wâh chún toh mah

spectacles wâirn dtah
แว่นตา

speed (noun) kwahm ray-o
ความเร็ว

speed limit ùt-dtrah kwahm
ray-o
อัตราความเร็ว

speedometer krêu-ung wút
kwahm ray-o
เครื่องวัดความเร็ว

spell: how do you spell it? sa-

gòt yung-ngai?
สะกดอย่างไร

spend chái ngern
ใช้เงิน

spider mairng moom
แมงมุม

spin-dryer krêu-ung bpùn pâh
hâi hâirng
เครื่องปั่นผ้าให้แห้ง

splinter sa-gèt mái
สะเก็ดไม้

spoke (in wheel) sêe lór rót
ซี่ล้อรถ

spoon chórn
ช้อน

sport gee-lah
กีฬา

sprain: I've sprained my ... pǒm
(chún) tum ... klèt
ผม(ฉัน)ทำเคล็ด ...

spring (season) réu-doo bai mái
plì ฤดูใบไม้ผลิ
in the spring dtorn réu-doo
bai mái plì ตอนฤดูใบไม้ผลิ

squid bplah-mèuk
ปลาหมึก

stairs bun-dai
บันได

stale mâi sòt
ไม่สด

stall: the engine keeps stalling
krêu-ung dùp bòy
เครื่องดับบ่อย

stamp (noun) sa-dtairm
แสตมป์

a stamp for England, please kòr sa-
dtairm sòng bpai ung-grìt

what are you sending? koon ja
sòng a-rai bpai?

this postcard bpóht-káht nêe

Post offices are the best places
to buy stamps, though hotels
and guesthouses often sell them
too, charging an extra baht per
stamp. All parcels must be officially boxed and sealed at special counters within main post
offices or in a private outlet just
outside – you can't just turn up
with a package and buy stamps
for it.

---

standby 'standby'

star dao
ดาว
(in film) dah-rah nǔng
ดาราหนัง

start (verb) rêrm
เริ่ม
when does it start? rêrm mêu-
rai?
เริ่มเมื่อไร
the car won't start rót sa-dtàht
mâi dtìt
รถสตาร์ทไม่ติด

starter (of car) bpòom sa-dtàht
ปุ่มสตาร์ท

starving: I'm starving pǒm
(chún) hěw jung ler-ee
ผม(ฉัน)หิวจังเลย

state (country) rút
รัฐ

the States (USA) sa-hǎh-rút
สหรัฐ

station sa-tǎh-nee rót fai
สถานีรถไฟ

statue rôop bpûn
รูปปั้น

stay: where are you staying?
koon púk yòo têe nǎi?
คุณพักอยู่ที่ไหน

I'm staying at ... pǒm (chún)
púk yòo têe
ผม(ฉัน)พักอยู่ที่ ...

I'd like to stay another two
nights pǒm (chún) yàhk ja
púk yòo èek sǒrng keun
ผม(ฉัน)อยากจะพักอยู่อีกสองคืน

steak néu-a sa-dték
เนื้อเสต็ก

steal ka-moy-ee
ขโมย

my bag has been stolen gra-
bpǎo tòok ka-moy-ee
กระเป๋าถูกขโมย

steep (hill) chun
ชัน

steering mǒon poo-ung mah-
lai
หมุนพวงมาลัย

step: on the steps têe kûn bun-

dai
ที่ขั้นบันได

stereo sa-dtay-ri-oh
สเตริโอ

sterling ngern bporn
เงินปอนด์

steward (on plane) pa-núk ngahn
krêu-ung bin
พนักงานเครื่องบิน

stewardess pa-núk ngahn
dtôrn rúp bon krêu-ung bin
พนักงานต้อนรับบนเครื่องบิน

sticking plaster plah-sa-dter
พลาสเตอร์

sticky rice kâo něe-o
ข้าวเหนียว

still: I'm still here pǒm (chún)
yung yòo têe nêe
ผม(ฉัน)ยังอยู่ที่นี่

is he still there? káo yung yòo
têe nûn mái?
เขายังอยู่ที่นั่นไหม

keep still! yòo nîng nîng!
อยู่นิ่ง ๆ

sting: I've been stung pǒm
(chún) tòok ma-lairng
dtòy
ผม(ฉัน)ถูกแมลงต่อย

stockings tǒong nôrng
ถุงน่อง

stomach tórng
ท้อง

stomach ache bpòo-ut tórng
ปวดท้อง

stone (rock) hǐn
หิน

stop (verb) yòot
หยุด

please stop here (to taxi driver
etc) yòot dtrong née krúp
(kâ)
หยุดตรงนี้ครับ(ค่ะ)

do you stop near ...? kOOn
yòot glâi glâi ... mái?
คุณหยุดใกล้ ๆ ... ไหม

stop it! yòot na!
หยุดนะ

stopover wáir
แวะ

storm pah-yóo
พายุ

straight: it's straight ahead yòo
dtrong nâh
อยู่ตรงหน้า

a straight whisky wít-sa-gêe
pee-o
วิสกี้เพียว

straightaway tun-tee
ทันที

strange (odd) bplàirk
แปลก

stranger kon bplàirk nâh
คนแปลกหน้า

I'm a stranger here pǒm
(chún) mâi châi kon têe nêe
ผม(ฉัน)ไม่ใช่คนที่นี่

strap sǎi
สาย

strawberry sa-dtor-ber-rêe
สตรอเบอร์รี่

stream lum-tahn
ลำธาร

street ta-nǒn
ถนน

on the street bon ta-nǒn
บนถนน

streetmap pǎirn-têe ta-nǒn
แผนที่ถนน

string chêu-uk
เชือก

strong kǎirng rairng
แข็งแรง

stuck dtìt
ติด

it's stuck mun dtìt
มันติด

student núk-sèuk-sǎh
นักศึกษา

stupid ngôh
โง่

suburb bor-ri-wayn chahn
meu-ung
บริเวณชานเมือง

suddenly tun-tee
ทันที

suede nǔng glùp
หนังกลับ

sugar núm dtahn
น้ำตาล

suit (noun) chóot
ชุด

it doesn't suit me (jacket etc)

mâi **mòr gùp** pǒm (chún)
ไม่เหมาะกับผม(ฉัน)

it suits you **mòr gùp** koon
dâi dee
เหมาะกับคุณได้ดี

suitcase gra-bpǎo dern tahng
กระเป๋าเดินทาง

summer nâh rórn
หน้าร้อน

in the summer dtorn nâh
rórn
ตอนหน้าร้อน

sun prá-ah-tít
พระอาทิตย์

in the sun dtàhk dàirt
ตากแดด

out of the sun nai rôm
ในร่ม

sunbathe àhp dàirt
อาบแดด

sunblock (cream) yah tah gun
dàirt
ยาทากันแดด

sunburn tòok dàirt
ถูกแดด

sunburnt tòok dàirt mâi
ถูกแดดไหม้

Sunday wun ah-tít
วันอาทิตย์

sunglasses wâirn gun dàirt
แว่นกันแดด

sun lounger máh nûng àhp
dàirt
ม้านั่งอาบแดด

sunny: it's sunny dàirt òrk
แดดออก

sunroof (in car) lǔng-kah gra-
jòk
หลังคากระจก

sunset ah-tít dtòk
อาทิตย์ตก

sunshade ngao dàirt
เงาแดด

sunshine dàirt òrk
แดดออก

sunstroke rôhk páir dàirt
โรคแพ้แดด

suntan pěw klúm dàirt
ผิวคล้ำแดด

suntan lotion kreem tah àhp
dàirt
ครีมทาอาบแดด

suntanned mee pěw klúm
dàirt
มีผิวคล้ำแดด

suntan oil núm mun tah àhp
dàirt
น้ำมันทาอาบแดด

super yôrt yêe-um
ยอดเยี่ยม

supermarket soo-bper-mah-get
ซูเปอร์มาร์เก็ต

supper ah-hǎhn yen
อาหารเย็น

supplement (extra charge) kâh
bor-ri-gahn pi-sàyt
ค่าบริการพิเศษ

sure: are you sure? koon nâir-

jai rĕu?
คุณแน่ใจหรือ
sure! nâir-norn!
แน่นอน
surname nahm sa-gOOn
นามสกุล
swearword kum sa-bòt
คำสบถ
sweater sêu-a sa-wet-dter
สเวตเตอร์
Sweden bpra-tâyt sa-wee-den
ประเทศสวีเดน
sweet (taste) wăhn
หวาน
 (noun: dessert) kŏrng wăhn
ของหวาน
sweets tórp-fêe
ท็อฟฟี่
swelling boo-um
บวม
swim (verb) wâi náhm
ว่ายน้ำ
 I'm going for a swim pŏm
 (chún) bpai wâi náhm
ผม(ฉัน)ไปว่ายน้ำ
 let's go for a swim bpai wâi
 náhm mái?
ไปว่ายน้ำไหม
swimming costume chóot àhp
 náhm
ชุดอาบน้ำ
swimming pool sà wâi náhm
สระว่ายน้ำ
swimming trunks gahng-gayng

wâi náhm
กางเกงว่ายน้ำ
switch (noun) sa-wít
สวิช
switch off bpìt
ปิด
switch on bpèrt
เปิด
Switzerland bpra-tâyt sa-wìt
ประเทศสวิส
swollen boo-um
บวม

T

table dtó
โต๊ะ
 a table for two dtó sŭm-rùp
 sŏrng kon
โต๊ะสำหรับสองคน
tablecloth pâh bpoo dtó
ผ้าปูโต๊ะ
table tennis bping bporng
ปิงปอง
tailback (of traffic) rót dtìt
รถติด
tailor châhng dtùt sêu-a pâh
ช่างตัดเสื้อผ้า
take (lead: something somewhere) ao
 ... bpai
เอา ... ไป
 (someone somewhere) pah ...
 bpai
พา ... ไป

take (accept) rúp
รับ

can you take me to the ...? pah bpai ... dâi mái?
พาไป ... ได้ไหม

do you take credit cards? rúp bùt kray-dìt rěu bplào?
รับบัตรเครดิตหรือเปล่า

fine, I'll take it oh kay, pǒm (chún) ao
โอเค ผม(ฉัน)เอา

can I take this? (leaflet etc) kǒr un née dâi mái?
ขออันนี้ได้ไหม

how long does it take? chái way-lah nahn tâo-rài?
ใช้เวลานานเท่าไร

it takes three hours chái way-lah sǎhm chôo-a mohng
ใช้เวลาสามชั่วโมง

is this seat taken? têe nêe wâhng mái?
ที่นี่ว่างไหม

can you take a little off here? (to hairdresser) dtùt dtrong née òrk nít-nòy dâi mái?
ตัดตรงนี้ออกนิดหน่อยได้ไหม

talcum powder bpâirng
แป้ง

talk (verb) pôot
พูด

tall sǒong
สูง

tampons tairm-porn
แทมพอน

tan (noun) klúm
คล้ำ

to get a tan hâi pěw klúm
ให้ผิวคล้ำ

tank (of car) tǔng núm mun
ถังน้ำมัน

tap górk náhm
กอกน้ำ

tape (for cassette) táyp
เทป

tape measure sǎi wút
สายวัด

tape recorder krêu-ung bun-téuk sěe-ung
เครื่องบันทึกเสียง

taste (noun) rót
รส

can I taste it? kǒr **lorng chim** nòy, dâi mái?
ขอลองชิมหน่อยได้ไหม

taxi táirk-sêe
แท๊กซี่

will you get me a taxi? chôo-ay rêe-uk táirk-sêe hâi nòy, dâi mái?
ช่วยเรียกแท๊กซี่ให้หน่อยได้ไหม

•••••• DIALOGUE ••••••

to the airport/to the Regent Hotel, please bpai sa-nǎhm bin/rohng rairm ree-yen

how much will it be? tâo-rài?

300 baht sǎhm róy bàht

that's fine right here, thanks jòrt dtrong née na

The three-wheeled open-sided **tuk-tuk** is the classic Thai vehicle and is very cheap to hire. Tuk-tuks are also sometimes known as **samlors** (literally: three wheels), but the real samlors are tricycle rickshaws propelled by pedal-power alone. Slower and a great deal more stately than tuk-tuks, samlors operate pretty much everywhere except in Bangkok. It is customary to negotiate the price before the journey begins.

Motorbike taxis feature in both big towns and out-of-the-way places. In remote spots, they are often the only alternative to hitching or walking and are especially useful for getting between bus stops on main roads and to national parks or ancient ruins. Within towns motorbike taxi fares are comparable to those for tuk-tuks, but for trips to the outskirts the cost rises steeply. Car taxis are generally available only in the biggest towns, and charge fares that begin at around B40; a few have air-conditioning.

see **bargaining**

---

taxi-driver kon kùp táirk-sêe
คนขับแท็กซี่

taxi rank têe jòrt rót táirk-sêe
ที่จอดรถแท็กซี่

tea (drink) núm chah
น้ำชา

tea for one/two, please kŏr núm chah tee nèung/sŏrng tee
ขอน้ำชาทีหนึ่ง/สองที

teabags chah tôong
ชาถุง

teach: could you teach me? sŏrn hâi dâi mái?
สอนให้ได้ไหม

teacher kroo
ครู

team teem
ทีม

teaspoon chórn chah
ช้อนชา

tea towel pâh chét jahn
ผ้าเช็ดจาน

teenager dèk wai rôon
เด็กวัยรุ่น

telegram toh-ra-lâyk
โทรเลข

telephone toh-ra-sùp
โทรศัพท์

see **phone**

television toh-ra-tút
โทรทัศน์

tell: could you tell him ...?
chôo-ay bòrk káo wâh ...

nòy, dâi mái?

ช่วยบอกเขาว่า ... หน่อยได้ไหม

temperature (weather) oOn-na-
ha-poom

อุณหภูมิ

(fever) kâi

ไข้

temple wút

วัด

tennis tay-nit

เทนนิส

tennis ball lôok ten-nít

ลูกเทนนิส

tennis court sa-năhm ten-nít

สนามเทนนิส

tennis racket mái dtee ten-nít

ไม้ตีเทนนิส

tent dten

เต็นท์

term term

เทอร์ม

terminus (rail) sa-tăh-nee

สถานี

terrible yâir

แย่

terrific yôrt yêe-um

ยอดเยี่ยม

Thai (adj) tai

ไทย

(language) pah-săh tai

ภาษาไทย

a Thai, the Thais kon tai

คนไทย

Thai attitudes

There are three specifically Thai concepts you're bound to come across. The first is **sanuk**, the wide-reaching philosophy of 'fun', which, crass as it sounds, Thais do their best to inject into any situation, even work. Hence the crowds of inebriated Thais who congregate at waterfalls and other beauty spots on public holidays, and the national waterfight which takes place every April on streets right across Thailand.

The Thais sometimes have a laissez-faire attitude to delayed buses and other inconveniences which can be explained by the concept of **jai yen** (literally: cool heart) and this is something everyone tries to maintain — most Thais hate raised voices, visible irritation and confrontations of any kind. Related to this is the oft-quoted response to a difficulty, **mâi bpen rai** (never mind, no problem, or it can't be helped), the verbal equivalent of an open-handed shoulder shrug which has its base in the Buddhist notion of karma.

Thailand (formal) bpra-tâyt tai
ประเทศไทย
(informal) meu-ung tai
เมืองไทย

than* gwàh
กว่า
smaller than lék gwàh
เล็กกว่า

thanks, thank you kòrp-kOOn
ขอบคุณ
thank you very much kòrp-
kOOn mâhk
ขอบคุณมาก
thanks for the lift korp-kOOn
tee mah ̩song
ขอบคุณที่มาส่ง
no thanks mâi ao kòrp-kOOn
ไม่เอาขอบคุณ

• • • • • • DIALOGUE • • • • • •

thanks kòrp-kOOn
that's OK, don't mention it mâi
bpen rai

that: that boy pôo-chai kon nún
ผู้ชายคนนั้น
that girl pôo-yǐng kon nún
ผู้หญิงคนนั้น
that one un nún
อันนั้น
I hope that … pǒm (chún)
wǔng wâh …
ผม(ฉัน)หวังว่า …
that's nice sǒo-ay
สวย

is that …? … châi mái?
… ใช่ไหม
that's it (that's right) châi láir-o
ใช่แล้ว

the*

theatre rohng la-korn
โรงละคร
their kǒrng káo
ของเขา
theirs kǒrng káo
ของเขา
them káo
เขา
for them sǔm-rùp káo
สำหรับเขา
with them gùp káo
กับเขา
to them gàir káo
แก่เขา
who? – them krai? – pôo-uk
káo
ใครพวกเขา

then (at that time) dtorn nún
ตอนนั้น
(after that) lǔng jàhk nún
หลังจากนั้น
there têe nûn
ที่นั่น
over there têe-nôhn
ที่โน่น
up there kâhng bon nún
ข้างบนนั้น
is/are there …? mee … mái?
มี … ไหม

there is/are ... mee ...
มี ...

there you are (giving something)
nêe krúp (kâ)
นี่ครับ(คะ)

thermometer bpròrt
ปรอท

Thermos flask® gra-dtìk náhm
กระติกน้ำ

these*: these men pôo-chai
pôo-uk lào née
ผู้ชายพวกเหล่านี้

these women pôo-yǐng pôo-
uk lào née
ผู้หญิงพวกเหล่านี้

I'd like these ao pôo-uk lào
née
เอาพวกเหล่านี้

they káo
เขา

thick nǎh
หนา

(stupid) ngôh
โง่

thief ka-moy-ee
ขโมย

thigh nôrng
น่อง

thin pǒrm
ผอม

thing kǒrng
ของ

my things kǒrng pǒm (chún)
ของผม(ฉัน)

think kít
คิด

I think so pǒm (chún) kít
wâh yung-ngún
ผม(ฉัน)คิดว่าอย่างนั้น

I don't think so pǒm (chún)
kít wâh kong mâi
ผม(ฉัน)คิดว่าคงไม่

I'll think about it pǒm (chún)
ja lorng kít doo gòrn
ผม(ฉัน)จะลองคิดดูก่อน

thirsty: I'm thirsty pǒm (chún)
hěw náhm
ผม(ฉัน)หิวน้ำ

this: this boy pôo-chai kon née
ผู้ชายคนนี้

this girl pôo-yǐng kon née
ผู้หญิงคนนี้

this one un née
อันนี้

this is my wife nêe pun-ra-
yah kǒrng pǒm
นี่ภรรยาของผม

is this ...? ... châi mái?
... ใช่ไหม

those: those men pôo chai pôo-
uk lào nún
ผู้ชายพวกเหล่านั้น

those women pôo yǐng pôo-
uk lào nún
ผู้หญิงพวกเหล่านั้น

which ones? – those un nâi? –
un nún
อันไหนอันนั้น

thread (noun) sên dâi
เส้นด้าย

throat kor hǒy
คอหอย

throat pastilles yah om gâir kor
jèp
ยาอมแก้คอเจ็บ

through pàhn
ผ่าน

does it go through ...? (train, bus)
pàhn ... rěu bplào?
ผ่าน ... หรือเปล่า

throw (verb) kwâhng
ขว้าง

throw away (verb) tíng
ทิ้ง

thumb néw hǒo-a mâir meu
นิ้วหัวแม่มือ

thunderstorm pah-yóo fǒn
พายุฝน

Thursday wun pá-réu-hùt
วันพฤหัส

ticket dtǒo-a
ตั๋ว

•••••• DIALOGUE ••••••

a return to Chiangmai dtǒo-a bpai
glùp chee-ung-mài

coming back when? glùp mêu-
rai?

today/next Tuesday wun née/wun
ung-kahn nâh

that will be 200 baht sǒrng róy
bàht

ticket office (bus, rail) têe jum-nài
dtǒo-a
ที่จำหน่ายตั๋ว

tie (necktie) nék-tai
เน็คไท

tight (clothes etc) kúp
คับ

it's too tight kúp gern bpai
คับเกินไป

tights tǒong yai boo-a
ถุงใยบัว

till (cash desk) têe gèp ngern
ที่เก็บเงิน

time* way-lah
เวลา

what's the time? gèe mohng
láir-o?
กี่โมงแล้ว

this time krúng née
ครั้งนี้

last time krúng têe láir-o
ครั้งที่แล้ว

next time krúng nâh
ครั้งหน้า

three times sǎhm krúng
สามครั้ง

timetable dtah-rahng way-lah
ตารางเวลา

tin (can) gra-bpǒrng
กระป๋อง

tinfoil gra-dàht a-loo-mi-nee-
um
กระดาษอลูมิเนียม

tin-opener têe bpèrt

gra-bpŏrng
ที่เปิดกระป๋อง

tiny lék
เล็ก

tip (to waiter etc) ngern típ
เงินทิป

In restaurants and coffee shops
it is usual to leave a small tip.
It is unnecessary to tip in 'noodle shops', 'curry shops' and
other cheap eating places; tip-
ping is not usual either in taxis
or tuk-tuks.

tired nèu-ay
เหนื่อย

I'm tired pŏm (chún) nèu-ay
ผม(ฉัน)เหนื่อย

tissues pâh chét meu
ผ้าเช็ดมือ

to: to Bangkok bpai groong-
tâyp
ไปกรุงเทพฯ

to Thailand bpai meu-ung tai
ไปเมืองไทย

to the post office bpai bprai-
sa-nee
ไปไปรษณีย์

toast (bread) ka-nŏm bpung
bpîng
ขนมปังปิ้ง

today wun née
วันนี้

toe néw táo
นิ้วเท้า

together dôo-ay gun
ด้วยกัน

we're together (in shop etc) rao
mah dôo-ay gun
เรามาด้วยกัน

toilet hôrng náhm
ห้องน้ำ

where is the toilet? hôrng
náhm yòo têe năi?
ห้องน้ำอยู่ที่ไหน

I have to go to the toilet pŏm
(chún) dtôrng bpai hôrng
náhm
ผม(ฉัน)ต้องไปห้องน้ำ

Public toilets are few and far
between in Thailand. Take ad-
vantage of the facilities before
you leave a restaurant!

toilet paper gra-dàht chum-rá
กระดาษชำระ

tomato ma-kěu-a tâyt
มะเขือเทศ

tomato juice núm ma-kěu-a
tâyt
น้ำมะเขือเทศ

tomato ketchup sórt ma-kěu-a
tâyt
ซอสมะเขือเทศ

tomorrow prôong née
พรุ่งนี้

tomorrow morning cháo
prôong née
เช้าพรุ่งนี้

the day after tomorrow wun
ma-reun née
วันมะรืนนี้

toner (cosmetic) toner
toner

tongue lín
ลิ้น

tonic (water) núm toh-ník
น้ำโทนิค

tonight keun née
คืนนี้

tonsillitis dtòrm torn-sin ùk-
sàyp
ต่อมทอนซิลอักเสป

too (excessively) ... gern bpai
... เกินไป

(also) dôo-ay
ด้วย

too hot rórn gern bpai
ร้อนเกินไป

too much mâhk gern bpai
มากเกินไป

me too pǒm (chún) gôr měu-
un gun
ผม(ฉัน)ก็เหมือนกัน

tooth fun
ฟัน

toothache bpòo-ut fun
ปวดฟัน

toothbrush bprairng sěe fun
แปรงสีฟัน

toothpaste yah sěe fun
ยาสีฟัน

top: on top of ... yòo bon ...
อยู่บน ...

at the top yòo kâhng bon
อยู่ข้างบน

top floor chún bon
ชั้นบน

topless bpleu-ay òk
เปลือยอก

torch fai chǎi
ไฟฉาย

total (noun) roo-um yôrt
รวมยอด

tour (noun) rai-gahn num
têe-o
รายการนำเที่ยว

is there a tour of ...? mee rai-
gahn num têe-o bpai ... mái?
มีรายการนำเที่ยวไป ... ไหม

tour guide múk-koo-tâyt
มัคคุเทศก์

tourist núk tôrng têe-o
นักท่องเที่ยว

tourist information office sǔm-
núk kào sǎhn núk tôrng
têe-o
สำนักงานข่าวสารนักท่องเที่ยว

tour operator pôo-jùt bor-ri-
gahn num têe-o
ผู้จัดการบริการนำเที่ยว

towards sòo
สู่

towel pâh chét dtoo-a
ผ้าเช็ดตัว

town meu-ung
เมือง

in town nai meu-ung
ในเมือง

just out of town nork meu-ung bpai noy
นอกเมืองไปหน่อย

town centre jai glahng meu-ung
ใจกลางเมือง

town hall tâyt-sa-bahn
เทศบาล

toy kŏrng lên
ของเล่น

track chahn chah-lah
ชานชาลา

which track is it for Chiangmai?
bpai chee-ung-mài chahn chah-lah a-rai?
ไปเชียงใหม่ชานชาลาอะไร

tracksuit chóot gee-lah
ชุดกีฬา

traditional bpen ka-nòp-tum nee-um
เป็นขนบธรรมเนียม

traffic ja-rah-jorn
จราจร

traffic jam rót dtìt
รถติด

traffic lights fai sŭn-yahn ja-rah-jorn
ไฟสัญญาณจราจร

trailer (for carrying tent etc) rót pôo-ung
รถพ่วง

train rót fai
รถไฟ

by train doy-ee rót fai
โดยรถไฟ

Although usually slower than buses, trains are safer and offer the possibility of sleeping during overnight trips; moreover, if travelling by day you're likely to follow a more scenic route by rail than by road.

Managed by the State Railway of Thailand (SRT), the rail network consists of four main lines and a few branch lines. Fares depend on the class of seat, whether or not you want air-conditioning, and on the speed of the train. All long-distance trains have dining cars, and rail staff will also bring meals to your compartment. Tourist menus are written in English but have inflated prices – ask for the similar but cheaper 'ordinary' version, the menu '**tum-ma-dah**'.

Advance booking of at least one day is essential for second-class and first-class seats on all lengthy journeys, and for sleepers needs to be done as far in advance as possible.

•••••• DIALOGUE ••••••

is this the train for Korat? rót fai née bpai koh-râht mái?

สูเร nâir-norn

no, you want that platform there mâi bpai koon dtôrng bpai chahn chah-lah un nún

trainers (shoes) rorng táo gee-lah
รองเท้ากีฬา

train station sa-tǎhn-nee rót fai
สถานีรถไฟ

translate bplair
แปล

could you translate that? chôo-ay bplair hâi nòy, dâi mái?
ช่วยแปลให้หน่อยได้ไหม

translation gahn bplair
การแปล

translator pôo bplair
ผู้แปล

trash can tǔng ka-yà
ถังขยะ

travel gahn dern tahng
การเดินทาง

we're travelling around rao dern tahng bpai rêu-ay rêu-ay
เราเดินทางไปเรื่อย ๆ

travel agent's trah-wern ay-yen
ทราเวิลเอเยนต์

traveller's cheque chék dern tahng
เช็คเดินทาง

tray tàht
ถาด

tree dtôn mái
ต้นไม้

tremendous wí-sàyt
วิเศษ

trendy tun sa-mǎi
ทันสมัย

trim: just a trim, please (to hairdresser) chôo-ay dtùt òrk nít-nòy tâo-nún krúp (ká)
ช่วยตัดออกนิดหน่อยเท่านั้นครับ(คะ)

trip (excursion) têe-o
เที่ยว

I'd like to go on a trip to ... pǒm (chún) yàhk ja bpai têe-o ...
ผม(ฉัน)อยากจะไปเที่ยว ...

trolley rót kěn
รถเข็น

trouble (noun) bpun-hǎh
ปัญหา

I'm having trouble with ... pǒm (chún) mee bpun-hǎh gùp ...
ผม(ฉัน)มีปัญหากับ ...

trousers gahng-gayng
กางเกง

true jing
จริง

that's not true mâi jing
ไม่จริง

trunk (US: car) gra-bprohng

tái rót
กระโปรงท้ายรถ

trunks (swimming) gahng-gayng
wâi náhm
กางเกงว่ายน้ำ

try (verb) pa-yah-yahm
พยายาม

can I try it? kŏr lorng nòy, dâi
mái?
ขอลองหน่อยได้ไหม

try on lorng sài doo
ลองใส่ดู

can I try it on? kŏr lorng sài
doo nòy, dâi mái?
ขอลองใส่ดูหน่อยได้ไหม

T-shirt sêu-a yêut
เสื้อยืด

Tuesday wun ung-kahn
วันอังคาร

tuna bplah too-nah
ปลาทูนา

tunnel OO-mohng
อุโมงค์

turn: turn left/right lée-o sái/
kwǎh
เลี้ยวซ้าย/ขวา

turn off: where do I turn off? ja
lée-o têe nǎi?
จะเลี้ยวที่ไหน

can you turn the air-
conditioning off? chôo-ay bpìt
krêu-ung bprùp ah-gàht nòy,
dâi mái?
ช่วยปิดเครื่องปรับอากาศ
หน่อยได้ไหม

turn on: can you turn the air-
conditioning on? chôo-ay
bpèrt krêu-ung bprùp ah-
gàht nòy, dâi mái?
ช่วยเปิดเครื่องปรับอากาศ
หน่อยได้ไหม

turning (in road) tahng lée-o
ทางเลี้ยว

TV tee-wee
ทีวี

tweezers bpàhk kêep
ปากคีบ

twice sŏrng krúng
สองครั้ง

twice as much mâhk sŏrng
tâo
มากสองเท่า

twin beds dtee-ung kôo
เตียงคู่

twin room hôrng kôo
ห้องคู่

twist: I've twisted my ankle kŏr
táo pŏm (chún) plík
ข้อเท้าผม(ฉัน)พลิก

type (noun) bàirp
แบบ

another type of ... ... èek bàirp
nèung
... อีกแบบหนึ่ง

typical bàirp cha-bùp
แบบฉบับ

tyre yahng rót
ยางรถ

U

ugly nâh glèe-ut
นาเกลียด

UK bpra-tâyt ung-grìt
ประเทศอังกฤษ

ulcer plăir gra-pór
แผลกระเพาะ

umbrella rôm
ร่ม

uncle (older brother of mother/father)
loong
ลุง
(younger brother of father) ah
อา
(younger brother of mother) náh
น้า

unconscious mòt sa-dtì
หมดสติ

under (in position) dtâi
ใต้
(less than) dtùm gwàh
ต่ำกว่า

underdone (meat) sòok-sòok
dìp-dìp
สุก ๆ ดิบ ๆ

underpants gahng-gayng nai
กางเกงใน

understand: I understand pŏm
(chún) kâo jai
ผม(ฉัน)เข้าใจ

I don't understand pŏm
(chún) mâi kâo jai
ผม(ฉัน)ไม่เข้าใจ

do you understand? kâo jai
mái?
เข้าใจไหม

United States sa-hà-rút a-may-
ri-gah
สหรัฐอเมริกา

university ma-hăh-wít-ta-yah-lai
มหาวิทยาลัย

unleaded petrol núm mun rái
săhn dta-gòo-a
น้ำมันไร้สารตะกั่ว

unlimited mileage mâi jum-gùt
ra-ya tahng
ไม่จำกัดระยะทาง

unlock kăi goon-jair
ไขกุญแจ

unpack gâir hòr
แก้ห่อ

until jon
จน

unusual pìt tum-ma-dah
ผิดธรรมดา

up kêun
ขึ้น

up there yòo bon nún
อยู่บนนั้น

he's not up yet (not out of bed)
káo yung mâi dtèun
เขายังไม่ตื่น

what's up? (what's wrong?) bpen
a-rai?
เป็นอะไร

upmarket rŏo-răh
หรูหรา

upset stomach tórng sěe-a
ท้องเสีย

upside down kwûm
คว่ำ

upstairs kâhng bon
ข้างบน

urgent dòo-un
ด่วน

us* rao
เรา

with us gùp rao
กับเรา

for us sǔm-rùp rao
สำหรับเรา

USA sa-hà-rút a-may-ri-
gah
สหรัฐอเมริกา

use (verb) chái
ใช้

may I use ...? kǒr chái ... dâi
mái?
ขอใช้ ... ได้ไหม

useful mee bpra-yòht
มีประโยชน์

usual tum-ma-dah
ธรรมดา

V

vacancy: do you have any
vacancies? (hotel) mee hôrng
wâhng mái?
มีห้องว่างไหม
see room

vacation wun yòot
วันหยุด

on vacation yòot púk pòrn
หยุดพักผ่อน

vaccination chèet wúk-seen
ฉีดวัคซีน

vacuum cleaner krêu-ung dòot
fòon
เครื่องดูดฝุ่น

valid (ticket etc) chái dâi
ใช้ได้

how long is it valid for? chái
dâi tĕung mêu-a rài?
ใช้ได้ถึงเมื่อไร

valley hòop kǎo
หุบเขา

valuable (adj) mee kâh
มีค่า

can I leave my valuables here?
ao kâo kǒrng tíng wái têe
nêe, dâi mái?
เอาข้าวของทิ้งไว้ที่นี่ได้ไหม

value (noun) kâh
ค่า

van rót dtôo
รถตู้

vanilla wá-ní-lah
วานิลา

a vanilla ice cream ait kreem
wá-née-lah

vary: it varies láir-o dtàir
แล้วแต่

vase jair-gun
แจกัน

vegetables pùk
ผัก

vegetarian (noun) kon mâi gin néu-a
คนไม่กินเนื้อ

vending machine dtôo
ตู้

very mâhk
มาก

very little for me kŏr nít dee-o tâo-nún
ขอนิดเดียวเท่านั้น

I like it very much pŏm (chún) chôrp mâhk
ผม(ฉัน)ชอบมาก

vest (under shirt) sêu-a glâhm
เสื้อกล้าม

via pàhn
ผ่าน

video (noun: film) wee-dee-o
วีดีโอ

(recorder) krêu-ung wee-dee-oh
เครื่องวีดีโอ

Vietnam bpra-tâyt wêe-ut-nahm
ประเทศเวียดนาม

Vietnamese (adj) wêe-ut-nahm
เวียดนาม

view wew
วิว

village mòo bâhn
หมู่บ้าน

vinegar núm sôm
น้ำส้ม

visa wee-sâh
วีซ่า

visit (verb: place) têe-o
เที่ยว

(person) yêe-um
เยี่ยม

I'd like to visit ... pŏm (chún) yàhk ja bpai têe-o/yêe-um ...
ผม(ฉัน)อยากจะไปเที่ยว/เยี่ยม ...

vital: it's vital that ... sŭm-kun mâhk têe ja dtôrng ...
สำคัญมากที่จะต้อง ...

vodka word-kâh
วอร์ดค่า

voice sĕe-ung
เสียง

voltage rairng fai fáh
แรงไฟฟ้า

Electricity is supplied at 220 volts and is available at all but the most remote villages and basic beach huts.

---

vomit ah-jee-un
อาเจียน

W

waist ay-o
เอว

waistcoat sêu-a gúk
เสื้อกั๊ก

wait ror
รอ

wait for me ror pǒm (chún)
nòy ná
รอผม(ฉัน)หน่อยนะ

don't wait for me mâi dtôrng
ror pǒm (chún) ná
ไม่ต้องรอผม(ฉัน)นะ

can I wait until my wife/partner
gets here? ror jon pun-ra-
yah/fairn mah dâi mái?
รอจนภรรยา/แฟนมาได้ไหม

can you do it while I wait?
pǒm (chún) ror ao dâi mái?
ผม(ฉัน)รอเอาได้ไหม

could you wait here for me?
ror pǒm (chún) têe nêe dâi
mái?
รอผม(ฉัน)ที่นี่ได้ไหม

waiter kon sérp
คนเสิร์ฟ

waiter! koon krúp (kâ)!
คุณครับ(ค่ะ)

waitress kon sérp
คนเสิร์ฟ

waitress! koon krúp (kâ)!
คุณครับ(ค่ะ)

wake: can you wake me up at

5.30? chôo-ay **bplòok** pǒm
(chún) way-lah dtee hâh
krêung dâi mái?
ช่วยปลุกผม(ฉัน)เวลาตีห้าครึ่งได้ไหม

Wales Wales
เวลส์

walk: is it a long walk? dern glai
mái?
เดินไกลไหม

it's only a short walk dern mâi
glai
เดินไม่ไกล

I'll walk pǒm (chún) dern
bpai
ผม(ฉัน)เดินไป

I'm going for a walk pǒm
(chún) bpai dern lên
ผม(ฉัน)ไปเดินเล่น

Walkman® walkman®
วอล์กแมน

wall (inside) fǎh
ฝา

(outside) gum-pairng
กำแพง

wallet gra-bpǎo sa-dtahng
กระเป๋าสตางค์

wander: I like just wandering
around pǒm (chún) chôrp
dern lên rêu-ay bpèu-ay bpai
ผม(ฉัน)ชอบเดินเล่นเรื่อยเปื่อยไป

want: I want a … pǒm (chún)
ao …
ผม(ฉัน)เอา …

I don't want any … pǒm

(chún) mâi yàhk dâi ...

ผม(ฉัน)ไม่อยากได้ ...

I want to go home pǒm
(chún) yàhk ja glùp bâhn

ผม(ฉัน)อยากจะกลับบ้าน

I don't want to pǒm (chún)
mâi yàhk ...

ผม(ฉัน)ไม่อยาก ...

he wants to ... káo yàhk ja ...

เขาอยากจะ ...

what do you want? kOOn
dtôrng-gahn a-rai?

คุณต้องการอะไร

ward (in hospital) hǒr pôo bpòo-
ay

หอผู้ป่วย

warm rórn

ร้อน

I'm so warm pǒm (chún)
rórn jung

ผม(ฉัน)ร้อนจัง

was*: he was káo bpen

เขาเป็น

she was káo bpen

เขาเป็น

it was (mun) bpen

มันเป็น

wash (verb) súk

ซัก

(oneself) láhng

ล้าง

can you wash these? súk un
née hâi nòy dâi mái?

ซักอันนี้ให้หน่อยได้ไหม

washer (for bolt etc) wong-wǎirn

วงแหวน

washhand basin àhng láhng
nâh

อ่างล้างหน้า

washing machine krêu-ung súk
pâh

เครื่องซักผ้า

washing powder pǒng súk fôrk

ผงซักฟอก

washing-up liquid núm yah
láhng

น้ำยาล้าง

wasp dtairn

แตน

watch (wristwatch) nah-li-gah

นาฬิกา

will you watch my things for
me? chôo-ay fâo kǒrng hâi
nòy dâi mái?

ช่วยเฝ้าของให้หน่อยได้ไหม

watch out! ra-wung!

ระวัง

watch strap sǎi nah-li-gah

สายนาฬิกา

water náhm

น้ำ

may I have some water? kǒr
náhm nòy dâi mái?

ขอน้ำหน่อยได้ไหม

waterproof (adj) gun náhm

กันน้ำ

waterskiing sa-gee náhm

สกีน้ำ

wave (in sea) klêun
คลื่น

way: it's this way bpai tahng née
ไปทางนี้

it's that way bpai tahng nóhn
ไปทางโน้น

is it a long way to ...? bpai ...
glai mái?
ไป ... ไกลไหม

no way! mâi mee tahng!
ไม่มีทาง

• • • • • • DIALOGUE • • • • • •

could you tell me the way to ...?
chôo-ay bòrk tahng bpai ... hâi
nòy, dâi mái?

go straight on until you reach the
traffic lights dern dtrong bpai jon
tĕung fai sŭn-yahn

turn left lée-o sái

take the first on the right lée-o
kwăh têe tahng yâirk un râirk

see where

we* rao
เรา

weak (person, drink) òrn-air
อ่อนแอ

weather ah-gàht
อากาศ

wedding pi-tee dtàirng ngahn
พิธีแต่งงาน

wedding ring wăirn dtàirng
ngahn
แหวนแต่งงาน

Wednesday wun póot
วันพุธ

week ah-tít
อาทิตย์

a week (from) today èek ah-tít
nèung jàhk wun née bpai
อีกอาทิตย์หนึ่งจากวันนี้ไป

a week (from) tomorrow èek
ah-tít nèung jàhk prôong née
bpai
อีกอาทิตย์หนึ่งจากพรุ่งนี้ไป

weekend wun săo wun ah-tít
วันเสาร์วันอาทิตย์

at the weekend wun săo ah-
tít
วันเสาร์อาทิตย์

weight núm-nùk
น้ำหนัก

weird bplàirk
แปลก

weirdo
คนแปลก

welcome: welcome to ... kŏr
dtôrn rúp ...
ขอต้อนรับ ...

you're welcome (don't mention it)
mâi bpen rai
ไม่เป็นไร

well: I don't feel well pŏm
(chún) róo-sèuk mâi kôy sa-
bai
ผม(ฉัน)รู้สึกไม่ค่อยสบาย

she's not well kăo mâi sa-bai
เขาไม่สบาย

you speak English very well
kOOn pôot pah-săh ung-grìt
dâi dee mâhk
คุณพูดภาษาอังกฤษได้ดีมาก
well done! dee mâhk!
ดีมาก
this one as well un née dôo-ay
อันนี้ด้วย
well well! (surprise) măir!
แหม

•••••• DIALOGUE ••••••

how are you? bpen yung-ngai
bâhng?
very well, thanks, and you? sa-bai
dee kòrp-kOOn, láir-o kOOn lâ?

well-done (meat) sòOk sòOk
สุก ๆ
Welsh: I'm Welsh pŏm (chún)
bpen kon Wales
ผม(ฉัน)เป็นคนเวลส์
were*: we were rao bpen
เราเป็น
you were kOOn bpen
คุณเป็น
they were káo bpen
เขาเป็น
west dta-wun dtòk
ตะวันตก
in the west dta-wun dtòk
ตะวันตก
West Indian (adj) mah jahk mòo
gòr in-dee-a dta-wun dtòk
มาจากหมู่เกาะอินเดียตะวันตก

wet bpèe-uk
เปียก
what? a-rai?
อะไร
what's that? nûn a-rai?
นั่นอะไร
what should I do? ja tum
yung-ngai dee?
จะทำอย่างไรดี
what a view! wew sŏo-ay
jung ler-ee!
วิวสวยจังเลย
what bus do I take? kêun rót
may săi năi?
ขึ้นรถเมล์สายไหน
wheel lór
ล้อ
wheelchair rót kĕn sŭm-rùp
kon bpòo-ay
รถเข็นสำหรับคนป่วย
when? mêu-rai?
เมื่อไร
when we get back mêu-a rao
glùp mah/bpai
เมื่อเรากลับมา/ไป
when's the train/ferry? rót fai/
reu-a òrk gèe mohng?
รถไฟ/เรือออกกี่โมง
where? têe-năi?
ที่ไหน
I don't know where it is pŏm
(chún) mâi sâhp wâh yòo
têe-năi
ผม(ฉัน)ไม่ทราบว่าอยู่ที่ไหน

•••••• DIALOGUE ••••••

where is the temple? wút yòo têe
năi?

it's over there yòo têe-nôhn

could you show me where it is on
the map? chôo-ay chée hâi hěn
wâh yòo têe năi nai păirn-têe

it's just here yòo dtrong née

see **way**

which: which bus? rót may săi
năi?
รถเมล์สายไหน

•••••• DIALOGUE ••••••

which one? un năi?

that one un nún

this one? un née, châi mái?

no, that one mâi châi un nún

while: while I'm here ka-nà têe
pŏm (chún) yòo têe née
ขณะที่ผม(ฉัน)อยู่ที่นี่

whisky lâo wít-sa-gêe
เหล้าวิสกี้

white sěe kǎo
สีขาว

white wine lâo wai kǎo
เหล้าไวน์ขาว

who? krai?
ใคร

who is it? nûn krai lâ?
นั่นใครล่ะ

the man who ... kon têe ...
คนที่ ...

whole: the whole week dta-lòrt
ah-tít
ตลอดอาทิตย์

the whole lot túng mòt
ทั้งหมด

whose: whose is this? nêe
kǒrng krai?
นี่ของใคร

why? tum-mai?
ทำไม

wide gwâhng
กว้าง

wife: my wife pun-ra-yah kǒrng
pǒm
ภรรยาของผม

will*: will you do it for me?
chôo-ay tum hâi nòy dâi mái?
ช่วยทำให้หน่อยได้ไหม

wind (noun) lom
ลม

window nâh-dtàhng
หน้าต่าง

near the window glâi nâh-
dtàhng
ใกล้หน้าต่าง

in the window (of shop) têe
nâh-dtàhng
ที่หน้าต่าง

window seat têe nûng dtìt nâh-
dtàhng
ที่นั่งติดหน้าต่าง

windscreen gra-jòk nâh rót
yon
กระจกหน้ารถยนต์

windscreen wiper têe bpùt núm
fǒn
ที่ปัดน้ำฝน

windsurfing gahn lên gra-dahn
dtôh lom
การเล่นกระดานโต้ลม

windy: it's so windy lom rairng
jung
ลมแรงจัง

wine lâo wai
เหล้าไวน

can we have some more wine?
kǒr wai èek dâi mái?
ขอไวน์อีกได้ไหม

Wine is not widely drunk in
Thailand and many people feel
it does not complement Thai
food very well. A cheap local
brand is produced but is not
generally served in restaurants.
Western wines will be available
only in the more expensive restaurants.

wine list rai-gahn lâo wai
รายการเหล้าไวน์

winter nâh nǎo
หน้าหนาว

in the winter nai nâh
nǎo
ในหน้าหนาว

wire lôo-ut
ลวด

(electric) sǎi fai fáh
สายไฟฟ้า

wish: best wishes dôo-ay
kwahm bprah-ta-nǎh dee
ด้วยความปรารถนาดี

with gùp
กับ

I'm staying with ... pǒm
(chún) púk yòo gùp ...
ผม(ฉัน)พักอยู่กับ ...

without doy-ee mâi
โดยไม่

witness pa-yahn
พยาน

will you be a witness for me?
chôo-ay bpen pa-yahn hâi
pǒm (chún) dâi mái?
ช่วยเป็นพยานให้ผม(ฉัน)ได้ไหม

woman pôo-yǐng
ผู้หญิง

women
On the whole, Thailand is a
fairly hassle-free destination for
women travellers. Though un-
palatable and distressing, the
high-profile sex industry is rela-
tively unthreatening for Western
women, with its energy focused
exclusively on foreign men;
it's also quite easily avoided,
being contained within certain
pockets of the capital and a
couple of beach resorts. As for →

harassment from Thai men, it's hard to generalize, but most Western tourists find it less of a problem in Thailand than they do back home. Outside the main tourist spots, you're more likely to be an object of interest as a foreigner rather than as a woman and, if travelling alone, as an object of concern rather than of sexual aggression.

wonderful yôrt yêe-um
ยอดเยี่ยม

won't*: it won't start mâi yorm dtìt
ไม่ยอมติด

wood (material) mái
ไม้

woods (forest) bpàh
ป่า

wool kŏn sùt
ขนสัตว์

word kum
คำ

work (noun) ngahn
งาน

it's not working mun sěe-a
มันเสีย

I work in ... pŏm (chún) tum ngahn têe ...
ผม(ฉัน)ทำงานที่ ...

world lôhk
โลก

worry: I'm worried pŏm (chún) bpen hòo-ung
ผม(ฉัน)เป็นห่วง

worse: it's worse yâir gwàh
แย่กว่า

worst yâir têe sòot
แย่ที่สุด

worth: is it worth a visit? nâh têe-o mái?
น่าเที่ยวไหม

would: would you give this to ...? chôo-ay ao nêe bpai hâi ... dâi mái?
ช่วยเอานี่ไปให้ ... ได้ไหม

wrap: could you wrap it up? chôo-ay hòr hâi nòy, dâi mái?
ช่วยห่อให้หน่อยได้ไหม

wrapping paper gra-dàht hòr kŏrng kwŭn
กระดาษห่อของขวัญ

wrist kôr meu
ข้อมือ

write kěe-un
เขียน

could you write it down? chôo-ay kěe-un long hâi nòy, dâi mái?
ช่วยเขียนลงให้หน่อยได้ไหม

how do you write it? kěe-un yung-ngai?
เขียนอย่างไร

writing paper gra-dàht kěe-un

jòt-măi
กระดาษเขียนจดหมาย

wrong: it's the wrong key gOOn-
jair pìt
กุญแจผิด

this is the wrong train rót fai
pìt ka-boo-un
รถไฟผิดขบวน

the bill's wrong kít bin pìt
คิดบิลผิด

sorry, wrong number kŏr-tôht
dtòr ber pìt
ขอโทษ ต่อเบอร์ผิด

sorry, wrong room kŏr-tôht,
pìt hôrng
ขอโทษ ผิดห้อง

there's something wrong with ...
... mee a-rai pìt
... มีอะไรผิด

what's wrong? bpen a-rai?
เป็นอะไร

X

X-ray 'X-ray'
เอ็กซ์เรย์

Y

yacht reu-a yórt
เรือยอชท์
yard*
year bpee
ปี

yellow sĕe lĕu-ung
สีเหลือง

yes* krúp (kâ); châi
ครับ(ค่ะ); ใช่

yesterday mêu-a wahn née
เมื่อวานนี้

yesterday morning cháo wahn
née
เช้าวานนี้

the day before yesterday wun
seun née
วันซืนนี้

yet yung
ยัง

•••••• DIALOGUE ••••••

is it here yet? mah láir-o rĕu
yung?

no, not yet yung

you'll have to wait a little longer yet
kOOn dtôrng koy èek sùk nòy

yoghurt yoh-gut
โยกัด

you* kOOn
คุณ

this is for you nêe sŭm-rùp
kOOn
นี่สำหรับคุณ

with you gùp kOOn
กับคุณ

young (man) nòOm
หนุ่ม

(woman) săo
สาว

young (child) dèk lék
เด็กเล็ก

your* kǒrng kOOn
ของคุณ

your camera glôrng tài rôop
kǒrng kOOn
กล้องถ่ายรูปของคุณ

yours kǒrng kOOn
ของคุณ

Z

zero sǒon
ศูนย์

zip sìp
ซิป

could you put a new zip on?
chôo-ay sài sìp mài dâi mái?
ช่วยใส่ซิปใหม่ได้ไหม

zip code ra-hùt bprai-sa-nee
รหัสไปรษณีย์

zoo sǒo-un sùt
สวนสัตว์

Thai - English

COLLOQUIALISMS

You might well hear the following expressions but you shouldn't be tempted to use any of the stronger ones – local people will not be amused or impressed by your efforts.

âi hàh! shit!
bpai (hâi pón)! go away!
bpai năi! hi!
chìp-hăi! damn!
dtai hàh! oh hell!
dtai jing! oh no!
mâi chêu-a! come on!, I don't believe you!
mâi mee tahng! no chance!, no way!
măir! goodness!
òrk bpai hâi pón! get out!
tôh! good heavens!
yÒÒt pôot ná! shut up!
yôrt! great!

Entries are listed alphabetically according to the first complete word, for example, entries beginning with **bâhn** precede those beginning with **bahng**.

A

ah uncle (younger brother of father); aunt (younger sister of father)

ah-fri-gah Africa; African

ah-gahn klêun hĕe-un nausea

ah-gahn ùk-sàyp infection

ah-gàht air; weather

ah-hăhn meal; food; cuisine; cooking

ah-hăhn bpen pìt food poisoning

ah-hăhn cháo breakfast

ah-hăhn glahng wun lunch

ah-hăhn kao savoury

ah-hăhn mâi yôy indigestion

ah-hăhn pí-sàyt speciality

ah-hăhn yen evening meal; supper; dinner

ah-jahn teacher

ah-kahn building

àhn read

àhng sink, basin

àhng àhp náhm bath

àhng láhng nâh washbasin

àhp dàirt sunbathe

ah-tít week

ah-tít dtòk sunset

ah-tít kêun sunrise

ah-yÓO age

k00n ah-yÓO tâo-rài? how old are you?

ai cough; shy

âi hàh! shit!

ai-lairn Ireland

ai-lairn nĕu-a Northern Ireland

air hóht-tet air stewardess

ai-rít Irish

airm amp

airt-pai-rin aspirin

a-lài spare part(s)

a-may-ri-gah America; American (person)

a-may-ri-gun American (adj)

a-nah-kót future

a-nÓO-săh-wa-ree monument; statue

ao like; want

ào bay

ao ... bpai take; remove

ao jing ao jung serious

ao krúp (kâ) yes please

ao lá! right!, OK!

ao ... mah fetch; bring

ao ... mái? do you want ...?

ào tai Gulf of Siam

a-páht-mén flat, apartment

a-rai something

a-rai? what?

a-rai èek something else

a-rai èek? what else?

a-rai gôr dâi anything

a-rai ná? pardon (me)?, sorry?; excuse me?

a-ròy nice, delicious

àyk-ga-săhn document; leaflet

ay-o waist

ay-see-a Asia

ay-see-a ah-ka-nay South East Asia

B

bâh mad, crazy

bâhn house; home
  têe bâhn at home

bâhn tùt bpai nextdoor

bahng thin; some

bâhng a few; some

bahng krúng bahng krao
  occasionally

bahng tee sometimes; maybe;
  perhaps

bàht baht (unit of currency)

bàht jèp injured

bàht plǎir wound

bàht wít-têe pavement,
  sidewalk

bài afternoon
  bài ... mohng ... p.m. (in the
  afternoon)
  bài née this afternoon
  bài prôông née tomorrow
  afternoon
  bài wahn née yesterday
  afternoon

bai bai ná cheerio, bye

bai báirng banknote, (US) bill

bai bplew leaflet

bai bpra-gàht kôht-sa-nah
  poster

bai kùp kèe driving licence

bai kùp kèe sǎh-gon
  international driving licence

bai mái leaf

bai mêet gohn razor blade(s)

bai reu-a sail

bai rúp bpra-gun guarantee

bai rúp-rorng guarantee;
  certificate

bai sèt rúp ngern receipt

bai sùng yah prescription

bai ùn-nOO-yâht licence,
  permit

bair-dta-rêe battery

bàirk carry

bairn flat (adj)

bàirng share; divide

bàirp sort, kind, type; pattern

bàirp cha-bùp typical

bàirp fa-rùng European-style

bàirp form form

bàirp ree-un pah-sǎh language
  course

bàirp yàhng pattern

bao light (not heavy)

ber toh-ra-sùp phone number

bèu-a bored

bin bill, (US) check; fly (verb)

bòhk rót hitchhike, hitch

boh-rahn ancient

boh-rahn wút-thOO antique

bon on; on top of
  bon péun din on the ground

bòn complain

bOOp-fay buffet

bOO-rèe cigarette(s)

bOO-rèe gôn grorng tipped
  cigarettes

bOO-rôOt gents' toilet, men's
  room

bòo-uk plus

boo-um swollen

bòrk say; tell

bòrk wâh say

bor-ri-gahn service

bor-ri-gahn ngern dòo-un
  cashpoint, ATM

bor-ri-gahn num têe-o

excursion

bor-ri-gahn rót châo car rental

bor-ri-gahn rúp chái nai hôrng
   púk room service

bor-ri-gahn sòrp tăhm ber toh-
   ra-sùp directory enquiries

bor-ri-sòot innocent

bor-ri-sùt company, firm

bor-ri-wayn bâhn backyard

bor-ri-wayn chahn meu-ung
   suburb

bòt ree-un lesson

bòy bòy often

bpà-dti-tin calendar

bpâh aunt (elder sister of mother/
   father)

bpàh jungle; forest

bpàh cháh cemetery

bpàh dong dìp forest, jungle

bpàh mái sùk teak forest

bpah-gee-sa-tăhn Pakistan

bpàhk mouth

bpàhk-gah pen

bpàhk-gah lôok lêun ballpoint
   pen

bpai to; go; go away

   bpai (hâi pón)! go away!

   bpai tèr let's go

bpâi label

bpai glùp wun dee-o day trip

bpai gùp pŏm (chún) come
   with me

bpai năi! hi!

bpâi rót may bus stop

bpâi séu kŏrng go shopping

bpâi ta-bee-un rót licence
   plates

bpâirng powder; face powder;
   talcum powder

bpàirt eight

bpa-rin-yah degree

bpây lŭng rucksack

bpee year

   bpee têe láir-o last year; a
   year ago

bpee mài New Year

bpèek wing

bpèe-uk wet

bpen be; is; in; can; be
   capable of

   bpen … it is …; it was …

   bpen a-rai? what's up?,
   what's wrong?

bpen bâi dumb (can't speak)

bpen bpai dâi possible

bpen bpai mâi dâi impossible

bpen bpra-yòht beneficial

bpen gun ayng informal

bpen hòo-ung worry

bpen it-sa-rá independent

bpen ka-nòp-tum nee-um
   traditional

bpen lom faint (verb); stroke;
   attack

bpen mun greasy

bpen nêe bŏOn-kOOn grateful

bpen nern hilly

bpen pèun heat rash

bpen pêu-un friendly

bpen pìt poisonous; polluted

bpen sai sandy

bpen sòht single, unmarried

bpen tahng gahn formal

bpen têe nâh por jai
   satisfactory

bpen têe nee-yom popular

bpen yung-ngai bâhng? how
   are you?

bper-sen per cent

bpèrt open (adj); on

bpèt duck

bpeun gun

bpeun pók pistol

bpeun yao rifle

bpìt close, shut; closed

bplah fish

bplah cha-lǎhm shark

bplah-sa-dter Elastoplast®,
    Bandaid®

bplah-sa-dtìk plastic

bplair interpret; translate

bplàirk strange, odd, funny,
    weird

bplàirk bpra-làht strange

bplay cot

bplèe-un change
    bplèe-un rót fai change
    trains

bpleu-ay naked

bplòrk condom

bplòrk mǒrn pillow case

bplòrt-pai safe

bplúk plug; adaptor

bplúk fai power point

bplúk krêu-ung gohn nòo-ut
    shaving point

bpoh-sa-dter poster

bpóht-gáht postcard

bpoo crab

bpòo grandfather (paternal)

bpôom dtìt krêu-ung ignition

bpôom sa-dtàht starter (of car)

bpòo-ut it aches

bpòo-ut fun toothache

bpòo-ut hǒo-a headache;
    hangover

bpòo-ut lǔng backache

bpòo-ut tórng stomachache

bpòrt lungs; nervous

bpra-chah-chon public;
    population

bpra-ch00m meeting

bpra-chót sarcastic

bpra-dtoo door; gate; goal

bpra-gun insurance

bprah-sàht castle

bprairng brush

bprairng pǒm hairbrush

bprairng sěe fun toothbrush

bprairng tah kreem gohn nòo-ut
    shaving brush

bprairng tǒo lép nailbrush

bprai-sa-nee post office; mail

bprai-sa-nee dòo-un express
    mail

bprai-sa-nee glahng central
    post office

bpra-jum deu-un period
    (menstruation)

bpra-làht jai suprised

bpra-mahn roughly, about,
    approximately

bpra-pay-nee custom

bpra-tahn director, president
    (of company)

bpra-tah-nah-tí-bor-dee
    president (of country)

bpra-tâyt country

bpra-tâyt bayl-yee-um Belgium

bpra-tâyt fa-rùng-sàyt France

bpra-tâyt fi-líp-bpin Philippines

bpra-tâyt gao-lěe Korea

bpra-tâyt gum-poo-chah
    Cambodia

bpra-tâyt hor-lairn Holland

bpra-tâyt ì-dtah-lee Italy

bpra-tâyt in-dee-a India

bpra-tâyt in-don-nee-see-a Indonesia

bpra-tâyt jeen China

bpra-tâyt kairn-nah-dah Canada

bpra-tâyt lao Laos

bpra-tâyt mah-lay-see-a Malaysia

bpra-tâyt new see-láirn New Zealand

bpra-tâyt pa-mâh Burma

bpra-tâyt sa-bpayn Spain

bpra-tâyt sa-górt-lairn Scotland

bpra-tâyt tai Thailand (formal)

bpra-tâyt ung-grìt England; Britain

bpra-tâyt wêe-ut-nahm Vietnam

bpra-tâyt yêe-bpÒÒn Japan

bpra-tâyt yer-ra-mun Germany

bpra-wùt-sàht history

bprêe-o sour; sharp (taste)

bprêe-up têe-up compare

bpròht favourite

bpròrt thermometer

bpúm núm mun petrol station, gas station

bpun-hǎh problem; trouble

bpùt-jOO-bun-née nowadays

brayk meu handbrake

bum-nahn pension

bun-dai ladder; stairs

bun-dai lêu-un escalator

bun-dai sǔm-rùp něe fai fire escape

bung-em quite by chance

bun-yai describe

bùt bpra-jum dtoo-a identity card

bùt chern invitation

bùt kray-dìt credit card

bùt têe-nùng boarding pass

C

cháh late; slow; slowly

cháh cháh slowly

chahm dish, bowl

chahn chah-lah platform, (US) track

chahn meu-ung outskirts

cháhng elephant

châhng bpra-bpah plumber

châhng dtùt pǒm hairdresser; barber

châhng dtùt sêu-a pâh tailor

châhng fai fáh electrician

châhng ngern silversmith

châhng tài rôop photographer

châhng torng goldsmith

chai man; male

chái use

chái dâi valid

chai dairn border

chai hàht beach

châi láir-o that's it, that's right

châi láir-o! exactly!

chái mái? isn't it?

chái ngern spend

chái ... rôo-um gun share

chai ta-lay seaside; coast

châir kǎirng deep-freeze; frozen

cha-làht clever, intelligent

cha-ná win

châo rent, hire

cháo morning

cháo née this morning

cháo prôong née tomorrow morning

cháo wahn née yesterday morning

chao bâhn villager

chao dtàhng bpra-tâyt foreigner

chao kǎo hill tribe

chao nah rice farmer

chao yÓO-rôhp European

chèet yah injection

chee-wít life

chék cheque, (US) check

chék dern tahng travellers' cheque

chék doo check (verb)

chên for example

chern choo-un invite

chern gòrn after you

chern kâo mah! come in!

chern krúp (kâ) ... please ...

cherng kǎo hillside

chêu first name

kOOn chêu a-rai? what's your name?

chêu lên nickname

chêu-a believe

chéu-a châht race (ethnic)

chéun humid; damp

chêu-uk rope; string

chêu-uk rorng táo shoelaces

chim taste

chín piece

chín yài a big bit

chip-hǎi! damn!

chôhk luck

chôhk dee fortunately; good luck!;

chôhk rái unfortunately; hard luck!

chon glÒOm nói ethnic minority

chon-na-bòt countryside

choo chêep lifebelt

chôo-a krao temporary

chôo-a mohng hour

chôo-a rá-yá period (of time)

chôo-ay help

chôo-ay ...? please ...?, could you please ...?

chôo-ay dôo-ay! help!

chÒOk chěrn emergency

chÒOk-la-hÒOk hectic

chÓOt suit

chÓOt ah-hǎhn course (of meal)

chÓOt àhp náhm swimming costume

chÓOt bpa-thǒm pa-yah-bahn first-aid kit

chÓOt fun tee-um false teeth

chÓOt norn nightdress

chórk shock-absorber

chórn spoon

chórn sôrm cutlery

chôrng lane (on motorway)

chôrng kâo gate

chôrng kǎo mountain pass

chôrp like

chôrp ... mâhk gwàh prefer

chun steep

chún I; me; myself (said by a woman); floor, storey

chún nèung first class; ground floor, (US) first floor

chún sǎhm third class; second floor, (US) third floor

chún sǒrng second class; first floor, (US) second floor

D

dâhm handle
dâi get, obtain; may; might;
  be able
dâi glìn smell
... dâi mái? can I/you ... ?
dâi yin hear
dàirt òrk sunny; sunshine
dao star
dee good; fine; nice
dee! good!
dee gwàh better
dee jai happy; pleased
dee kêun mâhk much better
dee láir-o! good!; that'll do
  nicely!
dee mâhk! well done!;
  magnificent!
dee têe sôot (the) best
dee-chún I; me (said by a woman)
dee-o just, only
dĕe-o soon
dĕe-o, dĕe-o just a minute
dĕe-o gòrn! just a second!
dĕe-o née now; at present
dèk child; children
dèk chai boy
dèk òrn baby; young child
dèk wai rôon teenager
dèk yĭng girl
dern walk
dern bpai on foot
dern tahng travel
dern tahng bpai tóo-rá gìt
  business trip
dèuk late
dèum drink (verb)
deung pull

deu-un in; month
din earth; land
din-sŏr pencil
dìp raw
dòht dèe-o secluded
don-dtree music
don-dtree péun meu-ung folk
  music
don-dtree pórp pop music
don-dtree tai derm Thai
  classical music
doo look (at); watch
doo lair take care of
doo mĕu-un look, seem; look
  like
dôo-ay too, also
dôo-ay gun together
dôo-ay kwahm bprah-ta-nah dee
  with best wishes
dòo-un urgent
dòrk gOO-làhp rose
dòrk-mái flower
doy-ee by
  doy-ee rót yon by car
doy-ee cha-pòr especially
doy-ee jay-dta-nah deliberately
doy-ee mâi without
dta-bai (fŏn) lép nailfile
dta-gèe-up chopsticks
dta-gla greedy
dta-gohn shout
dta-grâh basket
dta-grâh ka-yà wastepaper
  basket
dta-grai scissors
dtah eye; grandfather
  (maternal)
dtah bòrt blind
dtahm follow

dtahm tum-ma-dah as usual

dtàhng different

dtàhng bpra-tâyt abroad;
foreign

dtàhng dtàhng various

dtàhng hàhk separate

dtàhng jung-wùt up-country
(outside Bangkok)

dtah-rahng têe-o bin scheduled
flight

dtah-rahng way-lah timetable,
(US) schedule

dtai die; dead; kidneys (in
body)

dtâi south; under, below

dtai hàh! oh hell!

dtai jing! oh no!

dtàir but

dtàir la kon each of them
(people)

dtàir la krúng each time

dtàir la un each of them
(things)

dtàirk break

dtàirk láir-o broken

dtàirk ngâi fragile

dtâirm score

dtàirng ngahn láir-o married

dta-làht market

dta-làht náhm floating
market

dta-làht yen night market

dta-lòk funny, amusing; joke

dta-lòrt throughout; whole

dtao cooker

dtào turtle; tortoise

dtao òp oven

dtao rêet iron

dta-wun dtòk west

dta-wun dtòk chěe-ung dtâi
southwest

dta-wun dtòk chěe-ung něu-a
northwest

dta-wun òrk east

dta-wun òrk chěe-ung dtâi
southeast

dta-wun òrk chěe-ung něu-a
northeast

dtee hit

dtêe-a short

dteen bottom (of hill)

dtee-ung bed

dtee-ung dèe-o single bed

dtee-ung kôo twin beds

dtem, dtem láir-o full

dten tent

dtên rum dance

dterm fill

dtèuk block of flats,
apartment block

dtêun shallow

dtèun awake; wake up; get up

dtèun-dtên nervous

dtìt stuck

dtìt dtòr contact

dtìt gùp next to

dtó table

dtó jài ngern cash desk,
cashier

dtòk miss (bus etc)

dtòk jai shock

dtôn bpah palm tree

dtôn mái plant; tree

dtôo cupboard, closet;
compartment; kiosk

dtôo bprai-sa-nee letterbox,
mailbox

dtôo châir kăirng freezer

dtôo gèp gra-bpăo locker

dtôo jòt-măi letterbox, mailbox

dtôo norn sleeper, sleeping car

dtôo núng-sĕu pim newsstand

dtôo toh-ra-sùp phone box, phone booth

dtôo yen fridge; refrigerator

dtŏo-a ticket

dtŏo-a bpai single ticket, one-way ticket

dtŏo-a bpai glùp return ticket, round trip ticket

dtoo-a yàhng example

dtÔÔk-ga-dtah doll

dt00-lah-kom October

dtÔÔm hŏo earring(s)

dtòr connection

dtòr rah-kah bargain (verb)

dtòr wâh complain

dtorn bài afternoon

dtorn cháo morning

dtorn glahng keun evening; night

dtorn yen late afternoon

dtôrng must; have to

dtôrng-gahn need

dtòy sting (verb)

dtrah brand

dtreung krêe-ut serious

dtrong direct

dtrong dtrong straight

dtrong kâhm opposite

dtrong nâh straight ahead

dtrong née right here, just here

dtrong way-lah on time

dtrÔÔt jeen Chinese New Year

dtròo-ut examine

dtròo-ut chûng núm-nùk check-in

dtròrk lane (off a soi)

dtúk-dtúk tuk-tuk motorized three-wheeled taxi

dtùm low

dtùm gwàh under, less than

dtum-ròo-ut police; policeman

dtun blocked

dtûng-dtàir since (time)

dtùp liver

dtùp ùk-sàyp hepatitis

dtùt cut

dtùt fai power cut

dtùt pŏm haircut

dum dark (adj)

dum náhm dive

dung loud

E

èek more; again

èek bpra-dĕe-o in a minute

èek kon nèung the other one (person)

èek mâhk a lot more

èek ... nèung another ... ; the other ...

èek un nèung the other one (thing)

èun other; others; another

F

fáh sky

făh wall; lid

fáh lâirp lightning

fáh rórng thunder

fai fire; light
fâi cotton
fai chǎi torch, flashlight
fai cháirk cigarette lighter
fai fáh electric; electricity
fai kâhng sidelights
fai krêu-ung yon ignition
fai lée-o indicator
fai lǔng rót rear lights
fai mâi fire (blaze)
   fai mâi! fire!, it's on fire!
fai mòrk fog lights
fai nâh rót headlights
fairn boyfriend; girlfriend;
   partner
fàirt twins
fa-rùng European; Caucasian;
   Westerner; foreigner
fa-rùng-sàyt France; French
feem film (for camera); negative
feem sěe colour film
fláirt flat, apartment; flash
fók-chúm bruise
fǒn rain
   fǒn dtòk it's raining
fǒong kon crowd
fóot-born football
fùk boo-a shower
fun tooth
fung listen (to)
   fung sì! listen!
fùng shore; bank
... fùng dtrong kâhm across
   the ...

G

gah núm chah teapot
gahn bpa-tǒm pa-yah-bahn
   first aid
gahn bplair translation
gahn bpra-gun pai insurance
gahn chók dtòy fight
gahn dern tahng journey;
   travel
gahn dtai death
gahn dtôrn rúp kùp sôo
   hospitality
gahn dum náhm léuk skin-
   diving
gahn fórn rum péun meu-ung
   folk dancing
gahn jùp bplah fishing
gǎhn kàirng kǔn match; race
gahn lót rah-kah reduction
gahn meu-ung politics
gahn pàh dtùt operation
gahn rôo-um bpra-way-nee sex
gahn sa-dairng don-dtree
   concert
gahn sòrp exam
gahn sǔng ngót cancellation
gahn ta-hǎhn military
gahn wâi nahm swimming
gahng-gayng trousers, (US)
   pants
gahng-gayng kǎh sûn shorts
gahng-gayng nai underpants,
   underwear
gahng-gayng nai sa-dtree
   pants, panties
gahng-gayng wâi náhm
   swimming trunks
gahng-gayng yeen jeans

gàir strong; dark; old

gâir hòr unpack

gâirm cheek (on face)

gâir-o glass

gáirt gas

gao glue; scratch

gào old

gâo nine

gâo êe chair

gâo êe pâh bai deckchair

gâo êe rúp kàirk sofa

gâo êe sŏong highchair

ga-rúk-ga-dah-kom July

ga-see-un retired

gày găi smart

gáyt háot guesthouse

gèe? how many?

　gèe mohng láir-o? what time is it?

gee-a tŏy lŭng reverse gear

gee-lah sport

gee-lah náhm water sports

gèng well

... gern bpai too ...

gèrt kêun happen

　gèrt a-rai kêun? what's happening?

gèu-up nearly, almost

gin dâi edible

gin (kâo) eat

gin yòo prórm full board

glâh hăhn brave

glahng medium; middle

glahng jâirng outdoors

glahng keun night; overnight

glahng meu-ung central

glai far (away)

　glai gwàh farther (than)

glâi near; near here

... têe glâi têe sòot the nearest ...

glèe-ut hate

gler pal, mate

glom round

gloo-a afraid; fear

glôom group

glôom jai depressed

glôom kon party, group

glòrng carton

glòrng gee-a gearbox

glôrng tài nŭng movie camera

glôrng tài pâhp-pa-yon camcorder

glôrng tài rôop camera

glôrng yah sên, glôrng yah sòop pipe (for smoking)

glùp get back

glùp bâhn go home

glùp bpai go back

glùp mah come back

　glùp mah nêe! come back!

goh-hòk lie (tell untruth)

gohn shave

goh-roh-goh-sŏh junk, rubbish

gôn bottom (of body)

gôn grorng filter-tipped

g0om-pah-pun February

g0on-jair key; lock

gôr then

gòr island

gòr ai-lairn Ireland

gôr mĕu-un gun too, also

gôr yàhng nún làir so-so

górk náhm tap, faucet

gòrn ago; before

　săhm wun gòrn three days ago

gorng dtum-ròo-ut dùp plerng

fire brigade
górp golf
gòt-mǎi law
gra-bpǎo bag; briefcase; luggage, baggage; pocket
gra-bpǎo dern tahng suitcase; baggage
gra-bpǎo kwâi lǔng backpack
gra-bpǎo sa-dtahng purse; wallet, billfold
gra-bpǎo těu handbag, (US) purse; hand luggage, hand baggage
gra-bpǒrng can, tin
gra-bprohng skirt
gra-bprohng rót bonnet (of car), (US) hood
gra-bprohng tái (rót) boot (of car), (US) trunk
gra-dàht paper
gra-dàht chét meu, gra-dàht chét nâh paper handkerchiefs, Kleenex®
gra-dàht chum-rá toilet paper
gra-dàht hòr kǒrng kwǔn wrapping paper
gra-dàht kěe-un jòt-mǎi writing paper
gra-dìng bell
gra-dòok bone
gra-dòok hùk fracture
gra-dOOm button
gra-dtìk náhm vacuum flask
gra-jòk nâh rót yon windscreen
gra-jòk ngao mirror
gra-ter-ee gay, homosexual
grìng bell
gròht angry
grom dtròo-ut kon kâo meu-ung

Immigration Department
grOOng-tâyp Bangkok
grum gramme
gum-lai meu bracelet
... gum-lung pôot speaking
gum-pairng wall
gun chon bumper, (US) fender
gun-chah marijuana
gun-grai scissors
gun-yah-yon September
gùp with
gùp kâo dish; meal
gùt insect bite
gwàh than; more; over, more than
gwâhng wide

H

hâh five
hǎh look for
hǎh yâhk rare
hâhm prohibited, forbidden; prohibit
hâhm sòop bOO-rèe non-smoking
hâhng department store
hàhng glai remote
hâhng kǎi yah pharmacy
hàht beach
hâi give; for
hǎi lose
hǎi bpai disappear
hâi châo for hire, to rent
hǎir fishing net
hâirng dry
hàirng châht national
hǎi-ya-ná disaster
hàyt cause

hèep box
hĕn see
hĕn dôo-ay agree
hĕw hungry
hĕw carry
hĕw kâo hungry
hĕw náhm thirsty
hi-má snow
hĭn stone, rock
hîng shelf
hòk six
hŏo ear
hŏo nòo-uk deaf
hŏo-a head; corner
hŏo-a jai heart
hŏo-a jai wai heart attack
hŏo-a kào knee
hŏo-a láhn bald
hŏo-a m00m corner
hŏo-a nom lòrk dummy
hŏo-a rór laugh
hŏo-a tee-un spark plug
h00p kăo valley
hòr package, parcel
hŏr sa-m00t library
hôrng room
hôrng ah-hăhn dining room
hôrng air air-conditioned
   room
hôrng bprùp ah-gàht air-
   conditioned room
hôrng dèe-o single room
hôrng kôo twin-bedded room
hôrng kórk-tayn cocktail bar
hôrng kroo-a kitchen
hôrng náhm bathroom; toilet,
   rest room
hôrng náhm pôo-chai gents'
   toilet, men's room

hôrng náhm pôo-yǐng ladies'
   toilet, ladies' room
hôrng náhm sòo-un dtoo-a
   private bathroom
hôrng norn bedroom
hôrng pôo doy-ee săhn kăh òrk
   departure lounge
hôrng púk waiting room
hôrng rúp kàirk living room
hôrng rúp-bpra-tahn ah-hăhn
   dining room
hôrng sa-m00t library
hôrng tŏhng lounge
hŏy shell
hùk break; deduct
hŭn bpai tahng ... facing the ...
hun-loh hello

I

ì-sa-rá free

J

jàhk from
   jàhk .... bpai ... from ... to ...
jàhk bpai leave, go away
jàhk meu-ung 'Wales' Welsh
jahn dish; plate
jahn rorng tôo-ay saucer
jahn sĕe-ung record
jài pay
jai dee kind, generous
jai glahng meu-ung city centre
jair-gun vase
jàirm săi pleasant
ja-mòok nose
jâo-bào bridegroom
jâo-fáh chai prince

jâo-fáh yǐng princess
jâo-kǒrng owner
jâo kǒrng bâhn landlord
jâo nai boss
jâo-sǎo bride
ja-rah-jorn traffic
jay-dee pagoda
jeen China; Chinese
jèp sore; hurt
jèp bpòo-ut painful
jer find
jèt seven
jing true; real
jing jai sincere
jing jing lěr? honestly?
jǐng-jòk lizard
jìt-dta-gum fǎh pa-nǔng murals
jon until; poor
jòop kiss
jǒot-mǎi bplai tahng destination
jòp finish, end
jor-jair busy
jorng reservation; reserve
jor-ra-kây crocodile
jòrt park (verb)
jòt-mǎi letter; mail
jòt-mǎi ah-gàht aerogramme
jòt-mǎi long ta-bee-un registered letter
jùk-gra-yahn bicycle
jùk-sǒo pâirt optician
jum dâi remember; recognize
jum-bpen necessary
jung ler-ee so
jung-wùt changwat, province
jùp catch; arrest
jùp bplah fishing

jùt arrange; bright; strong
jùt gahn organize

K

kǎh leg
kâh kill; value
kǎh kâo arrival
kâh bor-ri-gahn service charge
kâh bor-ri-gahn pi-sàyt supplement (extra charge)
kâh châo rent
kâh doy-ee sǎhn fare
kâh mút-jum deposit
kǎh òrk departure
kâh pàhn tahng toll
kǎh-gun-grai jaw
kâhm ta-lay crossing
kahng chin
kâhng beside; side
kâhng bon above, over; upstairs
kâhng lâhng downstairs
kâhng lǔng back; behind; rear
kâhng nâh in front (of); at the front
kâhng nai indoors; inside
kâhng nôrk outside
kahng toom mumps
kài egg
kâi temperature, fever; feverish
kǎi sell
kǎi gоon-jair unlock
kâi jùp sùn malaria
kài móok pearl
kâi wùt flu
kàirk Indian; guest
kǎirn arm

kǎirn sêu-a sleeve

kair-nah-dah Canada; Canadian

kǎirng solid; hard

kǎirng rairng strong

kâirp narrow

ka-mǎyn Cambodian

ka-moy-ee steal; thief; burglar

ka-nà têe while

ka-nàht size; measurements

ka-nàht glahng medium-sized

ka-nòp-tum-nee-um tradition

káo he; him; she; her; they; them

kâo rice

kǎo hill; mountain

kào message; news

kâo bpai go in

kâo jai understand

   kâo jai láir-o I understand

kào-sǎhn information

ka-yà rubbish, litter, trash

kàyt district

kêe fôOn dirt

kêe gèe-ut lazy

kèet sǒong sòOt maximum

kĕe-un write

kem salty

kěm needle

kěm glùt sêu-a brooch

kěm kùt belt

kěm kùt ni-ra-pai seatbelt

kěm môOt pin

kěm-tít compass

ker-ee ever

kěrn embarrassed; embarrassing

keun night; give back

   keun la … … per night

kêun up

kêun bpai go up

keun née tonight; this evening

keun ngern refund

kêun rót may catch a bus

kew queue

kít think

klohn mud

klorng canal

kohm fai (fáh) lamp

koh-ték tampon

kǒhn classical masked drama

kòht hǐn rocky

kom sharp

kǒm bitter

kòm-kěun rape

kon person; people

kǒn hair (on the body)

kon bâh idiot

kon bpah-gee-sa-tǎhn a Pakistani; Pakistanis

kon bplàirk nâh stranger

kon châo tenant

kon cha-rah senior citizen

kon dee-o just, only; alone, by oneself

kon dern táo pedestrian

kon fâo bpra-dtoo doorman; porter

kon fâo dèk baby-sitter

kon fa-rùng-sàyt a French person; the French

kon hǒo-a sǒong snob

kon jai yen calm

kon jeen a Chinese person; the Chinese

kon jùp bplah fisherman

kon ka-mǎyn a Cambodian; the Cambodians

kon kùp (rót) driver

kon kùp táirk-sêe taxi-driver

kon lao a Lao; the Laos

kon lée-ung doo dèk child minder

kon mâi gin néu-a vegetarian

kon nâirn crowded

kon new see-láirn a New Zealander; New Zealanders

kon ngôh fool

kon nún chap

kon pa-mâh a Burmese person; the Burmese

kon sa-górt a Scot; the Scots

kon sérp waiter; waitress

kon sèrp yǐng waitress

kon sôrm rorng táo shoe repairer

kǒn sùt wool

kon tai a Thai person; the Thais

kon tèep jùk-ra-yahn cyclist

kon tum ka-nǒm-bpung baker

kon ung-grìt an English person; the English; a Briton; the British

kon yêe-bpÔ0n a Japanese person; the Japanese

kon yer-ra-mun a German; the Germans

kong (ja) probably

kôo pair

kôo meu num têe-o guidebook

kôo meu sǒn-ta-nah phrasebook

kôo mûn fiancé; fiancée

koo-ee chat

kÓ0k prison

k00n you

k00n krúp (kâ) excuse me

k00n-na-pâhp quality

koo-un ja should

kòo-ut bottle

kor neck; collar

kǒr please

  pǒm (chún) kǒr I would like

kor bpòk sêu-a collar

kôr glào hǎh complaint

kǒr hâi dern tahng doy-ee bplòrt-pai! have a safe journey!

kor hǒy throat

kôr meu wrist

kǒr ... nòy can I have ...?

kǒr rórng request

kǒr sa-dairng kwahm yin dee! congratulations!

kôr sòrk elbow

kôr táo ankle

kôr tét jing fact

kórn hammer

kórng gong

kǒrng thing; of

kǒrng bplorm fake

kǒrng bpròht favourite

kǒrng fÔ0m feu-ay luxury

kǒrng káo his; her; hers; their; theirs

kǒrng k00n your; yours

kǒrng kwǔn present, gift

kǒrng lên toy

kǒrng pǒm (chún) my; mine

  ... kǒrng pǒm (chún) ayng my own ...

kǒrng rao our; ours

kǒrng têe ra-léuk souvenir

kôrn-kàhng ja ... rather ...

kòrp-k00n thank; thanks,

thank you

kòrp-kOOn mâhk thank you very much

kŏr-tôht excuse me; sorry; I beg your pardon?

krai somebody

krai? who?

krai gôr dâi anybody

krao beard

kreem bum-rOOng pĕw moisturizer

kreem gohn nòo-ut shaving foam

kreem nôo-ut pŏm conditioner

kreem rorng péun foundation cream

kreem sa-măhn pĕw cold cream

kreem tah àhp dàirt suntan lotion

kreem tah nŭng dtah eye shadow

krêung half

krêung chôo-a mohng half an hour

krêung lŏh half a dozen

krêu-ung air air-conditioning

krêu-ung bàirp uniform

krêu-ung bin plane, airplane

krêu-ung bpào pŏm hairdryer

krêu-ung bplairng fai fáh adaptor (for voltage)

krêu-ung bpra-dùp ornament

krêu-ung bprùp ah-gàht air-conditioning

krêu-ung bpûn din păo pottery, earthenware

krêu-ung bun-téuk sĕe-ung tape recorder

krêu-ung chái sŏy equipment

krêu-ung chôo-ay fung hearing aid

krêu-ung dèum drink

krêu-ung dòot fŌOn vacuum cleaner

krêu-ung dùp plerng fire extinguisher

krêu-ung gohn nòo-ut shaver

krêu-ung kít lâyk calculator

krêu-ung kOOm gum-nèrt contraceptive

krêu-ung lên pàirn sĕe-ung record player

krêu-ung lên tâyp kah-set cassette player

krêu-ung reu-un furniture

krêu-ung súk pâh washing machine

krêu-ung sŭm-ahng make-up

krêu-ung wee-dee-oh videorecorder

krêu-ung wút OOn-na-ha-poom thermometer

krêu-ung yon motor; engine

krít Protestant

krít-dtung Roman Catholic

krít-sa-maht Christmas

kroo teacher

krôrp-kroo-a family

krúng time

krúng nèung once

krúp (kâ) yes

kum word

kûm dark

kum chern invitation

kum dtòrp answer

kum tăhm question

kun itch

kûn bun-dai step
kun gee-a gear lever
kun rêng accelerator
kun yôhk lever
kúp tight
kùp drive
kwǎh right (not left)
kwahm bpra-préut behaviour
kwahm bun-terng
  entertainment
kwahm chéun humidity
kwahm chôo-ay lěu-a help
kwahm dtai death
kwahm dtàirk dtàhng
  difference
kwahm fǔn dream
kwahm jèp bpòo-ay illness
kwahm jèp bpòo-ut pain
kwahm jing truth
kwahm kâo jai pìt
  misunderstanding
kwahm kít idea
kwahm lúp secret
kwahm ngêe-up silence
kwahm pìt fault; mistake
kwahm ray-o speed
kwahm rórn heat
kwahm rúk love
kwahm sǒong height
kwâhng throw
kwai water buffalo
kwûm upside down
kwun smoke

L

lah gòrn bye
láh sa-mǎi old-fashioned
lâhm interpreter

lǎhn chai grandson; nephew
lǎhn sǎo niece;
  granddaughter
láhng wash; develop (film)
lǎi several
lâi shoulder
lai sen signature
láir and
lâirk bplèe-un exchange (verb:
  money)
... láir-o already
láir-o dtàir it depends (on); it's
  up to you
la-korn play
lâo alcohol
lay-kǎh-nóo-gahn secretary
layn glôrng lens (of camera)
lée-o kwǎh turn right
lée-o sái turn left
lèe-um sǒong cheeky
lék small, little, tiny
lèk iron
lék nóy only a few
lên play
lép meu fingernail
ler-ee bpai further; beyond
  ler-ee bpai èek further on
lěu-a gern jing jing shocking
léuk deep
leum forget
lêun slippery
lêu-ut blood
líf lift, elevator
likay popular folk theatre
lín tongue
lít litre
lǒh dozen
loh-hà metal
loh-hà sǔm-rít bronze

lôhk world; earth
lom wind
lom òrn òrn breeze
long get off
long bpai go down
　　long bpai! get down!
long mah! get down!
long ta-bee-un register
lôok child; children (one's own)
lôok born ball
lôok bpùt beads
lôok chai son
lôok gwàht sweets, candies
lôok kĕr-ee son-in-law
lôok ra-bèrt bomb
lôok săo daughter
lôok sa-pâi daughter-in-law
lOOng uncle (older brother of father
　　or mother)
lôo-ung nâh in advance
lóp minus
lòr good-looking
lór wheel
lorng try; try out, test
lòrt fai fáh lightbulb
lum-tahn stream
lŭng after; back (of body)
lŭng jàhk nún then, after
　　that
lŭng-kah roof

M

mah come
măh dog
máh horse
mah gèp ... collect
máh glàirp pony
mah nêe come here

mah tĕung arrive
ma-hăh-wít-ta-yah-lai
　　university
mah-dtra-tăhn standard
mâhk a lot, lots; many; much;
　　very; very much
　　... mâhk plenty of ...
　　mâhk (gern) bpai too much;
　　excessive
màhk fa-rùng chewing gum
mâhk lĕu-a gern extremely
mâhk por sŏm-koo-un quite a
　　lot
màhk róOk chess
mâhn curtain
mai mile
măi silk
mái wood
mài new
mâi no; not
　　mâi ao ... no ...
　　mâi (ao) ... èek no more ...
mâi ao năi poor (quality);
　　disgusting
mâi bòy seldom
mâi bpen rai don't mention it;
　　it doesn't matter; never
　　mind; that's all right
mâi bpen rêu-ung nonsense
mâi chêu-a! come on!, I don't
　　believe you!
mâi dàirt sunburn
mâi dee bad
mái dtee racket
mâi dtôrng sĕe-a pah-sĕe duty-
　　free goods
mâi gin néu-a vegetarian
mái gwàht brush
mâi jing false

mâi jum-gùt ra-ya tahng
  unlimited mileage
mái kèet match
mâi ker-ee never
mâi kôy hardly
mâi lay-o it's not bad
mâi ler-ee not in the least
mâi mâhk not a lot, not much
  mâi mâhk gwàh ... no more
  than ...
  mâi mâhk tâo-rài not so
  much
mâi mao sober
mâi mee ... there isn't/aren't
  ...; no ...
mâi mee a-rai nothing
mâi mee bpra-sìt-ti-pâhp
  inefficient
mâi mee krai nobody, no-one
mâi mee lôo-ut lai plain
mâi mee mah-ra-yâht rude
mâi mee tahng! no chance!, no
  way!
mâi nâh chêu-a amazing
mái nèep (pâh) clothes peg
mái pài bamboo
mâi pèt mild
mâi rêe-up bumpy
mâi ròrk! certainly not!
mâi sài without
mái sùk teak
mâi těung ... less than ...
mâi wâhng engaged, occupied
măi-lâyk number, figure
mâir! well well!
máir dtàir ... even the ...
mâir (kŏrng) mother
mâir mái widow
mâir náhm river

máir wâh although
  máir wâh ... even if ...
mâir-náhm kŏhng Mekhong
  River
mairng ga-pr00n jellyfish
mair-o cat
ma-lairng insect
ma-lairng gùt insect bite
ma-lairng sàhp cockroach
ma-lairng wun fly
mao drunk
ma-reun-née the day after
  tomorrow
mâyk kréum cloudy
may-săh-yon April
máyt metre
mee have
  mee ... there is/are ...
  mee ... mái? have you got
  ...?; is/are there ...?
mee bpra-sìt-ti-pâhp efficient
mee bpra-yòht useful
mee chee-wít chee-wah lively
mee chee-wít yòo alive
mee chêu sĕe-ung famous
mee fûk boo-a with shower
mee hàyt-pŏn sensible
mee kâh valuable
mee kwahm pìt guilty
mee lom òrn òrn breezy
mee-nah-kom March
mee pĕw klúm dàirt suntanned
mee sa-này charming
mee sÒOk-ka-pâhp dee healthy
mee tórng pregnant
mêet knife
mêet gohn razor
mêet púp penknife
měn smell, stink

meu hand
mêu-a gòrn née once,
  formerly
mêu-a keun née last night
mêu-a rài? when?
mêu-a ray-o ray-o née lately,
  recently
mêu-a wahn née yesterday
mĕu-un similar, like
mĕu-un gun same
meu-ung city; town; country
meu-ung boh-rahn Ancient
  City
meu-ung gào old town
meu-ung lŏo-ung capital city
meu-ung tai Thailand (informal)
mí-cha-nún otherwise
mí-tOO-nah-yon June
mók-ga-rah-kom January
mŏo pig
moo-ay (săh-gon) boxing
  (international)
moo-ay tai Thai-style boxing
mòo-bâhn village
mòo-bâhn bon poo-kăo
  mountain village
mòo bâhn bpra-mong fishing
  village
mòo gòr in-dee-a dta-wun dtòk
  West Indies
môo-lêe blinds
mOOng mosquito net
mòo-uk hat; cap
móo-un tâyp kah-set cassette
mŏr doctor
mòr ideal
môr saucepan
mŏr fun dentist
mòr sŏm suitable, appropriate

mòrk mist
mòrk long foggy
mŏrn pillow; cushion
mor-ra-sOOm monsoon
mor-sor scruffy
mòt láir-o empty
mòt sa-dtì unconscious
múk-kOO-tâyt guide, courier
mun it; it is; they; fat (on
  meat); rich
  mun bpen it's
mûn engaged (to be married)
mun fa-rùng tôrt chips, French
  fries; crisps, (US) chips
mùt flea

N

năh thick
nah paddy field
náh uncle (younger brother of
  mother); aunt (younger sister of
  mother)
nâh face; front (part); page;
  season; next
nâh bèu-a boring
nâh dtèun dtên exciting
nâh fŏn rainy season
nâh glèe-ut ugly; horrible;
  disgusting
nâh năo winter
nâh nèu-ay nài tiring
nâh òk chest; bust
nâh rórn summer
nâh rung-gèe-ut unpleasant;
  revolting
nâh sĕe-a dai! what a shame!
nâh sêet pale
nâh sŏn jai interesting

nâh sŏng-sâhn! what a pity!

nâh têung impressive

nâh t00-râyt nasty

nâh-dtàhng window

nah-li-gah clock; watch

nah-li-gah bplÒòk alarm clock

nah-li-gah kôr meu watch

náhm water

nahm bùt business card

náhm dèum drinking water

nahm sa-g00n surname, last name

nahm sa-g00n derm maiden name

nahn a long time

nahng Mrs

nahng pa-yah-bahn nurse

nahng-săo Miss

nah-tee minute

nah-yók director, president

nah-yók rút-ta-mon-dtree prime minister

nai on; in; into; Mr

năi? which?

nai a-nah-kót in future

nai bpra-tâyt rao at home

nai lŏo-ung king

nai ra-wàhng during; among

nai têe sÒÒt eventually, at last

nâir jai certain, sure

nâir norn of course, certainly, definitely

nâirn crowded, busy

năo cold; feel cold

née this; these

nêe ... this is ...

  nêe a-rai? what's this?

nêe kŏrng krai? whose is this?

nêe krúp (kâ) there you are

nêe ngai here you are

nêe-o sticky; sultry

nék-tai tie, necktie

něu-a north

nèu-ay tired

nèung one

nèung nai sèe quarter

néw inch

néw hŏo-a mâir meu thumb

néw meu finger

néw táo toe

ngah cháhng tusk

ngahm sa-ngàh elegant

ngahn job; work; carnival; festival

ngahn lée-ung party

ngahn sa-dairng sĭn-káh trade fair

ngahn sòp funeral

ngâi easy; simple

ngao shadow

ngăo lonely

ngao dàirt sunshade

ngêe-up quiet; silent

ngêe-up ngêe-up nòy! be quiet!

ngern money; silver

ngern bporn sterling

ngern deu-un salary

ngern dorn-lâh dollar

ngern dtàhng bpra-tâyt foreign exchange

ngern rĕe-un coin

ngern sòt cash

ngern típ tip

ngèu-uk gum

ngêu-un kăi bpra-gun insurance policy

ngôh stupid, silly, dumb

ngoo snake

ngoo hào cobra
ngôo-ung norn sleepy
ngót cancel
nìm soft
nít dee-o tâo-nún just a little
ní-tahn story
ní-tá-sa-gahn exhibition
nít-nòy a little bit
nít-ta-ya-săhn magazine
nók bird
nom milk
nŏo mouse; rat
nÒOm young; young man
nÒOm nÒOm săo săo young
  people
nòo-uk hŏo noisy
nôo-ut massage
nòo-ut moustache
nôrk jàhk apart from
norn lie down
norn lùp sleep
norn lùp yòo asleep
nôrng thigh
nŏrng swamp
nórng chai younger brother
nórng săo younger sister
nórng sa-pái younger sister-
  in-law
nòy some
nóy few
nóy gwàh ... less than ...
nóy têe sÒOt minimum
nùk heavy; serious
núk don-dtree musician
núk moo-ay boxer
núk rórng singer
núk sa-dairng chai actor
núk sa-dairng yĭng actress
núk sèuk-săh student

núk tôrng têe-o tourist
núm dtòk waterfall
núm hŏrm toilet water;
  perfume
núm kăirng ice
núm mun oil; petrol, (US) gas
núm mun gáht petrol, (US)
  gas
núm mun krêu-ung oil (motor
  oil)
núm mun rót dee-sen diesel
  (fuel)
núm mun tah àhp dàirt suntan
  oil
núm nùk weight
núm nùk gern excess baggage
núm pÓO fountain
núm tôo-um flood
núm yah àhp náhm bubble
  bath
núm yah láhng chahm washing
  up liquid
nún that
nûn a-rai? what's that?
nûng sit
nŭng leather; film, movie
nŭng glùp suede
nŭng si sit down!
núng-sĕu book
núng-sĕu dern tahng passport
núng-sĕu num têe-o
  guidebook
núng-sĕu pim newspaper
nút appointment

O

oh-gàht chance, opportunity
ong-săh degree
òo sôrm rót garage
oo-bùt-dti-hàyt accident
ôo-ee! ouch!
ôom carry
oo-mohng tunnel
oon-na-ha-poom temperature
òop-bpa-gorn equipment
òot fun filling
òot-săh-ha-gum industry
ôo-un fat
òrk bpai go out
  òrk bpai hâi pón! get out!
òrk sĕe-ung pronounce
òrn weak (drink)
òrn-air weak (person)

P

pâh material, cloth
pah bpai take
pâh bpòo têe norn sheet; bed
  linen
pâh chét bpàhk napkin
pâh chét dtoo-a towel
pâh chét jahn tea towel
pâh chét meu napkin,
  serviette; tissues,
  Kleenex®
pâh chét nâh handkerchief;
  flannel
pâh hòm blanket
pâh kêe réw cloth, rag
pâh ôrm nappy, diaper
pâh pôhk sĕe-sà headscarf
pâh pun kor scarf (for neck)

pâh pun plăir bandage;
  dressing
pâh un-nah-mai sanitary
  towel, sanitary napkin
pâhk region
pâhk bung-kúp compulsory
pâhk dtâi southern region of
  Thailand
pâhk ee-săhn north-eastern
  region of Thailand
pâhk glahng central region of
  Thailand
pàhn through; via
pàhn bpai go through
pâhp kĕe-un painting; picture
pah-săh language
pah-săh tai Thai (language)
pah-săh tìn dialect
pah-săh ung-grìt English
  (language)
pah-sĕe duty; tax
pah-sĕe sa-năhm bin airport
  tax
pah-yóo storm
pah-yóo fŏn thunderstorm
pâi cards
páir goat; allergic to
páir dàirt heat stroke
pàirn slice
pàirn sĕe-ung record
pairng expensive
păirn-têe map
păirn-têe ta-nŏn road map,
  streetmap
pa-mâh Burma; Burmese
pa-nàirk dtôrn rúp reception;
  reception desk
pa-núk ngahn dtôrn rúp
  receptionist

pa-núk ngahn krêu-ung bin
  steward
pa-núk ngahn toh-ra-sùp
  operator
pa-nun gamble
pa-yah-yahm try; persevere
pay-dahn ceiling
pêe older brother/sister
pêe chai older brother
pêe săo older sister
pêe sa-pái older sister-in-law
pêrm increase
pèt hot, spicy
pét diamond
pét ploy jewellery
péun floor
  yòo bon péun on the floor
pèun rash (on skin)
péun din ground
péun rorng táo sole (of shoe)
pêu-un friend
pêu-un bâhn neighbour
pêu-un rôo-um ngahn partner
  (in business)
pêu-un tahng jòt-măi
  penfriend
pěw skin
pěw klúm dàirt suntan
pěw nŭng skin
pí-gahn disabled
pí-pít-ta-pun museum
pí-pít-ta-pun hàirng châht
  National Museum
pi-sàyt special; de luxe
pìt wrong; faulty
pìt gòt-măi illegal
pìt tum-ma-dah unusual
pìt wŭng disappointed
pi-tee dtàirng ngahn wedding

plăir bàht jèp injury
plăir gra-pór ulcer
plăir mâi burn
plăir porng blister
plăir wèr nasty
plăirng eccentric
playng song
playng póp pop song
plùk push
pŏm I; me; myself (said by a
  man); hair
pŏng súk fôrk soap powder
pŏn-la-mái fruit
pôo bplair translator
pôo doy-ee săhn passenger
pôo-chai boy; man
poo-gèt Phuket
pôo-jùt-gahn manager
poo-kăo mountain
poo-mi-bpra-tâyt scenery;
  landscape
pôot speak; talk
pôot èek tee repeat
pôot lên joke
pôo-uk group
pôo-uk née these
pôo-uk nún those
pôo-uk pôo-yĭng women
poo-ung mah-lai sái left-hand
  drive
poo-ung ma-lai kwăh right-
  hand drive
pôo-yài adult
pôo-yài bâhn village headman
pôo-yĭng woman; lady; girl
pôo-yĭng bah hostess (in bar)
pôo-yĭng ung-grìt English girl/
  woman
por enough

pôr father
pôr dtah father-in-law (of a man)
pôr dtah mâir yai parents-in-law (wife's parents)
por jai satisfied
por láir-o no more; that's enough
pôr mái widower
pôr mâir parents
pôr pǒo-a father-in-law (of a woman)
pôr pǒo-a mâir pǒo-a parents-in-law (husband's parents)
por sǒm-koo-un quite, fairly
pǒrm thin, skinny
pòt prickly heat
pót-ja-nah-nóo-grom dictionary
prá monk; priest
prá-ah-tít sun
prá-jâo God
prá-jun moon
prá-pÓot-ta-jâo Buddha
prá-pÓot-ta-rôop Buddha image
prá-rah-chi-nee queen
prá-râht-cha-wung palace
prá-tÓo-dong mendicant monk
pree-o slim
préut-sa-jìk-gah-yon November
préut-sa-pah-kom May
prom carpet; rug
prôong née tomorrow
prór because
prórm ready
púk stay
pùk vegetables
púk krêung interval

púk pòrn rest
púm núm mun petrol station, gas station
pun-ra-yah wife
pút fan (handheld)
pùt stir-fry
pút lom fan (mechanical)

R

ra-bee-ung patio; terrace; balcony
rah-kah cost; price
rah-kah tòok downmarket
ráhn shop, store
ráhn ah-hǎhn restaurant
ráhn ah-hǎhn jeen Chinese restaurant
ráhn gǒo-ay dtěe-o café; noodle shop
ráhn kǎi dòrk-mái florist
ráhn kǎi kǒrng chum food store
ráhn kǎi kǒrng gào antique shop
ráhn kǎi krêu-ung lèk hardware store
ráhn kǎi krêu-ung pét ploy jeweller's
ráhn kǎi lâo liquor store, shop selling wines and spirits
ráhn kǎi núng-sěu bookshop, bookstore
ráhn kǎi pâhp kěe-un art gallery
ráhn kǎi pùk greengrocer's
ráhn kǎi yah chemist's, pharmacy
ráhn kǎi yah sòop

tobacconist's, tobacco store
ráhn néu-a butcher's
ráhn sĕrm sŏo-ay beauty salon
ráhn súk hâirng dry-cleaner's
ráhn súk (sêu-a) pâh laundry
ráhn tum ka-nŏm-bpung
  bakery
râhng-gai body
rahng-wun prize
ra-hùt toh-ra-sùp dialling code
rai-gahn schedule
rai-gahn num têe-o tour
râirk first
rairng fai fáh voltage
ra-kung bell
rao we; us
ra-wàhng between
ra-wung! be careful!; look
  out!
  ra-wung ná! look out!
ra-yá tahng distance
ray-o early; quick, fast;
  quickly
ray-o ray-o kâo! hurry up!
ray-o ray-o nòy! come on!
rêep rêep nòy! hurry up!
rêe-uk call; be called
ree-un learn
rêe-up smooth
rêe-up róy neat
rêrm begin, start
rĕu or
  ... rĕu ... either ... or ...
reu-a ship; boat
reu-a bpra-mong fishing boat
reu-a choo chêep lifeboat
reu-a hăhng yao long-tailed
  boat
reu-a kâhm fâhk ferry

reu-a pai rowing boat
reu-a ray-o speedboat
reu-a sŭm-bpûn sampan
reu-a sŭm-pao junk
reu-a yon motorboat
reu-a yórt yacht
rêu-ay rêu-ay so-so
reu-doo season
reu-doo bai mái plì spring
réu-doo bai-mái rôo-ung
  autumn, (US) fall
rêu-ung story
  rêu-ung a-rai gun? what's
  going on?
rim fĕe bpàhk lip
rôhk disease
rôhk áyd Aids
rôhk bìt dysentery
rôhk bpòo-ut nai kôr
  rheumatism
rôhk gloo-a náhm rabies
rôhk hèut hay fever; asthma
rôhk hùt measles
rôhk hùt yer-ra-mun German
  measles
rôhk páir dàirt sunstroke
rôhk sâi dtìng appendicitis
rohng la-korn theatre
rohng ngahn factory
rohng nŭng cinema, movie
  theater
rohng pa-yah-bahn hospital
rohng rairm hotel
rohng ree-un school
rohng rót garage
rohng rúp jum-num pawnshop
rohng yim gym
rôm umbrella; parasol
  nai rôm in the shade

rôm gun dàirt beach umbrella

roo hole

róo know

róo-a fence

rôo-a leak

roo-ay rich

róo-jùk know

rôOng dawn

  rôOng cháo at dawn

rôop picture

rôop gàir sa-lùk carving

rôop lòr handsome

rôop-song figure

rôop tài photograph

rŏo-răh posh; luxurious; upmarket

róo-sèuk feel

róo-sèuk ja ah-jee-un feel sick

róo-sèuk kòrp-kOOn feel grateful

róo-sèuk mâi sa-bai feel unwell

roo-um include

roo-um yòo dôo-ay included

roo-um yôrt total

róp-goo-un disturb

ror wait

rórn hot; warm

rórng hâi cry

rórng playng sing

rorng táo shoe(s); boot(s)

rorng táo dtàir sandal(s)

rorng táo gee-lah trainer(s)

rorng táo ma-nÓOt gòp flipper(s)

rót car; taste; flavour

rót air air-conditioned bus

rót bprùp ah-gàht air-conditioned bus

rót bun-tÓOk lorry, truck

rót châo rented car

rót dtôo van

rót fai train

rót fai dòo-un express train

rót kĕn pushchair

rót kĕn sŭm-rùp kon bpòo-ay wheelchair

rót may bus

rót may bprùp ah-gàht air-conditioned bus

rót mor-dter-sai motorbike; moped

rót norn sleeping car

rót num têe-o coach trip

rót pa-yah-bahn ambulance

rót sa-bee-ung dining car

rót sa-góot-dter scooter

rót săhm lór trishaw

rót sa-năhm bin airport bus

rót too-a tour bus

rót yon car

rúk love

rûm roo-ay wealthy

rum tai Thai classical dancing

rum-kahn annoying; annoy

rum-wong ramwong dance (popular Thai folk dance)

rúp accept; receive

rút state

rút-ta-bahn government

S

sà pond; wash

sà pŏm wash one's hair

sà wâi náhm swimming pool

sa-àht clean

sa-bai well, in good health

  sa-bai dee OK, all right

sa-bòo soap

sa-bòo gohn nòo-ut shaving soap

sa-bpay chèet pŏm hairspray

sa-dòo-uk convenient; comfortable

sa-dtahng satang (unit of currency)

sa-dtairm stamp

sa-dtree ladies' toilet, ladies' room

sa-gee náhm waterskiing

sa-górt táyp Sellotape®, Scotch tape®

sa-hà-rút a-may-ri-gah United States

săh-gon international

sâhk sa-lùk hùk pung remains, ruins

săh-lah pavilion

săhm three

săhm lèe-um torng kum Golden Triangle

săh-mee husband

sâhp know

sàh-sa-năh religion

sàh-sa-năh póot Buddhism; Buddhist

săh-tah-ra-ná public

sai sand

sài put

sái left

săi late; telephone line; strap

săi fai fáh wire; lead

sài gOOn-jair lock

săi pahn fanbelt

săi rút fastener

săi yahng yêut elastic

sairng overtake

sa-lai slide

sa-lĕung salung (unit of currency)

sa-lùk nâh-dtàhng shutter

sa-mĕr always

sa-moh-sŏrn club, clubhouse

sa-mOOn prai herbs (medicinal)

sa-mÒOt notebook

sa-mÒOt bun-téuk bpra-jum wun diary

sa-mÒOt măi lâyk toh-ra-sùp phone book

sa-mÒOt yay-loh páyt yellow pages

sa-năhm playing field; pitch

sa-năhm bin airport

sa-năhm gee-lah hàirng châht National Stadium

sa-năhm górp golf course

sa-năhm ten-nít tennis court

sa-năhm yâh lawn

sa-ngòp calm

sa-nÒOk pleasant

sa-nÒOk dee enjoyable, fun

sâo sad

săo young (girl)

sa-pahn bridge

sa-tăhn bor-ri-gahn rót châo car rental company

sa-tăhn gong-sOOn consulate

sa-tăhn lée-ung dèk lék nursery

sa-tăhn sùk-gah-rá shrine

sa-tăhn tôot embassy

sa-tăhn-na-gahn situation

sa-tăh-nee terminus; station

sa-tăh-nee dtum-ròo-ut police station

sa-tăh-nee rót fai railway station

sa-tǎh-nee rót may bus station

sa-tǎhn-têe place

sa-wàhng bright

sa-wít switch

sa-wít fai switch

sa-wùt dee hello

sa-wùt dee bpee mài! happy
New Year!

sa-wùt dee kâ hello

sa-wùt dee krúp hello

sàyt sa-dtahng small change

sèe four

sěe colour; paint

sěe chom-poo pink

sěe dairng red

sěe dum black

sěe kǎo white

sěe kěe-o green

sěe krohng rib

sěe lěu-ung yellow

sěe lěu-ut mǒo scarlet

sěe mǒo-ung purple

sěe néu-a beige

sěe núm dtahn brown

sěe núm ngern blue

sěe òrn pale

sěe sôm orange

sěe tao grey

sěe tao gairm lěu-ung fawn

sèe yâirk crossroads,
intersection

sěe-a broken, faulty, out of
order; polluted

sěe-a jai sorry

sěe-a láir-o damage; damaged

sěe-o sharp

sèe-ung risky

sěe-ung sound, noise; voice

sên line

sên dâi thread, cotton

sên lôo-ut wire

sèt ready; over, finished

séu buy

sêu dtrong honest

sêu-a chért shirt

sêu-a choo chêep lifejacket

sêu-a chôot dress

sêu-a fǒn raincoat

sêu-a gahng-gayng norn
pyjamas

sêu-a glâhm vest (under shirt)

sêu-a gúk waistcoat

sêu-a kloom coat, overcoat

sêu-a kloom chôot norn
dressing gown

sêu-a nôrk jacket

sêu-a pâh clothes

sêu-a pâh chún nai underwear

sêu-a pôo-yǐng blouse

sêu-a sa-wet-dter sweater;
sweatshirt

sêu-a yêut T-shirt

sêu-a yók song bra

si-gah cigar

sîn sòot end

sǐng-hǎh-kom August

sǐn-la-bpà art

sǐn-la-bpà sa-mǎi mài modern
art

sǐn-la-bpin artist

sìp ten; zip

sìp-hâh nah-tee quarter of an
hour

sǒh-pay-nee prostitute

sòht single (unmarried)

sòk-ga-bpròk dirty

sôn rorng táo heel (of shoe)

sôn táo heel (of foot)

sòng send

sòng dtòr forward

sòng jòt-măi post, mail

sòng jòt-măi dtahm bâhn
delivery

sòng tahng ah-gàht by airmail

sông-grahn Thai New Year

sŏng-krahm war

sòo towards

sŏo-ay beautiful

sòOk ripe

sòOk sòOk well-done (steak)

sòOk sòOk dìp dìp rare (steak)

sòOk-ka-pâhp health

sòOk-ka-pâhp mâi dee
unhealthy

sòOk-ka-pâhp sŏm-boon fit,
healthy

sôOm sâhm clumsy

sŏon zero

sŏon glahng centre

sŏong tall; high

sOOn-la-gah-gorn Customs

sOO-pâhp polite

sOO-pâhp bOO-rôOt gentleman

sOO-pâhp sa-dtree lady

sòop bOO-rèe smoke

sóOt bottom (of road)

sôOt tái last

sŏo-um săh-tah-ra-ná public
convenience

sòo-un part

sŏo-un garden

sòo-un dtoo-a private

sòo-un mâhk most (of)

sòo-un pa-sŏm mixture

sŏo-um săh-tah-ra-ná park

sŏo-un sùt zoo

sòo-ut mon pray

sŏrm repair, mend; fork

sŏrn teach

sôrn hide

sorng pack, packet

sŏrng two

sŏrng ah-tít fortnight

sorng jòt-măi envelope

sŏrng krúng twice

sŏrng tâir-o van with two
benches used as a bus

sòt fresh

sòt chêun refreshing

soy side street; lane; soi

sôy kor necklace, chain

súk wash

... sùk nít nèung a little ...

súk pâh wash clothes; laundry

sŭm-kun important; main

sŭm-lee cotton wool,
absorbent cotton

sŭm-núk kào săhn núk tôrng
têe-o tourist information
office

sŭm-núk ngahn office

sŭm-núk ngahn kào săhn
information office

sŭm-rùp for

sŭm-rùp kOOn for you

sûn short

sŭn-châht nationality

sùng order

sŭn-yah promise

sŭn-yahn fay mâi fire alarm

sùp-sŏn complicated

sùt animal

T

ta-bee-un rót car registration
  number

tâh if

tâh reu-a docks; harbour,
  port; jetty; quay(side)

tâh yàhng nún then, in that
  case

tăhm ask

tahn (kâo) eat

tahng direction; path; route;
  way

tahng ah-gàht by air

tahng dern corridor

tahng dòo-un motorway,
  highway, freeway

tahng kâo entrance

tahng kóhng bend

tahng kwăh on the right

tahng lée-o turning

tahng lŏo-ung highway

tahng máh-lai pedestrian
  crossing

tahng òrk exit

tahng ôrm detour

tahng rót fai railway

tahng rót fai pàhn level
  crossing

tahng sái on the left

tahng yâirk junction; fork

tàht tray

tai Thai (adj)

tái tights, pantyhose

tài rôop photograph

táir genuine; original

tairm-porn tampon

tairn instead

  tairn têe ja ... instead of ...

tăir-o queue

ta-lay sea

ta-lay sàhp lake

ta-nah-kahn bank

ta-nai kwahm lawyer

ta-nŏn street; road

ta-nŏn yài main road

ta-nùt meu sái left-handed

táo foot

tâo-nún just; only

tâo-rài? how much?

tâyp nĕe-o Sellotape®, Scotch
  tape®

tee time

têe at

  têe bâhn at home

têe bpèrt gra-bpŏrng can-
  opener

têe bpèrt kòo-ut bottle-opener;
  corkscrew

têe bpùt núm fŏn windscreen
  wipers

têe èun somewhere else

têe fàhk gra-bpăo left luggage,
  baggage check

têe fàhk kŏrng cloakroom

têe hâhm rót kâo pedestrian
  precinct

têe jâirng kŏrng hăi lost
  property office

têe jòrt rót car park, parking
  lot

têe jòrt rót táirk-sêe taxi rank

têe jum-nài dtŏo-a ticket office

têe kèe-a b00-rèe ashtray

têe láir-o last, previous

tee la nóy gradually

têe lĕu-a rest

tee lŭng afterwards; later,

later on
tê nǎi somewhere
tê nǎi? where?
tê nêe here; over here
tê nôhn there; over there
tê norn mattress; berth
tê nûn there
tê nûng seat
tê nûng dtìt nâh-dtàhng
  window seat
tê nûng kâhng lǔng back seat
tê nûng rúp kàirk couch
tê pìt error
tê púk accommodation(s)
tê râhp lôom plain
tee râirk at first
tê rúk darling
tê rút kěm kùt seatbelt
tê sǒrng second (adj)
tê sòrp tǎhm information
  desk
tê tum ngahn office
tê yòo address
tê-o visit; trip
tê-o bin flight
tê-o bin mǎo charter flight
tê-o hâi sa-nòok! enjoy
  yourself!
tê-o sa-nòok ná! have fun!;
  have a good journey!
tee-um imitation
tee-un candle
tê-ung keun at midnight
tê-ung wun midday
tee-wee TV
tén tent
ter you
těu carry
těung reach

tíng throw away
tíng wái leave behind
tôh! good heavens!
toh tahng glai long distance
  call
toh-ra-lâyk telegram
toh-ra-sùp phone
toh-ra-sùp gèp ngern bplai
  tahng reverse charge call,
  collect call
toh-ra-sùp sǎh-tah-ra-ná
  payphone
toh-ra-tút television
tong flag
too-a bus tour
tòo-a peanuts; peas; beans
tôo-a bpai everywhere
tôo-ay cup
tôo-ay chahm crockery
tóok every
tòok right, correct; cheap,
  inexpensive
tòok dàirt mâi sunburnt
tòok gòt-mǎi legal
tòok ka-moy-ee robbed;
  stolen
tóok kon everyone
tòok láir-o that's right
tóok yàhng everything
tòok-dtôrng accurate
... tôom ... p.m. (in the evening)
t00ng bag
t00ng bplah-sa-dtìk plastic bag
t00ng gra-dàht paper bag
t00ng meu gloves
t00ng norn sleeping bag
t00ng nôrng stocking(s)
t00ng táo sock(s)
t00ng yahng condom

tOOng yai boo-a tights,
  pantyhose
tÔO-rá business
tÔO-ra-gìt deal
tôr pipe
torng gold
tórng stomach
tórng pòok constipated
tórng sĕe-a diarrhoea; upset
  stomach
tórp-fĕe sweet(s), candy,
  candies
tôrt deep-fry
trah-wern ay-yen travel
  agency
tum make; do
tûm cave
tum dôo-ay meu handmade
tum hâi cause
tum hâi ôo-un fattening
tum kwahm sa-àht clean
tum lép manicure
tum ngahn work
tum tĕe bâhn home-made
tum-ma-châht nature;
  natural
tum-ma-dah normal; usually,
  normally; ordinary; plain
tum-mai? why?
tûn you
tun sa-măi fashionable;
  modern
tŭng bucket
tŭng dtàirk broke
tŭng ka-yà dustbin, trashcan
túng mòt all; altogether;
  completely
tŭng núm mun petrol tank,
  gas tank

túng sŏrng both of them
tun-tee at once, immediately;
  suddenly
tun-wah-kom December

U

um-per amphoe (sub-division of
  province)
un thing
un nǎi? which one?
un née this one
un nún that one
un-dta-rai harm; danger;
  dangerous
ung-grìt English (adj); British
un-nÔO-yâht allowed
ùt-dta-noh-mút automatic
ùt-dtrah rate
ùt-dtrah lâirk bplèe-un
  exchange rate
ùt-ta-noh-mút automatic
ùt-ti-bai explain

W

wâh say
wǎhn sweet
wahn seun née the day before
  yesterday
wahng put
wâhng empty; deserted
wâhng bplào empty, vacant
wâhng ngahn unemployed
wâi náhm swim
wáir stopover
wǎirn ring
wǎirn dtah glasses, (US)
  eyeglasses

wăirn dtàirng ngahn wedding
  ring
wâirn gun dàirt sunglasses
wăirn mûn engagement ring
wai-yah-gorn grammar
wâo kite
way-lah time
way-lah sòo-un mâhk most of
  the time
way-lah-nún then, at that time
wĕe comb
wee-sah visa
wèet rórng scream
wew view
wí-nah-tee second (in time)
wîng run
wí-sàyt incredible,
  tremendous
wí-sàyt jung ler-ee fantastic
wít-ta-yah-lai college
wít-ta-yah-sàht science
wít-ta-yÓÓ radio
wít-tee method
wong don-dtree orchestra
wong glom circle
woo-a cow
wun day
wun ah-tít Sunday
wun gèrt birthday
wun gòrn ... the day before ...
wun jun Monday
wun lŭng jàhk têe ... the day
  after ...
wun ma-reun née the day after
  tomorrow
wun née today
wun pa-réu-hùt Thursday
wun pÓÓt Wednesday
wun prá Buddhist holy day

wun săo Saturday
wun săo ah-tít weekend
wun seun née the day before
  yesterday
wun sĭn bpee New Year's Eve
wun sÒÒk Friday
wun têe date
wun ung-kahn Tuesday
wun yÒÒt holiday, vacation
wun yÒÒt râht-cha-gahn public
  holiday
wung palace
wŭng hope
wút temple; monastery
wùt cold (illness)
wút-ta-na-tum culture

Y

yah medicine
yâh grandmother (paternal);
  grass
yàh! don't!
yah dùp glin dtoo-a deodorant
yah glôrng pipe tobacco
yàh gun láir-o divorced
yah gun ma-lairng insect
  repellent
yah kâh chéu-a antiseptic
yah kâh chéu-a rôhk
  disinfectant
yah kOOm gum-nèrt
  contraceptive pill
yah kùt polish
yah kùt rorng táo shoe polish
yah kwin-neen quinine
yah láhng make-up remover
yah mét tablet
yah pít poison

yah ra-ngúp bpòo-ut painkiller
yah sà pŏm shampoo
yah sàyp-dtìt drug, narcotic
yah sĕe fun toothpaste
yah sòop tobacco
yah tah lotion; ointment
yah tah gun dàirt sunblock
yah tah lŭng àhp dàirt aftersun cream
yah tah lŭng gohn nòo-ut aftershave
yah tài laxative
yâhk hard, difficult
yàhk dâi want
yàhk (ja) I'd like to
yahng rubber
yahng a-lài spare tyre
yahng dtàirk puncture
yahng lóp rubber, eraser
yahng nai inner tube
yàhng née this way, like this
yàhng nóy at least
yahng rót tyre
yahng rút rubber band
yâht relatives
yai grandmother (maternal)
yài big, large
yài bêr-rêr enormous
yai sŭng-krór synthetic
yâir terrible, dreadful
yâir jung! too bad!
yâir long worse
yâir mâhk awful, terrible
yâir têe sòot worst
yâirk gun separate; separately
yao long
yêe hôr brand
yêe-bpòOn Japan; Japanese
yeen jeans

yêe-um excellent, brilliant; visit
yêe-um ler-ee lovely, excellent
yêe-um yôrt fantastic
yen cold; cool
yen née this afternoon
yen prôOng née tomorrow evening
yép sew
yer-ra-mun Germany; German
yeun stand
yèu-uk jug
yím smile
yin dee glad
yĭng rúp chái maid, chambermaid
yók wáyn except
yòo live; still; in, at home
káo mâi yòo he/she's not in
... yòo têe năi? where is ...?
yòo bon ... on top of ...; at the top of ...
yòo dtrong glahng in the middle
yòo dtrong nâh straight ahead
yòo glâi nearby
yòo kâhng bon at the top
yOOng mosquito
yOO-rohp Europe; European
yòOt stop
yòOt pôot ná! shut up!
yòOt-dti-tum fair, just
yôrt smashing, fabulous
yôrt! great!
yôrt yêe-um splendid, super
yung still; not yet
yung mâi sèt finish
yung-ngai? how?

Thai-English:
Signs and Notices

Contents

ABBREVIATIONS

ป.อ. bprùp ah-gàht air-
conditioned

อ. um-per Amphoe, district

ก.ท.ม. grOOng-tâyp-ma-hǎh-na-
korn Bangkok

พ.ศ. pÓOt-ta-sùk-ga-ràht
Buddhist Era (BE) (543 years
ahead of AD)

ค.ศ. krít-dta-sùk-ga-ràht
Christian Era (AD)

ช.ม. chôo-a mohng hours

น. nah-li-gah hours

ก.ม. gi-loh-mét kilometre

ช. chai men

จ. jung-wùt province

ถ. ta-nǒn road

ต. dtum-bon sub-district,
Tambon

ญ. yǐng women

GENERAL SIGNS

ระวัง ra-wung caution

อันตราย un-dta-rai danger

ห้าม ... hâhm ... ... forbidden

อย่า yàh ... do not ...

สอบถาม sòrp tǎhm enquiries

โรงพยาบาลห้ามใช้เสียง rohng
pa-yah-bahn: hâhm chái sěe-
ung hospital: no noise

ห้ามผ่าน hâhm pàhn no
admission

ห้ามเข้า hâhm kâo no entry

ห้ามทิ้งขยะ hâhm tíng ka-yà no
litter

ห้ามจอด hâhm jòrt no parking

ห้ามถ่ายรูป hâhm tài rôop no
photographs

ห้ามสูบบุหรี่ hâhm sòop bOO-rèe
no smoking

กรุณาอย่าส่งเสียงดัง ga-rOO-nah
yàh sòng sěe-ung dung please
don't make a noise

โปรดทอดรองเท้า bpròht tòrt
rorng táo please remove
shoes

ตำรวจ dtum-ròo-ut police

โปรดเงียบ bpròht ngêe-up
silence, please

AIRPORT, PLANES

ที่ทำการบริษัทการบิน têe tum
gahn bor-ri-sùt gahn bin
airline company offices

ท่าอากาศยาน tâh ah-gàht-sa-
yahn airport

ถึง tǔeng arrives

ประชาสัมพันธ์
ท่าอากาศยานกรุงเทพฯ bpra-
chah sǔm-pun tâh-ah-gàht-sa-
yǎhn grOOng-tâyp public

relations, Bangkok Airport

ศุลกากร s00n-la-gah-gorn
Customs

สุขาชาย sòo-kǎh chai gent's
toilets, men's room

ชาย chai gents

ตรวจคนเข้าเมือง dtròo-
ut kon kâo meu-ung
immigration

ประชาสัมพันธ์ bpra-chah sǔm-
pun information

สุขาหญิง sòo-kǎh yǐng ladies'
toilets, ladies' room

หญิง yǐng ladies

ออก òrk leaves

ฝากกระเป๋า fàhk gra-bpǎo left
luggage, baggage
checkroom

ลิฟท์ lif lift, elevator

จุดนัดพบ jòot nút póp meeting
point

ห้ามสูบบุหรี่ hâhm sòop b00-rèe
no smoking

จุดตรวจค้นผู้โดยสาร jòot dtròo-
ut kón pôo doy-ee sǎhn
passenger check-point

เฉพาะผู้โดยสารและลูกเรือเท่านั้น
cha-pòr pôo-doy-ee sǎhn láir
lôok reu-a tâo-nún passengers and crew only

ตรวจหนังสือเดินทาง dtròo-ut

นังสือ เดินทาง núng-sěu dern tahng passport
control

ภัตตาคาร pút-dtah-khan
restaurant

ตรวจสอบบัตรผู้โดยสารและกระเป๋า
dtròo-ut sòrp bùt pôo-doy-ee-
sǎhn láir gra-bpǎo ticket and
baggage check

ที่จำหน่ายตั๋ว têe jum-nài dtǒo-a
ticket office

เวลา way-lah time

ผู้มาส่งผู้โดยสาร pôo mah
sòng pôo-doy-ee-sǎhn
visitors

ที่พักผู้มาส่งผู้โดยสาร têe púk
pôo mah sòng pôo-doy-ee-
sǎhn visitors waiting area

ทางเข้า tahng kâo way in,
entrance

ทางออก tahng òrk way out

BANKS, MONEY

บาท bàht baht

ธนาคาร ta-nah-kahn bank

ฝากประจำ fàhk bpra-jum
deposit account, savings
account

ฝากเงิน fàhk ngern deposits

อัตราแลกเปลี่ยนเงิน ùt-dtrah
lâirk bplèe-un ngern exchange
rate

อัตราแลกเปลี่ยนเงินตราต่าง
ประเทศ ùt-dtrah lâirk
bplèe-un ngern dtrah dtàhng
bpra-tâyt foreign exchange
rate

สอบถาม sòrp tăhm enquiries

แลกเปลี่ยนเงินตราต่างประเทศ
lâirk bplèe-un ngern dtrah
dtàhng bpra-tâyt bureau de
change

เปิดบัญชีใหม่ bpèrt bun-chee
mài new accounts

ถอนเงิน tŏrn ngern
withdrawals

BUS TRAVEL

รถปรับอากาศ rót bprùp ah-gàht
air-conditioned bus

ถึง tĕung arrives

ออก òrk departs

สุขาชาย sòO-kăh chai gent's
toilets, men's room

ประชาสัมพันธ์ bpra-chah sŭm-
pun information

สอบถาม sòrp tăhm informa-
tion, enquiries

สุขาหญิง sòO-kăh yĭng ladies'
toilets, ladies' room

รับฝากของ rúp fàhk kŏrng left
luggage, baggage
checkroom

ห้ามสูบบุหรี่ hâhm sòop bOO-rèe
no smoking

ห้องพักผู้โดยสาร hôrng púk pôo
doy-ee săhn passengers'
waiting room

ทางเข้าเฉพาะผู้ถือตั๋วโดยสาร
tahng kâo cha-pòr pôo tĕu
dtŏo-a doy-ee săhn passengers with tickets only

ที่จำหน่ายตั๋ว têe jum-nài dtŏo-a
ticket office

กำหนดเวลาเดินรถ gum-nòt
way-lah dern rót timetable,
(US) schedule

รถทัวร์ rót too-a tour bus

COUNTRIES, NATIONALITIES

อาฟริกา ah-fri-gah Africa;
African

อีก้อ ee-gôr Akha
(hill tribe)

อเมริกา a-may-ri-gah America;
American

เอเชีย ay-see-a Asia

ออสเตรเลีย òrt-sa-dtray-lee-a
Australia; Australian

พม่า pa-mâh Burma,
Myanmar; Burmese

กัมพูชา gum-poo-chah
Cambodia

แคนาดา kair-nah-dah Canada; Canadian

จีน jeen China; Chinese

ประเทศ bpra-tâyt country

อังกฤษ ung-grìt England; Britain; UK; English; British

ยุโรป yoo-rôhp Europe; European

ฝรั่งเศส fa-rùng-sàyt France; French

ประเทศเยอรมัน bpra-tâyt yer-ra-mun Germany

ชาวเขา chao kǎo hill-tribe person; hill-tribe people

แม้ว máy-o Hmong, Meo (hill tribe)

ฮอลแลนด์ horn-lairn Holland; Dutch

อินเดีย in-dee-a India; Indian

แขก kàirk Indian; Malaysian

อินโดนีเซีย in-doh-nee-see-a Indonesia; Indonesian

ไอร์แลนด์ ai-lairn Ireland

ประเทศอิตาลี bpra-tâyt i-dtah-lee Italy

ญี่ปุ่น yêe-bpòon Japan; Japanese

กะเหรี่ยง ga-rèe-ung Karen (hill tribe)

เขมร ka-mǎyn Khmer; Cambodian

เกาหลี gao-lěe Korea; Korean

ลาว lao Laos; Lao

มาเลเซีย mah-lay-see-a Malaysia; Malaysian

นิวซีแลนด์ new see-lairn New Zealand

ไอร์แลนด์เหนือ ai-lairn něu-a Northern Ireland

ปากิสถาน bpah-gi-sa-tǎhn Pakistan

ฟิลิปปินส์ fin-lip-bpin Phillipines; Fillipino

สกอตแลนด์ sa-gort-lairn Scotland

สิงคโปร์ sǐng-ka-bpoh Singapore

ประเทศสเปน bpra-tâyt sa-bpayn Spain

ไทย tai Thai

เมืองไทย meu-ung tai Thailand (informal)

ประเทศไทย bpra-tâyt tai Thailand (formal)

สหรัฐอเมริกา sa-hà-rút a-may-ri-gah United States of America

เวียดนาม wêe-ut-nahm Vietnam; Vietnamese

เย้า yáo Yao (hill tribe)

CUSTOMS

ศุลกากร sŏon-la-gah-gorn
Customs

มีของต้องสำแดง mee kŏrng
dtôrng sŭm-dairng goods to
declare

ตรวจคนเข้าเมือง dtròo-ut kon
kâo meu-ung immigration

ไม่มีของต้องสำแดง mâi mee
kŏrng dtôrng sŭm-dairng
nothing to declare

เฉพาะหนังสือเดินทางไทย
cha-pòr núng-sĕu dern-tahng
tai Thai passport holders
only

DAYS

วัน wun day

อาทิตย์ ah-tít week

วันเสาร์อาทิตย์ wun săo ah-tít
weekend

วันจันทร์ wun jun Monday

วันอังคาร wun ung-kahn
Tuesday

วันพุธ wun póot Wednesday

วันพฤหัส wun pa-réu-hùt
Thursday

วันศุกร์ wun sòok Friday

วันเสาร์ wun săo Saturday

วันอาทิตย์ wun ah-tít Sunday

ENTERTAINMENT

... บาท ... bàht ... baht

ถุงละ ... บาท tŏong la ... bàht
... baht per bag

ถ้วยละ ... บาท tôo-ay la ... bàht
... baht per cup

ชิ้นละ ... บาท chín la ... bàht ...
baht per piece

บริการ ๒๔ ช.ม. bor-ri-gahn
yêe-sip sèe chŏo-a mohng 24-
hour service

รอบ ๑๗.๐๐ น. rôrp 17.00 n(ah-
li-gah) 5 p.m. show

บาร์ bah bar

โบว์ลิ่ง bohn-lîng bowling

ที่จำหน่ายตั๋ว têe jum-nài dtŏo-a
box office

โรงภาพยนตร์ rohng pâhp-pa-
yon cinema, movie theater

เร็วๆนี้ ray-o ray-o née coming
soon

ดิสโก้ dít-sa-gôh disco

ทางเข้า tahng kâo entrance

ทางออก tahng òrk exit

เต็ม dtem full

อาบอบนวด àhp òp nôo-ut
massage

รายการหน้า rai-gahn nâh next
programme

อาทิตย์หน้า ah-tít nâh next
week

ไนทคลับ náit klúp nightclub

ฉายวันนี้ chǎi wun née now showing

ราคา rah-kah price

รอบ rôrp showing

FORMS

ที่อยู่ têe yòo address

อายุ ah-yóo age

พ.ศ. por sŏr (year) ... BE (543 years later than AD)

สีตา sěe dtah colour of eyes

สีผม sěe pŏm colour of hair

เกิดวันที่ gèrt wun-têe date of birth

ชื่อ chêu first name

ตั้งแต่ ... ถึง ... dtûng-dtàir ... tĕung ... from ... until ...

ความสูง kwahm sŏong height

บ้านเลขที่ bâhn lâyk têe house number

ตรอก dtròrk lane

ซอย soy lane, soi

บันทึก bun-téuk memo

เดือน deu-un month

สัญชาติ sŭn-châht nationality

หมายเหตุ mǎi-hàyt note, n.b.

อาชีพ ah-chêep occupation

หนังสือเดินทางหมายเลข núng-sěu dern tahng mǎi-lâyk passport number

จังหวัด jung-wùt Province

เชื้อชาติ chéu-a châht race

อยู่ที่ yòo têe residing at

ถนน ta-nŏn road

เพศ pâyt sex

ลายเซ็น lai sen signature

ลงชื่อ long chêu signed

พักที่ púk têe staying at

นามสกุล nahm sa-gOOn surname

ตำบล dtum-bon Tambon, sub-district

หมู่บ้าน mòo-bâhn village

น้ำหนัก núm nùk weight

พยาน pa-yahn witness

GARAGES

บริการ ๒๔ ช.ม. bor-ri-gahn yêe-sìp sèe chôo-a mohng 24-hour service

บริการซ่อมรถ bor-ri-gahn sôrm rót car repairs

บริการล้างรถ bor-ri-gahn láhng rót car wash

ดีเซล dee-sen diesel

เปลี่ยนหม้อกรอง bplèe-un môr grorng filters changed

อู่ òo garage

ห้ามสูบบุหรี่ hâhm sòop bOO-rèe no smoking

เปลี่ยนน้ำมันเครื่อง bplèe-un

núm mun krêu-ung oil changed

บริการอัดฉีด bor-ri-gahn ùt chèet pressurized air

ปะยาง bpà yahng punctures repaired

เครื่องอะไหล่ krêu-ung a-lài spare parts

GEOGRAPHICAL TERMS

คลอง klorng canal

เมืองหลวง meu-ung lǒo-ung capital city

ชนบท chon-na-bòt country-side

ป่าดงดิบ bpàh dong dìp forest, jungle

เขา kǎo hill

เกาะ gòr island

ป่า bpàh jungle, forest

ที่ราบลุ่ม têe râhp lôom plain

แม่น้ำ mâir-náhm river

ทะเล ta-lay sea

ชายทะเล chai ta-lay seaside

เมือง meu-ung town; city; country

หมู่บ้าน mòo-bâhn village

HAIRDRESSER'S, BEAUTY SALONS

เสริมสวย sěrm sǒo-ay beauty care

เครื่องสำอาง krêu-ung sǔm-ahng cosmetics

นวดหน้า nôo-ut nâh facial massage

ตัดผม dtùt pǒm hair cut

เป่าผม bpào pôm hair drying

ไดผม dai pǒm hair drying

สระผม sà pǒm wash

ตัดเล็บ dtùt lép manicure

ดัดผม dùt pǒm perm

เซทผม sét pǒm set

โกนหนวด gohn nòo-ut shave

HEALTH

รถพยาบาล rót pa-yah-bahn ambulance

คุมกำเนิด koom gum-nèrt birth control

คลีนิค klee-ník clinic

ห้องคลอด hôrng klôrt delivery room

ทันตแพทย์ tun-dta-pâirt dentist

ทำฟัน tum fun dentist's

จำหน่ายยา jum-nài yah dispensary

แพทย์หญิง pâirt yǐng doctor (female)

พ.ญ. pâirt yĭng doctor (female)

น.พ. nai pâirt doctor (male)

นายแพทย์ nai pâirt doctor (male)

ตรวจสายตา dtròo-ut sǎi dtah eye test

ตรวจสายตา dtròo-ut sǎi dtah dtròo-ut sǎi-dtah eye-testing

โรงพยาบาล rohng pa-yah-bahn hospital

ฉีดยา chèet yah injections

นางพยาบาล nahng pa-yah-bahn nurse

ห้างขายยา hâhng kǎi yah pharmacy, drugstore

ตรวจปัสสาวะ dtròo-ut bpùt-sǎh-wá urine test

เอ็กซเรย์ X-ray X-ray

HIRING, RENTING

ชั่วโมงละ ... บาท chôo-a mohng la ... bàht ... baht per hour

เดือนละ ... บาท deu-un la ... bàht ... baht per month

วันละ ... บาท wun la ... bàht ... baht per month

อพาร์ตเม้นท์ให้เช่า ah-paht-mén hâi châo apartment for rent

บาท bàht baht (unit of currency)

รถให้เช่า rót hâi châo car for hire, car to rent

เงินมัดจำ ngern mút-jum deposit

แฟลตให้เช่า flàirt hâi châo apartment for rent

ให้เช่า hâi châo for hire, to let, to rent

บ้านให้เช่า bâhn hâi châo house to let, house for rent

รถมอเตอร์ไซค์/
รถจักรยานให้เช่า rót mor-dter-sai/rót jùk-ra-yahn hâi châo motorcycle/bicycle for hire

จ่ายล่วงหน้า jài lôo-ung nâh pay in advance

ค่าเช่า kâh châo rental, fee

ห้องให้เช่า hôrng hâi châo room for rent

HOTELS

คอฟฟี่ช็อบ kòrp-fêe chórp café serving coffees, alcoholic drinks, snacks and meals

ห้องคู่ hôrng kôo double room

ห้องคูปรับอากาศ hôrng kôo bprùp ah-gàht double room with air-conditioning

ทางออก tahng òrk exit

ชั้น chún floor

เกสท์เฮาส์ gàyt háot guest-
house

สอบถาม sòrp tăhm
enquiries

ห้องน้ำสตรี hôrng náhm sa-
dtree ladies' toilet, ladies'
room

หญิง yĭng ladies

ลิฟท์ lif lift, elevator

บริการรถรับส่ง bor-ri-gahn rót
rúp sòng limousine service

ห้องน้ำบุรุษ hôrng náhm b00-
rôot men's toilet, men's
room

ชาย chai men

ห้ามสูบบุหรี่ hâhm sòop b00-rèe
no smoking

แผนกต้อนรับ pa-nàirk dtôrn rúp
reception

ห้องอาหาร hôrng ah-hăhn
restaurant

ห้อง hôrng room

ห้องให้เช่า hôrng hâi châo
rooms to let

บริการนำเที่ยว bor-ri-gahn num
têe-o sight-seeing tours

ห้องเดี่ยว hôrng dèe-o single
room

ห้องเดี่ยวปรับอากาศ hôrng
dèe-o bprùp ah-gàht single
room with air-conditioning

สระว่ายน้ำ sà wâi náhm
swimming pool

สุขา sòo-kăh toilet

ห้องน้ำ hôrng náhm toilets

ห้องว่าง hôrng wâhng vacancies

ยินดีต้อนรับ yin dee dtôrn rúp
welcome

LIFTS

ลง long down

ชั้น chún floor

ลิฟท์ lif lift, elevator

ไม่เกิน ... คน mâi gern ... kon
maximum load ... people

ห้ามสูบบุหรี่ hâhm sòop b00-rèe
no smoking

ขึ้น kêun up

MEDICINES

หลังอาหาร lŭng ah-hăhn after
meals

ทา tah apply (ointments)

ก่อนนอน gòrn norn before
going to bed

ก่อนอาหาร gòrn ah-hăhn
before meals

ยาอันตราย yah un-dta-rai
dangerous medicine

วิธีใช้ wí-tee chái instructions
for use

กินเกินขนาดเป็นอันตราย gin gern ka-nàht bpen un-dta-rai it is dangerous to exceeed the stated dose

ยา yah medicine

เม็ด mét tablet, pill

รับประทาน rúp-bpra-tahn take (orally)

ช้อนชา chórn chah teaspoon

วันละ ... ครั้ง wun la ... krúng times ... times per day

วันละ ... เม็ด wun la ... mét tablets ... tablets per day

MONTHS

เดือน deu-un month

มกราคม mók-ga-rah-kom January

กุมภาพันธ์ gOOm-pah-pun February

มีนาคม mee-nah-kom March

เมษายน may-săh-yon April

พฤษภาคม préut-sa-pah-kom May

มิถุนายน mí-tOO-nah-yon June

กรกฎาคม ga-rúk-ga-dah-kom July

สิงหาคม sĭng-hăh-kom August

กันยายน gun-yah-yon September

ตุลาคม dtOO-lah-kom October

พฤษจิกายน préut-sa-jìk-gah-yon November

ธันวาคม tun-wah-kom December

NOTICES ON DOORS

เฉพาะเจ้าหน้าที่ cha-pór jâo-nâh-têe authorized personnel only

กริ่ง grìng bell

หมาดุ măh dOO beware of the dog

ปิด bpìt closed

ทางเข้า tahng kâo entry

ทางออก tahng òrk exit

ห้ามจอดรถขวางประตู hâhm jòrt rót kwăhng bpra-dtoo no parking in front of the gate

เข้า kâo in

ห้ามเข้า hâhm kâo no entry

ไม่มีกิจห้ามเข้า mâi mee gìt hâhm kâo no entry to unauthorized persons

ห้ามจอด hâhm jòrt no parking

ห้ามกลับรถ hâhm glùp rót no turning

เปิด bpèrt open

ออก òrk out

กรุณาถอดรองเท้า ga-rOO-nah tòrt rorng táo please remove your shoes

กรุณากดกริ่ง ga-r00-nah gòt grìng please ring

กด gòt press

ถนนส่วนบุคคล ta-nŏn sòo-un bòok-kon private road

ดึง deung pull

ผลัก plùk push

ระวังสุนัขดุ ra-wung s00-núk dò0 beware of the dog

NUMBERS

ศูนย์ sŏon zero

หนึ่ง nèung one

สอง sŏrng two

สาม săhm three

สี่ sèe four

ห้า hâh five

หก hòk six

เจ็ด jèt seven

แปด bpàirt eight

เก้า gâo nine

สิบ sìp ten

สิบเอ็ด sìp-èt eleven

สิบสอง sìp-sŏrng twelve

สิบสาม sìp-săhm thirteen

สิบสี่ sìp-sèe fourteen

สิบห้า sìp-hâh fifteen

สิบหก sìp-hòk sixteen

สิบเจ็ด sìp-jèt seventeen

สิบแปด sìp-bpàirt eighteen

สิบเก้า sìp-gâo nineteen

ยี่สิบ yêe-sìp twenty

ยี่สิบเอ็ด yêe-sìp-èt twenty-one

สามสิบ săhm-sìp thirty

สามสิบเอ็ด săhm-sìp-èt thirty-one

สี่สิบ sèe-sìp forty

ห้าสิบ hâh-sìp fifty

หกสิบ hòk-sìp sixty

เจ็ดสิบ jèt-sìp seventy

แปดสิบ bpàirt-sìp eighty

เก้าสิบ gâo-sìp ninety

หนึ่งร้อย nèung róy one hundred

หนึ่งพัน nèung pun one thousand

สองพัน sŏrng pun two thousand

หนึ่งหมื่น nèung mèun ten thousand

สองหมื่น sŏrng mèun twenty thousand

หนึ่งแสน nèung săirn one hundred thousand

สองแสน sŏrng săirn two hundred thousand

หนึ่งล้าน nèung láhn one million

หนึ่งร้อยล้าน nèung róy láhn one hundred million

๐ sŏon 0

๑ nèung 1

๒ sŏrng 2

๓ săhm 3

๔ sèe 4

๕ hâh 5

๖ hòk 6

๗ jèt 7

๘ bpàirt 8

๙ gâo 9

๑๐ sìp 10

๑๑ sìp-èt 11

๑๒ sìp-sŏrng 12

๑๓ sìp-săhm 13

๑๔ sìp-sèe 14

๑๕ sìp-hâh 15

๑๖ sìp-hòk 16

๑๗ sìp-jèt 17

๑๘ sìp-bpàirt 18

๑๙ sìp-gâo 19

๒๐ yêe-sìp 20

๒๑ yêe-sìp-èt 21

๓๐ săhm-sìp 30

๓๑ săhm-sìp-èt 31

๔๐ sèe-sìp 40

๕๐ hâh-sìp 50

๖๐ hòk-sìp 60

๗๐ jèt-sìp 70

๘๐ bpàirt-sìp 80

๙๐ gâo-sìp 90

๑๐๐ nèung róy 100

๑๐๐๐ nèung pun 1,000

๒๐๐๐ sŏrng pun 2,000

๑๐๐๐๐๐ nèung săirn 100,000

๒๐๐๐๐๐ sŏrng săirn 200,000

๑๐๐๐๐ nèung mèun 10,000

๒๐๐๐๐ sŏrng mèun 20,000

๑๐๐๐๐๐๐ nèung láhn
   1,000,000

๑๐๐๐๐๐๐๐๐ nèung róy láhn
   100,000,000

ORDINALS

ที่หนึ่ง têe nèung first

ที่สอง têe sŏrng second

ที่สาม têe săhm third

ที่สี่ têe sèe fourth

ที่ห้า têe hâh fifth

ที่หก têe hòk sixth

ที่เจ็ด têe jèt seventh

ที่แปด têe bpàirt eighth

ที่เก้า têe gâo ninth

ที่สิบ têe sìp tenth

PHONES

บาท bàht baht (unit of currency)

รหัส ra-hùt code

เหรียญ rĕe-un coin

ต่อ dtòr extension

โทรศัพท์ทางไกล toh-ra-sùp
   tahng glai long distance
   telephone

เสีย sĕe-a out of order
ตำรวจ dtum-ròo-ut police
ตู้โทรศัพท์สาธารณะ dtôo toh-ra-sùp săh-tah-ra-ná public telephone box
โทร. toh tel.
โทรศัพท์ toh-ra-sùp telephone
สมุดเบอร์โทรศัพท์ sa-mòot ber toh-ra-sùp telephone directory
เบอร์โทรศัพท์ ber toh-ra-sùp telephone number

PLACE NAMES

อยุธยา a-yóot-ta-yah Ayutthaya
บางปะอิน bahng-bpà-in Bang Pa-In
กรุงเทพฯ gròong-tâyp Bangkok
บางลำภู bahng-lum-poo Banglamphu
เชียงใหม่ chêe-ung-mài Chiangmai
อนุสาวรีย์ประชาธิปไตย a-nóo-săh-wa-ree bpra-chah-típ-bpa-dtai Democracy Monument
หาดใหญ่ hàht yài Hat Yai
หัวหิน hŏo-a hin Hua Hin
หัวลำโพง hŏo-a lum-pohng Hua Lampong

กาญจนบุรี gahn-ja-na-bOO-ree Kanjanaburi
ขอนแก่น kŏrn-gàirn Khonkaen
เกาะสมุย gòr sa-mŏo-ee Koh Samui
สวนลุมพินี sŏo-un lOOm-pi-nee Lumpini Park
นครปฐม na-korn bpa-tŏm Nakhorn Pathom
พัทยา pút-ta-yah Pattaya
ภูเก็ต poo-gèt Phuket
ประตูน้ำ bpra-dtOO náhm Pratu Nam
แม่น้ำแคว mâir-náhm kwair River Kwai
สนามหลวง sa-năhm lŏo-ung Sanam Luang
สยามแสควร์ sa-yăhm sa-kwair Siam Square
สงขลา sŏng-klăh Songkhla
สุโขทัย sOO-kŏh-tai Sukhothai
ธนบุรี ton-bOO-ree Thonburi
อุบลราชธานี OO-bon râht-cha-tah-nee Ubonratchathani
อนุสาวรีย์ชัยสมรภูมิ a-nÓO-săh-wa-ree chai sa-mŏr-ra-poom Victory Monument
เยาวราช yao-wa-râht Yaowarat (China Town area of Bangkok)

POST OFFICE

ผู้รับ pôo rúp addressee

ทางอากาศ tahng ah-gàht airmail

กรุงเทพฯ gr00ng-tâyp Bangkok

ตู้จดหมาย dtôo jòt-mãi letter box, mail box

ที่อื่น têe èun other places

พัสดุ pút-sa-d00 parcels

รหัสไปรษณีย์ ra-hùt bprai-sa-nee postcode

ที่ทำการไปรษณีย์ têe tum gahn bprai-sa-nee post office

ลงทะเบียน long ta-bee-un registered mail

ผู้ส่ง pôo sòng sender

ไปรษณียากร bprai-sa-nee-yah-gorn stamps

ทางเรือ tahng reu-a surface mail

โทรเลข toh-ra-lâyk telegrams

โทรศัพท์ toh-ra-sùp telephone

PUBLIC BUILDINGS

สนามบิน sa-nãhm bin airport

ธนาคาร ta-nah-kahn bank

สนามมวย sa-nãhm moo-ay boxing stadium

สถานีรถเมล์ sa-tãhn-nee rót may bus station

โรงภาพยนตร์ rohng pâhp-pa-yon cinema, movie theater

คลีนิค klee-ník clinic

วิทยาลัย wít-ta-yah-lai college

กรมศุลกากร grom s00n-la-gah-gorn Customs Department

กรม grom department (government)

ที่ว่าการอำเภอ têe wâh gahn um-per district office

กอง gorng division (government)

สถานทูต sa-tãhn tôot embassy

โรงพยาบาล rohng pa-yah-bahn hospital

โรงแรม rohng rairm hotel

กองตรวจคนเข้าเมือง gorng dtròo-ut kon kâo meu-ung Immigration Department

กรมแรงงาน grom rairng ngahn Labour Department

ศาล sãhn law court

ห้องสมุด hôrng sa-mòot library

ตลาด dta-làht market

กระทรวง gra-soo-ung ministry

พิพิธภัณฑ์ pí-pít-ta-pun museum

สนามกีฬาแห่งชาติ sa-nãhm gee-lah hàirng châht National Stadium

ร้านขายยา ráhn kǎi yah
pharmacy

สถานีตำรวจ sa-tǎhn-nee dtum-
ròo-ut police station

ไปรษณีย์ bprai-sa-nee post
office

โรงเรียน rohng ree-un
school

ร้าน ráhn shop, store

ศูนย์การค้า sǒon gahn káh
shopping centre

ห้าง hâhng store, shop

องค์การส่งเสริมการท่องเที่ยวแห่ง
ประเทศไทย ong-gahn sòng
sěrm gahn tôrng têe-o hǎirng
bpra-tâyt TAT – Tourist
Organisation of Thailand

กรมสรรพากร grom sǔn-pah-
gorn Tax Department

วัด wút temple

โรงละคร rohng la-korn
theatre

สถานีรถไฟ sa-tǎhn-nee rót fai
train station

มหาวิทยาลัย ma-hǎh-wít-ta-
yah-lai university

PUBLIC HOLIDAYS

วันพระ wun prá Buddhist holy
day

วันหยุดราชการ wun yòot râht-
cha-gahn official public
holiday

วันขึ้นปีใหม่ wun kêun bpee mài
New Year's Day

วันสงกรานต์ wun sǒng-grahn
Songkran Day (Thai New Year)

RAIL TRAVEL

จองตั๋วล่วงหน้า jorng dtǒo-a
lôo-ung nâh advance
bookings

ถึง těung arrives

ออก òrk departs

แผนกสอบถาม pa-nàirk sòrp
tǎhm enquiries

สุขาชาย sòo-kǎh chai gent's
toilets, men's room

สุขาหญิง sòo-kǎh yǐng ladies'
toilets, ladies' room

รับฝากของ rúp fàhk kǒrng left
luggage, baggage
checkroom

ชานชาลา chahn-chah-lah
platform, (US) track

ประชาสัมพันธ์ bpra-chah sǔm-
pun public relations

สถานีรถไฟ sa-tǎhn-nee rót fai
railway station, train
station

ที่จำหน่ายตั๋ว têe jum-nài dtǒo-a
ticket office

กำหนดเวลาเดินรถ gum-nòt way-lah dern ròt timetable, (US) schedule

รถไฟ rót fai train

ห้องพักผู้โดยสาร hôrng púk pôo doy-ee sähn waiting room

REGIONS, PROVINCES ETC

ชายแดน chai dairn border

เขต kàyt boundary; area

ภาคกลาง pâhk glahng central region

แม่น้ำเจ้าพระยา mâir-náhm jâo pra-yah Chao Phraya River

ประเทศ bpra-tâyt country

อำเภอ um-per district, Amphoe

แม่โขง mâir-köhng Mekhong River

ภาคอีสาน pâhk ee-sähn north-eastern region

ภาคเหนือ pâhk nëu-a north-ern region

จังหวัด jung-wùt province

ภาคใต้ pâhk dtâi southern region

ตำบล dtum-bon sub-district, Tambon

บ้านนอก bâhn-nôrk up-country

ต่างจังหวัด dtàhng jung-wùt up-country

RESTAURANTS, BARS

บริการ ๒๔ ชั่วโมง bor-ri-gahn 24 chôo-a mohng 24-hour service

ห้องแอร์ hôrng-air air-conditioned room

ร้านอาหารโต้รุ่ง ráhn ah-hähn dtôh rôong all-night restau-rant

บาร์ bah bar

ชาม chahm bowl, dish

อาหารเช้า ah-hähn cháo breakfast

คอฟฟี่ช็อป kórp-fêe chórp café serving coffees, alcoholic drinks, snacks and meals

อาหารจีน ah-hähn jeen Chinese food

อาหารเย็น ah-hähn yen evening meal

อาหาร ah-hähn food

อาหารญี่ปุ่น ah-hähn yêe-bpôon Japanese food

อาหารกลางวัน ah-hähn glahng wun lunch

อาหารมุสลิม ah-hǎhn móo-sa-lim Muslim food

อาหารอีสาน ah-hǎhn ee-sǎhn North-Eastern food

สวนอาหาร sǒo-un ah-hǎhn open-air restaurant

ชามละ ... chahm la ... ... per bowl/dish

จานละ ... jahn la ... ... per plate/dish

จาน jahn plate, dish

ราคา rah-kah price

ภัตตาคาร pút-dtah-kahn restaurant

ร้านอาหาร ráhn ah-hǎhn restaurant

ห้องอาหาร hôrng ah-hǎhn restaurant

อาหารทะเล ah-hǎhn ta-lay seafood

เชลล์ชวนชิม chen choo-un chim Shell® recommended, seal of approval, equivalent to Good Food Guide

อาหารปักษ์ใต้ ah-hǎhn bpùk dtâi Southern food

อาหารไทย ah-hǎhn tai Thai food

อาหารฝรั่ง ah-hǎhn fa-rùng Western food

ROAD SIGNS

ทางโค้ง tahng kóhng bend

ระวังทางขวางหน้าเป็นทางเอก ra-wung tahng kwǎhng nâh bpen tahng àyk caution: major road ahead

ระวัง ra-wung caution

อันตราย un-dta-rai danger

ทางเบี่ยง tahng bèe-ung diversion

ขับช้าๆ kùp cháh cháh drive slowly

๔๐ ก.ม. sèe sìp gi-loh-mét 40 kilometres

๔ ตัน sìi dtun 4 tons

หยุด เ ตรวจ yòOt - dtròo-ut halt - checkpoint

โรงพยาบาลห้ามใช้เสียง rohng pa-yah-bahn hâhm chái sěe-ung hospital: no sounding horns

ชิดซ้าย chít sái keep left

ห้ามเข้า hâhm kâo no entry

ห้ามแซง hâhm sairng no overtaking, no passing

ห้ามจอดรถ hâhm jòrt rót no parking

ห้ามเลี้ยว hâhm lée-o no turning

ห้ามกลับรถ hâhm glùp rót no U-turns

ห้ามรถทุกชนิด hâhm rót tóok cha-nít no vehicles

ทางรถไฟ tahng rót fai railway

โรงเรียน rohng ree-un school

หยุด yòot stop

๓ ม. sahm mét 3 metres

SHOPPING

บาท bàht baht (unit of currency)

ลูกละ … บาท lôok la … bàht … baht each (e.g. for large fruit)

ใบละ … บาท bai la … bàht … baht each (e.g. for eggs, fruit)

ตัวละ … บาท dtoo-a la … bàht … baht each (e.g. items of clothing)

โลละ … บาท loh la … bàht … baht per kilo

คู่ละ … บาท kôo la … bàht baht per pair (e.g. shoes)

ชิ้นละ … บาท chín la … bàht … baht per piece/ portion

สุขภัณฑ์ sòok-ka-pun bathroom accessories

ที่จ่ายเงิน têe jài ngern cash desk, cashier

พนักงานเก็บเงิน pa-núk ngahn gèp ngern cashier

แผนกเด็ก pa-nàirk dèk children's department

แผนกไฟฟ้า pa-nàirk fai fáh electrical goods

เครื่องเรือน krêu-ung reu-un furniture

ราคา rah-kah price

วิทยุทีวี wít-ta-yóo - tee-wee radio - TV

ลดราคา lót rah-kah sale; reduced

รองเท้า rorng-táo shoes

ลดพิเศษ lót pi-sàyt special reductions

อุปกรณ์กีฬา òo-bpa-gorn gee-lah sports equipment

ของเล่น kŏrng lên toys

นาฬิกา nah-li-gah watches

SPORT

กรีฑา gree-tah athletics

มวย moo-ay boxing

ฟุตบอล fóot-born football

ประตู bpra-dtoo goal

กอล์ฟ górp golf

สนามกอล์ฟ sa-năhm górp golf course

สนามม้า sa-năhm máh race course

กีฬา gee-lah sport

สนามกีฬา sa-năhm gee-lah stadium

ว่ายน้ำ wâi náhm swimming

ทีม teem team
เทนนิส ten-nít tennis
สนามเทนนิส sa-nǎhm ten-nít tennis court
มวยไทย moo-ay tai Thai boxing

STREETS AND ROADS

ตรอก dtròrk lane (off a soi)
ซอย soy lane, soi
ถนน ta-nǒn road

THAI CULTURE

เมืองโบราณ meu-ung boh-rahn Ancient City
กรมศิลปากร grom sǐn-la-bpa-korn Department of Fine Arts
ตลาดน้ำ dta-làht náhm Floating Market
พิพิธภัณฑ์ pi-pít-ta-pun museum
พิพิธภัณฑ์สถานแห่งชาติ pi-pít-ta-pun sa-tǎhn hàirng châht National Museum
โรงละครแห่งชาติ rohng la-korn hàirng châht National Theatre
พระปฐมเจดีย์ prá-bpa-tǒm jay-dee Pra Pathom Jedi (Buddhist monument)
พระบรมมหาราชวัง prá-ba-rom-ma-hǎh-râtch-a-wung Royal Palace
วังสวนผักกาด wung sǒo-un pùk-gàht Suan Pakkard Palace
วัด wút temple
วัดพระแก้ว wút pra-kâir-o Temple of the Emerald Buddha
มวยไทย moo-ay tai Thai boxing
รำไทย rum tai Thai dancing
วัดโพธิ์ wút poh Wat Po

TIMETABLES

ถึง těung arrives
วันที่ wun-têe date
วัน wun day
ออก òrk departs
วันหยุด wun yòot holiday
นาฬิกา nah-li-gah hours
เวลา way-lah time
กำหนดเวลาเดินรถ gum-nòt way-lah dern rót timetable, (US) schedule
วันนี้ wun née today
พรุ่งนี้ prôong née tomorrow
วันเสาร์อาทิตย์ wun sǎo ah-tít weekend
เมื่อวานนี้ mêu-a wahn née yesterday

TOILETS

ไม่ว่าง mâi wâhng engaged

บุรุษ bOO-ròot gentlemen

ชาย chai gents

หญิง yǐng ladies

สตรี sa-dtree ladies

ผู้ชาย pôo-chai men

ช. chor men

ห้องน้ำ hôrng náhm toilet, rest
  room

สุขา sòO-kǎh toilet, rest room

ว่าง wâhng vacant

ญ. yor women

ผู้หญิง pôo-yǐng women

Contents

Menu Reader:

Food

ESSENTIAL TERMS

bowl chahm ชาม
chopsticks dta-gèe-up ตะเกียบ
cup tôo-ay ถ้วย
dessert kŏrng wǎhn ของหวาน
fish bplah ปลา
fork sôrm ส้อม
glass gâir-o แก้ว
knife mêet มีด
meat néu-a เนื้อ
menu may-noo เมนู
noodles gŏo-ay dtĕe-o ก๋วยเตี๋ยว
pepper prík tai พริกไทย
plate jahn จาน
rice kâo ข้าว
salt gleu-a เกลือ
set menu ah-hǎhn chóot อาหารชุด
soup sóop ซุป
spoon chórn ช้อน
table dtó โต๊ะ

another ... èek ... nèung อีก ... หนึ่ง
excuse me! (to call waiter/waitress) kOOn krúp (kâ)! คุณครับ(ค่ะ)
could I have the bill, please? chék bin เช็คบิล

BASIC FOODS

เนยสด ner-ee sòt butter

เนยแข็ง ner-ee kǎirng cheese

น้ำพริก núm prík chilli paste

กะทิ ga-tí coconut milk

น้ำปลา núm bplah fish sauce

แป้งสาลี bpâirng sǎh-lee flour

น้ำผึ้ง núm pêung honey

แยม yairm jam; marmalade

น้ำมันพืช núm mun pêut oil

น้ำมันมะกอก núm mun ma-gòrk
  olive oil

น้ำมันหอย núm mun hǒy
  oyster sauce

น้ำจิ้ม núm jîm sauce

น้ำซีอิ๊ว núm see éw soy sauce

น้ำตาล núm dtahn sugar

น้ำส้ม núm sôm vinegar

โยกัด yoh-gut yoghurt

BASIC MAIN MEALS

ข้าวผัดไก่ kâo pùt gài chicken
  fried rice

ข้าวมันไก่ kâo mun gài chicken
  rice

ข้าวผัดปู kâo pùt bpoo crab
  fried rice

บะหมี่แห้ง ba-mèe hâirng 'dry'
  egg noodles, served without
  soup

ก๋วยเตี๋ยวแห้ง gǒo-ay dtěe-o

hâirng 'dry' noodles, served
  without soup

ข้าวหน้าเป็ด kâo nâh bpèt
  duck rice

บะหมี่น้ำ ba-mèe náhm egg
  noodle soup

ก๋วยเตี๋ยวผัดซีอิ๊ว gǒo-ay dtěe-o
  pùt see éw noodles fried in
  soy sauce

ก๋วยเตี๋ยวราดหน้า gǒo-ay
  dtěe-o pùt râht nâh noodles
  with fried meat, vegetables
  and thick gravy

ก๋วยเตี๋ยวน้ำ gǒo-ay dtěe-o
  náhm noodle soup

ข้าวผัดหมู kâo pùt mǒo pork
  fried rice

ข้าวหมูแดง kâo mǒo dairng
  'red' pork rice (pork soaked in a
  red marinade)

ข้าวคลุกกะปิ kâo klóok ga-bpì
  rice and shrimp paste fried
  together and served with
  pork and shredded omelette

ข้าวผัดกุ้ง kâo pùt gôong
  shrimp fried rice

ผัดไทย pùt tai Thai-style fried
  noodles

ขนมจีนแกงไก่ ka-nǒm jeen
  gairng gài Thai vermicelli
  with chicken curry

BEEF AND BEEF DISHES

เนื้อผัดน้ำมันหอย néu-a pùt núm mun hǒy beef fried in oyster sauce

เนื้อผัดพริก néu-a pùt prík beef fried with chillies

เนื้อผัดกระเทียมพริกไทย néu-a pùt gra-tee-um prík tai beef fried with garlic and pepper

เนื้อผัดขิง néu-a pùt kǐng beef fried with ginger

เนื้อสับผัดพริกกระเพรา néu-a sùp pùt prík gra-prao minced beef fried with chillies and basil

เนื้อเสต็ก néu-a sa-dték steak

BREAD

ขนมปัง ka-nǒm-bpung bread; roll

ปอนด์ bporn loaf

ขนมปังปิ้ง ka-nǒm bpung bpîng toast

CAKES AND BISCUITS, SWEET PASTRIES

คุกกี้ kóok-gêe biscuit, cookie

ขนมเค้ก ka-nǒm káyk cake

แป้งขนม bpâirng ka-nǒm pastry (dough)

ขนม ka-nǒm pastry, small cake

CONDIMENTS AND SEASONINGS, HERBS AND SPICES

ใบกระเพรา bai gra-prao basil

พริก prík chilli

ผักชี pùk chee coriander

ข่า kàh galangal (similar to ginger)

ขิง kǐng ginger

เครื่องเทศ krêu-ung tâyt herbs

ตะไคร้ dta-krái lemon grass

พริกไทย prík tai pepper

เกลือ gleu-a salt

COOKING METHODS AND TYPICAL COMBINATIONS

... ต้ม ... dtôm boiled ...

... ย่าง ... yâhng charcoal-grilled ...

... ทอด ... tôrt deep-fried ...

... ผัดหน่อไม้ ... pùt nòr-mái ... fried with bamboo shoots

... ผัดใบกระเพรา ... pùt bai gra-prao ... fried with basil leaves

... ผัดพริก ... pùt prík ... fried with chillies

... ทอดกระเทียมพริกไทย ... tôrt

gra-tee-um prík tai ... fried
with garlic and pepper

... ผัดขิง ... pùt kĭng ... fried
with ginger

... อบ ... òp oven-cooked ...

... ผัด ... pùt stir-fried ...

... เปรี้ยวหวาน ... bprêe-o wăhn
sweet and sour ...

ปิ้ง bpîng toasted

CURRIES

แกงเนื้อ gairng néu-a beef
curry

แกงเขียวหวาน gairng kĕe-o
wăhn beef curry made using
green curry paste, made
from green chilli peppers

ข้าวแกง kâo gairng curry and
rice

แกงไก่ gairng gài chicken
curry

พะแนง pa-nairng 'dry' curry
(in thick curry sauce)

พะแนงเนื้อ pa-nairng néu-a
'dry' beef curry (in thick curry
sauce)

พะแนงไก่ pa-nairng gài 'dry'
chicken curry (in thick curry
sauce)

พะแนงหมู pa-nairng mŏo 'dry'
pork curry (in thick curry sauce)

แกงกาหรี่ gairng ga-rèe Indian-
style curry made with beef
and potatoes cooked in
coconut milk with yellow
curry paste

แกงมัสหมั่น gairng mút-sa-mùn
'Muslim' curry containing
beef, potatoes and peanuts

แกงเผ็ด gairng pèt spicy curry

แกงจืด gairng jèut vegetable
soup or stock (an accompaniment
to curries)

แกง gairng 'wet' curry – meat
cooked in coconut milk and
served in a bowl full of liquid

DESSERTS

กล้วยบวชชี glôo-ay bòo-ut chee
banana in sweet coconut-
milk sauce

ของหวาน kŏrng wăhn dessert

ไอศครีม ai-sa- kreem ice
cream

ข้าวเหนียวมะม่วง kâo nĕe-o
ma-môo-ung sweet sticky
rice, mango and coconut
cream

ตะโก้ dta-gôh Thai-style jelly
with coconut cream

EGGS AND EGG DISHES

ไข่ต้ม kài dtôm boiled egg

ไข่ kài egg

ไข่พะโล้ kài pa-lóh egg stewed in soy sauce and spices

ไข่ยัดไส้ kài yút sâi filled omelette

ไข่ดาว kài dao fried egg

ไข่เจียว kài jee-o omelette

ไข่ลูกเขย kài lôok kěr-ee 'son-in-law' eggs – hard-boiled eggs with various condiments

ไข่ลวก kài lôo-uk very soft boiled egg (eaten, or rather 'drunk' almost raw)

FISH AND SEAFOOD

ปู bpoo crab

ปลา bplah fish

กุ้งใหญ่ gôong yài lobster

หอยแมงภู่ hǒy mairng pôo mussels

ปลาหมึกยักษ์ bplah-mèuk yúk octopus

หอยนางรม hǒy nahng rom oyster

อาหารทะเล ah-hǎhn ta-lay seafood

หอย hǒy shellfish

กุ้ง gôong shrimp, prawn

ปลาหมึก bplah-mèuk squid

FISH AND SEAFOOD DISHES

กุ้งเผา gôong pǎo barbecued prawns

กุ้งทอดกระเทียมพริกไทย gôong tôrt gra-tee-um prík tai prawns fried with garlic and pepper

กุ้งผัดใบกระเพรา gôong pùt bai gra-prao shrimps fried with basil leaves

กุ้งผัดพริก gôong pùt prík shrimps fried with chillies

ทอดมันกุ้ง tôrt mun gôong shrimp 'tort mun', finely minced shrimps, fried in batter with spices

ปลาหมึกผัดพริก bplah-mèuk pùt prík squid fried with chillies

ปลาหมึกทอดกระเทียมพริกไทย bplah-mèuk tôrt gra-tee-um prík tai squid fried with garlic and pepper

ปลาเปรี้ยวหวาน bplah bprêe-o wǎhn sweet and sour fish

FRUIT

แอปเปิล air-bpêrn apple

กล้วย glôo-ay banana

มะพร้าว ma-práo coconut

น้อยหน่า nóy-nàh custard apple – green heart-shaped fruit with white flesh

อินทผาลัม in-ta-păh-lum dates

ทุเรียน tOO-ree-un durian – large green fruit with spiny skin, yellow flesh and a pungent smell

ผลไม้ pŏn-la-mái fruit

องุ่น a-ngÒOn grapes

ฝรั่ง fa-rùng guava – green-skinned fruit with white flesh

ขนุน ka-nOOn jackfruit – large melon-shaped fruit with thick, green skin and yellow flesh

มะนาว ma-nao lemon; lime

ลำใย lum-yai longan – like a lychee

ลิ้นจี่ lín-jèe lychee

มะม่วง ma-môo-ung mango

มังคุด mung-kÓOt mangosteen – round fruit with a thick, purplish-brown skin and white flesh

แตงไทย dtairng tai melon

ส้ม sôm orange

มะละกอ ma-la-gor papaya – green or yellow-skinned oblong-shaped fruit with reddish-orange flesh

ลูกพีช lôok pêech peach

ลูกแพร์ lôok pair pear

สับปะรด sùp-bpa-rót pineapple

ลูกพลัม lôok plum plum

ส้มโอ sôm oh pomelo – similar to grapefruit

เงาะ ngór rambutan – small fruit with reddish prickly skin and white flesh

ชมพู่ chom-pôo rose apple – red, pink or white strawberrry-shaped fruit

ละมุด la-mÓOt sapodilla – small brown-skinned fruit, similar in taste and texture to a pear

สตรอเบอรี่ sa-dtror-ber-rêe strawberry

แตงโม dtairng moh water melon

MEAT

เนื้อ néu-a beef; meat

ไก่ gài chicken

เป็ด bpèt duck

เครื่องใน krêu-ung nai kidneys

ไต tai kidneys

เนื้อแกะ néu-a gàir lamb

ตับ dtùp liver

หมู mŏo pork
เนื้อหมู néu-a mŏo pork

MENU TERMS

อาหารจีน ah-hăhn jeen
Chinese food
อาหาร ah-hăhn cuisine,
cooking; meal; food
กับข้าว gùp kâo dish, meal
เมนู may-noo menu
รายการอาหาร rai gahn ah-
hăhn menu
ราคา rah-kah price

MISCELLANEOUS DISHES

ทอดมัน tôrt mun deep-fried
fish-cakes
ขนมจีบ ka-nŏm jèep 'dim-
sum' – steamed balls of
minced pork in dough
ปอเปี๊ยะทอด bpor bpêe-a tôrt
Thai spring roll

PORK AND PORK DISHES

หมูสับผัดพริกกระเพรา mŏo sùp
pùt prík gra-prao minced pork
fried with chillies and basil
หมู mŏo pork
เนื้อหมู néu-a mŏo pork
หมูผัดใบกระเพรา mŏo pùt bai
gra-prao pork fried with basil

leaves
หมูผัดพริก mŏo pùt prík pork
fried with chillies
หมูทอดกระเทียมพริกไทย mŏo
tôrt gra-tee-um prík tai pork
fried with garlic and pepper
หมูผัดขิง mŏo pùt kĭng pork
fried with ginger
หมูพะโล้ mŏo pa-lóh pork
stewed in soy sauce
ซี่โครง sêe krohng mŏo spare
ribs
หมูเปรี้ยวหวาน mŏo bprêe-o
wăhn sweet and sour pork
หมูสะเต๊ะ mŏo sa-dtáy thin
strips of charcoal-grilled
pork

POULTRY AND POULTRY DISHES

ไก่ย่าง gài yâhng barbecued or
roast chicken
ไก่ gài chicken
ไก่ต้มข่า gài dtôm kàh chicken
boiled in spicy stock
ไก่ผัดหน่อไม้ gài pùt nòr-mái
chicken fried with bamboo
shoots
ไก่ผัดใบกระเพรา gài pùt bai
gra-prao chicken fried with
basil leaves

ไก่ผัดเม็ดมะม่วงหิมพานต์ gài pùt mét ma-môo-ung hǐm-ma-pahn chicken fried with cashew nuts

ไก่ผัดพริก gài pùt prík chicken fried with chillies

ไก่ทอดกระเทียมพริกไทย gài tôrt gra-tee-um prík tai chicken fried with garlic and pepper

ไก่ผัดขิง gài pùt kǐng chicken fried with ginger

ไก่ผัดหน่อไม้ฝรั่ง gài pùt nòr-mái fa-rùng chicken with asparagus

เป็ด bpèt duck

เป็ดย่าง bpèt yâhng roast duck

ไก่ผัดเปรี้ยวหวาน gài pùt brêe-o wǎhn sweet and sour chicken

RICE AND NOODLES

ข้าวสวย kâo sǒo-ay boiled rice

หมี่กรอบ mèe gròrp crispy noodles

บะหมี่ ba-mèe egg noodles

ข้าวผัด kâo pùt fried rice

เส้นใหญ่ sên yài large (width of noodles)

ผัดราดหน้า pùt râht nâh noodles with fried vegetables and meat, served with a thick gravy

ก๋วยเตี๋ยว gǒo-ay dtěe-o rice-flour noodles

ข้าว kâo rice

ข้าวต้ม kâo dtôm rice porridge

เส้นเล็ก sên lék small (width of noodles)

ข้าวเหนียว kâo něe-o sticky rice

ขนมจีน ka-nǒm jeen Thai vermicelli

วุ้นเส้น wóon-sên transparent noodles

เส้นหมี่ sên mèe very small (width of noodles)

SALADS

ส้มตำ sôm dtum papaya salad made with unripe green papaya, chillies, lime juice, fish sauce and dried shrimps

สลัด sa-lùt salad

ยำ yum Thai salad

SNACKS AND SWEETS

ช็อกโกเลต chórk-goh-let chocolate

มันฝรั่งทอด mun fa-rùng tôrt crisps, (US) potato chips

ไอศครีม ai-sa-kreem ice cream

ไอศกรีมแท่ง ai-sa-kreem tâirng
ice lolly

อมยิ้ม om-yím lollipop

ถั่ว tòo-a nuts; peanuts

ถั่วลิสง tòo-a li-sŏng peanuts

ท็อฟฟี่ tórp-fêe sweets, candies

ลูกกวาด lôok gwàht sweets,
candies

SOUPS

ต้มยำไก่ dtôm yum gài chicken
'tom yam' spicy soup

บะหมี่น้ำ ba-mèe náhm egg
noodle soup

ต้มยำปลา dtôm yum bplah fish
'tom yam' spicy soup

ต้มยำโป๊ะแตก dtôm yum bpó
dtàirk mixed seafood 'tom
yam' spicy soup

ก๋วยเตี๋ยวน้ำ gŏo-ay dtĕe-o
náhm noodle soup

ต้มยำกุ้ง dtôm yum gôOng
shrimp 'tom yam' spicy
soup

แกงส้ม gairng sôm spicy
vegetable soup

VEGETABLES AND VEGETABLE DISHES

หน่อไม้ฝรั่ง nòr-mái fa-rùng
asparagus

มะเขือ ma-kĕu-a aubergine,
eggplant

หน่อไม้ nòr mái bamboo
shoots

ถั่วงอก tòo-a ngôrk bean
sprouts

กะหล่ำปลี ga-lùm-bplee
cabbage

หัวผักกาดแดง hŏo-a pùk-gàht
dairng carrot

ดอกกะหล่ำปลี dòrk ga-lùm-
bplee cauliflower

พริก prík chilli

มันฝรั่งทอด mun fa-rùng tôrt
chips, French fries

แตงกวา dtairng-gwah cucumber

ผัดผักบุ้งไฟแดง pùt pùk bôOng
fai dairng fried morning-
glory (type of greens)

กระเทียม gra-tee-um garlic

ขิง kĭng ginger

พริกหยวก prík yòo-uk green
pepper

ผักกาด pùk-gàht lettuce

ถั่วลันเตา tòo-a lun-dtao
mange-tout

ผักบุ้ง pùk bôông morning-
glory (type of greens)

เห็ด hèt mushrooms

หัวหอม hŏo-a hŏrm onion

ถั่ว tòo-a peas; beans; lentils

มันฝรั่ง mun fa-rùng potato

พริกยวกแดง prík yôo-uk dairng
red pepper

ผักคะน้า pùk ka-náh spring
greens

ต้นหอม dtôn hŏrm spring
onions

ข้าวโพด kâo pôht sweet corn,
maize

มะเขือเทศ ma-kĕu-a tâyt
tomato

ผัก pùk vegetables

Menu Reader:

Drink

Contents

ESSENTIAL TERMS

beer bee-a เบียร์

bottle kòo-ut ขวด

　another bottle of ..., please kŏr ... èek kòo-ut nèung ขอ ...
อีกขวดหนึ่ง

coconut juice núm ma-práo น้ำมะพร้าว

coffee gah-fair กาแฟ

cup tôo-ay ถ้วย

　a cup of ..., please kŏr ... tôo-ay nèung ขอ ... ถ้วยหนึ่ง

fruit juice núm pŏn-la-mái น้ำผลไม้

gin lâo yin เหล้ายิน

　a gin and tonic, please kŏr yin toh-nik ขอยินโทนิค

glass gâir-o แก้ว

milk nom นม

mineral water núm râir น้ำแร่

soda (water) núm soh-dâh น้ำโซดา

soft drink náhm kòo-ut น้ำขวด

sugar núm dtahn น้ำตาล

tea núm chah น้ำชา

tonic (water) núm toh-ník น้ำโทนิค

water náhm น้ำ

whisky lâo wít-sa-gêe เหล้าวิสกี้

wine lâo wai เหล้าไวน

wine list rai-gahn lâo wai รายการเหล้าไวน์

BEER, SPIRITS, WINE etc

เหล้า lâo alcohol, liquor
เบียร์ bee-a beer
ขวด kòo-ut bottle
เหล้าบรั่นดี lâo brùn-dee
 brandy
ค็อกเทล kórk-tayn cocktail
แก้ว gâir-o glass
เหล้ายิน lâo yin gin
ยินโทนิค yin toh-nik gin and
 tonic
น้ำแข็ง núm kǎirng ice
แม่โขง mâir-kǒhng Mekhong®
 whisky
เบียร์สิงห์ bee-a sǐng Singha®
 beer
วอดก้า word-gâh vodka
เหล้าวิสกี้ lâo wít-sa-gêe
 whisky, scotch
เหล้าไวน์ lâo wai wine

COFFEE, TEA etc

คาฟีน kah-feen caffeine
เย็น yen chilled
โกโก้ goh-gôh cocoa
กาแฟ gah-fair coffee
โอเลี้ยง oh-lée-ung iced black
 coffee
กาแฟเย็น gah-fair yen iced
 coffee
ชาใส่มะนาว chah sài ma-nao
 lemon tea
กาแฟผง gah-fair pǒng instant
 coffee
น้ำชา núm chah tea
ไม่ใส่นม mái sài nom without
 milk
ไม่ใส่น้ำตาล mái sài núm dtahn
 without sugar

SOFT DRINKS

น้ำมะพร้าว núm ma-práo
 coconut juice
โค้ก kóhk Coke®
เครื่องดื่ม krêu-ung dèum
 drinks
ซ่า sâh fizzy, carbonated
น้ำส้มคั้น núm sôm kún fresh
 orange juice
น้ำแข็ง núm kǎirng ice
น้ำผลไม้ náhm pǒn-la-mái juice
นม nom milk
น้ำมะนาว núm ma-nao
 lemonade
น้ำแร่ núm râir mineral water
น้ำส้ม núm sôm orange juice
 (bottled)
น้ำสับปะรด núm sùp-bpa-rót
 pineapple juice
น้ำโซดา núm soh-dah soda
 water
น้ำขวด náhm kòo-ut soft drink

นมกระป๋อง nom gra-bpŏrng
  tinned milk
น้ำมะเขือเทศ núm ma-kĕu-a
  tâyt tomato juice
น้ำ náhm water